Fashioning Society

fb

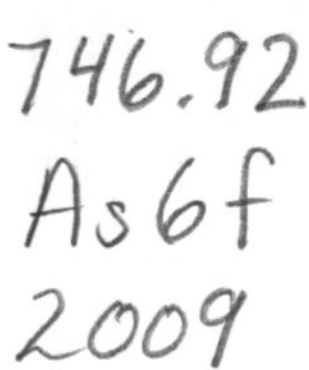

Fashioning Society

A Hundred Years of
HAUTE COUTURE
by Six Designers

KARL ASPELUND
UNIVERSITY OF RHODE ISLAND

FAIRCHILD BOOKS, **NEW YORK**

Executive Editor: Olga T. Kontzias
Acquisitions Editor: Joseph Miranda
Editorial Development Director: Jennifer Crane
Development Editor: Sylvia L. Weber
Associate Art Director: Erin Fitzsimmons
Production Director: Ginger Hillman
Senior Production Editor: Elizabeth Marotta
Photo Research: Sarah Silberg, Erin Fitzsimmons
Copyeditor: Joanne Slike
Cover Design: Erin Fitzsimmons

Library of Congress Catalog Card Number: 200792751
ISBN: 978-1-56367-597-3
GST R 133004424
Printed in the United States of America
TP09

I dedicate this volume
to the memory of an elegant tailor and sharp mind,
my student, colleague, and friend,
Indridi Gudmundsson,
who passed away just as I began writing.

Debating with him the ideas herein
would have benefited the work and been a pleasure.
Better than anyone I've known, he would,
from his student days onward, repeatedly demonstrate
the importance to scholarship and creativity
of a well-placed
question.

CONTENTS

EXTENDED CONTENTS

PREFACE

Our society speaks of itself with clothing. However, when studying high fashion in apparel design, there is often a tendency to neglect the dialogue of society and clothes and focus on the individual designers and their creations, as if they were not responsive to the world around them, except by careful and artful choice. When considering apparel design and the charismatic characters involved, one can easily get caught up in the short-term view of seasonal trends or the artifice of decades and not consider the larger undercurrents and waves of history.

With *Fashioning Society*, I wish to show how the designers of what has been called "the hundred years of fashion"—spanning roughly 1860 to1970—operated within, were influenced by, and influenced the hustle and bustle of the world. High-fashion design cannot be separated from the swirl of history and society any more than the politics and commerce from which the discipline grew.

I have come to believe that students need to quickly realize that the discipline they are heading into is *of* the world and *in* the world, but also *shapes* the world. To treat high-fashion design as an art form, separate from any reality outside the studio, is ultimately to miss a major force in its development and ignore a core element of the discipline's origin: it came into being as a tool of a society in need of identity and, right from the start, with varying degrees of consciousness, served a political purpose.

Both the fashion business and the discipline of fashion design are in a fragmented state and lack forward-looking vision. It is of vital importance for students of fashion to consider the place, effect, and interaction of fashion design in the world in order to assess the shape of the long-term trend of the discipline. The discipline, as it was known (or at least presented) for over a hundred years is indeed transformed. Mass production, mass media, and global markets have altered the shape of the world. The world is shrinking, not only metaphorically in the sense that communications are making everything smaller, but our relative share of it is becoming smaller. The fashion market, as it was ruled from Paris before expanding to New York, London, and Milan, is now a relatively smaller part of a global market that is less centralized. To understand what happened to high-fashion design is the first step to fathoming what may happen next.

With high-fashion design currently in a decades-long transition, if not at a crisis point, it is necessary to examine its nature as a part of society, and not just study it within its own boundaries. Much energy has been spent on creating myths of great designers and their magical designs, but the complex reality is actually much more exciting and interesting. To see high fashion as what it is—society's mirror, self-portrait, and representation of its longing for perfection—makes the study of it the study of society's undercurrents. This approach allows for more than the analysis of seasonal trends. Here is the material for the study of long-term trends, over years and decades. As you will see in this book, the entire hundred years' fashion is indeed itself a long-term trend that may have had its day.

I have attempted to place the narrative of high-fashion design into the context of the happening world, with its politics and cultural undercurrents, so that the current shift in the world balance of economy and politics may perhaps be read in terms of its long-term effects and the larger trends.

I have tried to keep the frame large, as I know from my students that diving into the specific historical and sociological aspects of this story without having let one's eyes first wander over the big picture can be misleading, if not confusing. Therefore, I have limited the discussion for the most part to the six designers who have most obviously and popularly driven the story of the hundred years of high fashion design: Charles Worth, Paul Poiret, Coco Chanel, Elsa Schiaparelli, Christian Dior, and Yves Saint Laurent. Presenting each of them as a representation and embodiment of the history is not meant to imply anything about other designers. This is simply a way to keep the narrative moving. These six most prominent profiles became the picture, and for the purpose of this story, they suffice as the frame on which to drape the narrative.

We begin in France, mid-nineteenth century, at the Second Empire court of Emperor Napoleon III and the empress Eugénie. There the groundwork for the rest of the story is laid in Chapters 1 and 2, and we stay at court for a while observing the politics and rituals. Then it's on to Paul Poiret, the star character of Chapter 3, and from there to Chanel and Schiaparelli (in Chapter 4). These take us clear through to World War II, after which the torch is picked up by Christian Dior (who is introduced in Chapter 4) and then passed on to Yves Saint Laurent (introduced in Chapter 7), who carries it to the end. Along the way, beginning in Chapters 5 and 6, we stop to consider the effects of media, art, philosophy, and politics, notably anarchism and youthful revolt, which lead us to the interesting topic of punk rock and style. I claim that punk style, in being the ultimate anti-design, both contributed to and signified the end of high-fashion culture. As such, it warrants a close look in Chapter 7, for the cultural force that overwhelms another often contains the clues as to what will happen next. Chapters 8 through 14 reflect upon the decades following the hundred years of high fashion and explore the ways in which the spirit and influence of our six archetypes survived beyond the lifetimes of these designers.

Most of the literature in this field is written for the graduate student or is specific to a period, area, or style. What seems to be lacking is a broad overview of the scene, and it is this I hope to have provided. I would hope that this book is a source of material for much classroom discussion and discovery, in both studies of fashion theory and hands-on design studies.

The chapters are presented in chronological order, albeit loosely, as the story is not really linear. To represent this history as a series of events on a timeline neglects a very important element of high-fashion history: it is a story that loops in and back on itself, with each period repeating and picking up on the previous ones, and different groups responding in the same way to the same set of circumstances through the years. I have allowed the narrative go where it wanted to go in order to emphasize this, skipping back and forth a bit. As you read, use this to break from the linear mode of thinking and consider it a panorama. (There is a timeline at the end of the book to assist in keeping track of the chronology for those who are not familiar with the details of nineteenth- and twentieth-century history.)

This "time traveling" is essential to the understanding of the story, and to further underscore this, each chapter includes two additional features that should make for interesting classroom use or to ponder when reading. Boxes within each chapter, labeled "Looking Forward/Looking Back," pick up on points in the chapters and relate them to a larger discussion, in particular, placing elements of the narrative in the context of high fashion's longing for a mythical past. Thematically, these boxes serve to underscore the nonlinear nature of the story, and overall they clarify the notion that past, present, and future are continually entangled in high-fashion design and possibly that the entanglement is inherent in the discipline.

In addition, a box at the end of each chapter contains excerpts from a newspaper article. Most of these articles appeared while I was writing the book; three are older, from a collection of hundreds of articles I've clipped or downloaded over the years. I have appended questions to each box to prompt discussion about the chapter's materials in relation to news from our time (again time goes back and forth).

Finally, there is the previously mentioned timeline, which serves to illustrate a linear structure of the events recounted in this book. In this I have also included a sprinkling of other events, some whimsical but others linked to a larger context of technology, science, inventions, and political developments. It is my hope that this timeline will spark even deeper and more involved discussions about the place of fashion design in shaping the world.

The images in the book show designers' works, key historical players, and events and places mentioned. In the color insert are key examples from the six designers who form the core of the narrative. It is my hope that all these images add a dimension to the reading and ground the information in the reality of each period, connecting the information in the text to the world.

The material in both types of boxes and in the main text is further amplified in the instructor's guide, where additional study questions, projects, and discussion topics are suggested. A PowerPoint presentation is also available to instructors.

This is a book to be read with an eye on connections. Take time to connect what you are reading to what you have already read, and relate the material to the boxes and discussion questions. Build an image in your mind of the story as it gets layered, and see the patterns emerging from one chapter to the next. Pick up magazines and newspapers to find the themes from the book echoed there. Keep an eye on fashion weeks and developments in the fashion business: who's being hired where? Who's in; who's out? What are the kids wearing? What's going on in London, Moscow, New Delhi, and Beijing? Then relate this back to the book. Look at the study questions and think of variations or questions of your own. This whole book rose from one simple question: What happened to high-fashion design?

ACKNOWLEDGMENTS

Fashioning Society springs from nearly 20 years of pondering high fashion while teaching students of tailoring and apparel design. I have been inspired by hundreds of wonderful, inquisitive students to try to answer the question: "What is happening to high fashion design?" Thanks to all of them, too numerous to name, all remembered fondly.

I owe a continuing debt to Dr. Linda Welters, who chairs the Department of Textiles, Fashion Merchandising and Design at the University of Rhode Island. Her support is as encouraging as her scholarship and writings are inspiring. I am also in much debt to Professor Adam Seligman at Boston University for his powerful thoughts on ritual in society that guided my development of Chapter 1. His engaging style of teaching and inquiry were an inspiration throughout this work.

Then there is the team at Fairchild Books, whose positive energy, enthusiasm, and dedication is continually impressive: Olga Kontzias, executive editor; Joe Miranda, acquisitions editor; Jennifer Crane, editorial development director; Liz Marotta, senior production editor; Adam Bohannon, director of creative services, who served as art director; and Erin Fitzsimmons, associate art director, who is responsible for the photo research. I must also acknowledge the merry band of sales professionals in advance, knowing that they will be equally forceful.

Fairchild Books is truly a magnificent team, without whom nothing would appear, and with whom I am grateful and honored to work. I'm sure they will forgive me as I single out one of the team for my deepest gratitude: my development editor Sylvia Weber. Her good humor and patience know no bounds; her gentle guidance has improved every aspect of this book.

To the following reviewers, selected by the publisher, many thanks for their time, attention, and input, which were encouraging and challenging and made for a better text:

Darlene Kness, University of Central Oklahoma; Yoo Jin Kwon, Washington State University; Dana Legette-Traylor, American Intercontinental University; Jeanie Lisenby, Miami International University; Elizabeth Cole Sheehan, Mount Ida College; and Susan Stark, San Francisco State University.

My wife, Brenda, deserves special thanks for having now twice put up with the stretches of pontificating, general disarray, and hermitlike behavior that go with my writing. I am in awe of her capacity to not only deal with this, but all the while to provide invaluable support.

All of these, named and unnamed, have made this book richer. My own failings are to blame for what is amiss.

Fashioning Society

CHAPTER 1

Modernity Rising

The Age of Worth

A story begins only where the storyteller decides to begin telling. Events lead up to this beginning and other happenings lead to those events and on and on in a long receding chain back into the past. The moment chosen may illustrate a significant event or bring specific people into the foreground. We might therefore begin our story in Paris in early 1860, when the Princess Pauline von Metternich arrived at the Palace de Tuilleries for a ball given by the Emperor Napoleon III and the Empress Eugénie. The weekly balls of the Second Empire were amazing scenes of ostentatious display. Thousands of guests would attend, the men in formal military garb or ceremonial dress, the women in couture gowns, a new one every week and each one different (Figure 1.1). The princess wore a dress made of white tulle and silver lamé, trimmed with flowers, and a belt of white satin. All around the twenty-four-year-old, heavily jeweled ladies with fans and bouquets would be wearing huge crinolines with trains, covered with lace, feathers, ribbons, fringes, and frills. The princess's dress was modest, by the standards of the day, but therein was its strength: it was designed to achieve its effect through masterful cutting and the relatively simple elegance of its composition.

The empress was quite impressed and inquired after the maker of the dress, then asked that Metternich instruct the dressmaker to visit her at ten o'clock the very next morning.[1] The dressmaker was a little-known Englishman, Charles Frederick Worth, who had arrived in Paris a few years before, hoping to make his fortune.

The spirits of Empress Eugénie and Charles Worth still haunt high fashion today. Their meeting brought fashion, politics, and class structure together in such a way that all else that has happened in high fashion design since has been a reaction or reflection of what they set in motion. In addition, Worth's operation created the myth and image of the *couturier*, which has been in effect since. But there was much already set in place for their meeting to cause such an effect. We therefore have to set the stage for our story some

FIGURE 1.1. The Empress Eugénie and her ladies-in-waiting. Portrait by Winterhalter (1855). The dresses are from Gagelin, very likely created by Charles Worth.

decades earlier, as the events of the nineteenth century up until then had created the place into which Eugénie and Worth would fit perfectly. A swift political history may be in order.

Fashion and Politics in Nineteenth-Century France

Paris in the middle of the nineteenth century was a place of much uncertainty and turmoil. The largest part of the adult generation at that time had not yet lived through a single decade free of political unrest, uprisings, revolution, or even war. Governments were toppled, regimes changed—the monarch along with a host of nobles had been reviled and executed 60 years earlier—and a rising current of socialism and anarchism was both reacting to and threatening the rapidly growing urban middle class. Large-scale industrialization and the urbanization of culture were redrawing the social and cultural landscape leading to much confusion and question of generations-old practices and norms. Nothing seemed sacred. Artists of all stripes were redefining themselves and their arts, breaking boundaries, becoming autonomous, socially conscious, and in many cases politically vocal. Revolutionary ideas in religion and philosophy were turning the ancient world on its head. Even science, which in the eighteenth century had seemed to be on its way to explaining the world and all things in it rationally, was beginning to hint at new disturbing areas of study that questioned all ideas of nature and human existence itself.

Four major factions were vying for control of the French: On one side were the Republicans, left-wingers who advocated the principles of the Revolution, and on the other, three that were all monarchist, traditionalist, and right-wing. These were the Bourbons (or Legitimists) and the Orleanists, royalist factions both, and then the Bonapartists, who advocated a lineage of descendants of Emperor Napoleon I. The three monarchist factions could unite only against the working class, and their ultimate goal was to restore and maintain monarchy in France.

After the revolution of 1848 in Paris, Louis-Napoleon Bonaparte (Figure 1.2), a nephew of the late Emperor Napoleon, returned from England. He had fled to England, having escaped from imprisonment in France following an attempted coup in 1840 (his second such effort, having also attempted to seize power in 1836). He was elected president of the newly established Second Republic and, with the two royalist factions now united as

FIGURE 1.2. Napoleon III (Louis-Napoleon Bonaparte, 1808–1873), Emperor of the French from 1851 to 1871.

the "Party of Order," formed a government. Of this time, Karl Marx writes in "The 18th Brumaire of Louis Bonaparte":

> Never did [Louis-Napoleon] enjoy in fuller measure the contempt of all classes than at this period. Never did the bourgeoisie rule more absolutely; never did it more boastfully display the insignia of sovereignty.[2]

Indeed, the fashions of mid-century Parisian bourgeoisie worked hard to create boundaries of class and display. This is the period when we see not only the beginning of conspicuous consumption in all industrial societies but also the greatest differentiation in male and female fashions and an enormous difference between classes in every element of apparel: shape, fabric, decoration, color, and accessorizing. In fact, the nineteenth century saw all over Europe the invention and establishment of all manner of "traditions" of ceremony, dress, and social behavior in response to the new reality of urban life and nationalistic, centralized mass politics.

At the midpoint of his presidential term, Louis-Napoleon proposed a change in the constitution to allow him more than a single term in office. This was meant to allow him to continue his "reforms" and the fight against disorder and to combat the encroaching anarchists and socialists. On being rebuffed in his quest by parliament, he staged a coup d'état (with financing from his English mistress, Harriet Howard), dissolved the Republic in late 1851, and assumed dictatorial powers. Soon after, he declared himself Emperor of the French and, continually playing on fears of anarchy and the strong pro-Bonapartist sentiment outside the cities, submitted this decision to plebiscite and won.

The fear of anarchy and chaos, of the enemy at the doorstep, was a crucial element in his victory, and it was this fear that his regime had to seem to counterbalance:

> . . .you will comprehend why in this unspeakable, deafening chaos of fusion, revi-

> sion, prorogation, constitution, conspiration, coalition, emigration, usurpation and revolution, the bourgeois madly snorts at his parliamentary republic: "Rather an end with terror than terror without end!"[3]

Louis-Napoleon, despite his authoritarian tendencies, attempted to better the lives of the working classes, with programs in education and health care, among other things, but the breathtaking corruption of his regime and the general failure of his "trickle-down" economics to trickle down, resulted in a constant widening of the social gap between the workers and the enriched bourgeoisie.[4]

The Ghost of Fashions Past: Marie Antoinette

Louis-Napoleon's lack of legitimacy severely threatened his status as emperor. Even within the ranks of Bonapartists, there were voices grumbling that he was nowhere near the stature of his uncle, and many thought him too liberal. Others in France saw him as a usurper with no right to the title at all. To the royal families of Europe he was twice suspect: being a Napoleon meant that he could, at any moment, revive the dream of his uncle's empire. But more importantly to the deep-rooted aristocracy, Louis-Napoleon had no lineage. He was only two generations away from common blood, and worse still, from the southern island of Corsica. Corsicans, newly part of greater France, were not considered to be truly French and hence not worthy to join the ranks of the aristocracy of Paris. Not surprisingly, when Louis-Napoleon went around the courts of Europe looking for a bride, he was humiliatingly turned down by the royal families of Sweden, Spain, Portugal, Bavaria, and Russia. After being refused by three or four lesser families, Louis Napoleon decided to marry Eugénie de Montijo, a young Spanish woman of noble ancestry but rumored to have a somewhat "adventurous" background. This marriage, although the emperor declared it to be for love, was widely derided and considered embarrassing for the new French Empire, both from within and outside the court.

Eugénie, despite the wildness of her youth, took her ceremonial role as empress very seriously and quickly learned from the French the tradition of fashion as political leverage. She idolized the former queen Marie Antoinette (1755–1793), who had been executed after the French Revolution half a century before. Eugénie had good reason to feel a kinship with her unfortunate predecessor on the French throne. Both, young and pretty, came to the court at Paris into an established and very defensive elite, where they were considered outsiders and not welcome. Both had troubled marriages, and both had trouble conceiving an heir to the throne. Marie Antoinette's father-in-law, Louis XIV, had set in place very strict practices involving courtly dress and advised his young daughter-in-law to fight the ladies of the French court with fashion. Marie had, in fact, been introduced rather aggressively to the fashion codes of the French court when she was stripped of her Austrian clothes on arriving at the border to France and dressed in appropriate gowns for the court at Versailles. This was meant to symbolize the future queen's transition from an Austrian princess to being the French *dauphine* but was also a quick introduction for her to the power games involved in courtly dress and the power of fashion to direct political behavior. Antoinette's ghost, called up by Eugénie, has haunted high fashion since, along with those of Worth and Eugénie herself.

High Fashion: An Epideictic Display

Louis XIV (1638–1715) had his "fashion wars" with Charles II of England (1639–1685) when they vied to be the arbiter of men's fashion in Europe. The detail in which courtiers followed the whims of dress of these two kings is sometimes astonishing, but at the same time, it shows that the control over fashion had a much stronger political and social significance than is often realized.[5] The signals and methods have become somewhat more subtle in the intervening 350 years, but not by much. We may not have courtly living, but we can recognize in fashionable gatherings what is called an *epideictic display.* This is an event that serves the purpose of communicating to the participants information concerning the size or density of the group.[6] An epideictic display can be, for example, mass dances or a pep rally or any such gathering of a social group or tribe. The display creates group solidarity at the same time as it affirms the vitality and strength of the social organization. Periodically, a group, epecially at times of uncertain future, crisis, or transition, will need to affirm its own existence in this way. Life at the courts of Europe—and particularly France—was one big epideictic display, dedicated to communicating the power of the regime to itself and those aiming to challenge it.[7] The king and other royalty were seen to be creating fashion, being both icon and arbiter. Charles II, for an illuminating example, attempted to force the development of men's fashion at his court by incorporating a less cumbersome fashion. Samuel Pepys wrote on October 18, 1666:

> To Court, it being the first time his Majesty put himself solemnly into the Eastern fashion of vest, changing doublet, stiff collar, bands and cloak, into a comely dress after the Persian mode, with girdles of straps, and shoestrings and garters into buckles, of which some were set with precious stones, resolving never to alter it, and to leave the French mode, which had hitherto obtained to our great expense and reproach. Upon which divers courtiers and gentlemen gave his Majesty gold by way of wager that he would not persist in this resolution.[8]

The king who came out ahead in the fashion struggle would not only have the distinction of being at the center of the epideictic display at his own court but would also have the victory of being the source for the code at the center of the displays at other courts, establishing a presence, as it were, at the heart of the adversary's kingdom. In addition (and not peripherally) as Pepys points out, these garments were often bought at great expense. Establishing a local fashion meant supporting local trade. Furthermore, if the trend could be exported then local industries would benefit from the export trade. This fight was not without humor, as when Louis answered Charles's initiative with a swift "put-down." Samuel Pepys writes on November 22, 1666:

> . . . the King of France hath, in defiance to the King of England, caused all his footmen to be put into vests, and that the noblemen of France will do the like; which . . . is the greatest indignity ever done by one prince to another, and would incite a stone to be revenged.[9]

He who became the fashion arbiter of Europe would not only be strengthening his internal political status, but he would also be encouraging a strong trade in textiles, which was a leading export commodity for both nations at a time when free trade was replacing mercantilism as the guiding principle of national economics. As things went, France and England each took the prize they were entitled to; France for female attire and England for men's tailoring. The split made perfect economic sense in a free-trade market, as the French had established industries in silk, embroidery, and lace, whereas the English had developed a tradition in wool and through that an expertise in tailoring. To compete on all fronts would make less sense than specializing in the production of local commodities and then exchanging goods. Only later, when the consumer society brought the allure of variety into the market would countries begin importing goods that were also locally produced.

Despite the impression that the kings and queens were creating fashion, there were various couturiers, *modistes*, and *stylistes* behind the scenes. As the urbanization of culture progressed, the couturiers became more visible through having premises in the fashionable districts as well as developing a larger clientele among the urban elite. Dressmakers and milliners, like the artists and other creative professions of the day, were achieving greater autonomy and were becoming individual voices of authority. One must also remember that at this time manufacturing and marketing, both at the local level of individual sewing machines as well as the transnational level of international commerce and mass production of consumer goods, were undergoing a rapid transformation. The rise of an autonomous designer was called for to counterbalance the arrival of mass-produced clothing. The knowledge that the garment had been personally approved by the "master" and had been created specifically for the client, even though the design was based on a premade model, created an aura about the garment and its wearer. The signature of the designer served the same purpose as the signature of the artist on a painting—the name provides authentication. (Here are the seeds of twentieth-century branding and logo mania.)

Both Marie Antoinette and later the first Napoleon's empress, Josephine, had their *modistes*. Rose Bertin, Marie Antoinette's dressmaker, was very much in the public eye but was not considered *the* authority in the way Charles Worth and later designers would be. For cues on how to dress, the system still tended toward one looking to the icon herself rather than the designer (this tendency would continue alongside the designer culture). Fashion would appear on the iconic figure and then propagate outward to the court and the new bourgeoisie and then outward still in increasingly watered-down versions.

Ladies and Gentlemen: Fashion and Symbols

In 1855, after some political back-and-forth, Queen Victoria and Prince Albert of Britain welcomed Napoleon and Eugénie to a full state visit to England (Figure 1.3). It was during

FIGURE 1.3. Queen Victoria and Prince Albert with their children. Portrait by Winterhalter.

this visit to the court of Victoria that Eugénie came into her own as a fashion icon. She and Victoria became instant and firm friends. From Victoria, Eugénie learned methods of behaving like true royalty, and Victoria, who had until then been the fashion icon for European high-fashion, was inspired by Eugénie's style and the fashions she wore. Eugénie may have brought in her vast luggage the first cage crinolines seen in England. She had recently adopted and popularized instantly at her own court the new cage crinoline, which allowed dresses to become wider and more voluminous than ever, by replacing heavy petticoats with a lightweight steel frame.

Eugénie's visit actually had a rather unfortunate beginning, as it was found upon arrival at Windsor Castle that that her hairdresser, Felix, and her mountain of luggage had somehow been left behind in London. After some hysteria, she borrowed a gown from one of her ladies-in-waiting, who also helped her with a simple styling of her hair. (Meanwhile

Felix, no less hysterical, was at the train station threatening to kill himself if he were not taken to Windsor immediately.) As it turned out, Eugénie without her luggage thereby appeared with elegant simplicity, which was in marked contrast to the English ladies' overloaded style. She created a lasting impression on her hosts and won the fashion contest in the first round.

Being held up to scrutiny by Queen Victoria herself and meeting the approval of the most powerful court in Europe was a great coup and a large step toward legitimacy. And it was not only Eugénie who achieved greater social status. Queen Victoria had admitted Napoleon III into the fold of European royalty by conferring on him the Most Noble Order of the Garter, the highest order of the English honors system.[10] On exiting the throne room at Windsor after the ceremony, Napoleon whispered to Victoria: "At last, I am a gentleman."[11] Napoleon and Eugénie returned to France greatly empowered at home and abroad.

The Role of Princess Pauline Metternich

Having set the stage, we come back to the point of our beginning. Early in 1860, Charles Worth's wife, Marie, took sketches of her husband's dresses to Princess Metternich, a friend and confidant of the empress. Pauline Metternich had arrived in Paris the year before, the wife of the Austrian ambassador, who was also her uncle. The Austrians had great political ambitions related to France and the Metternich's wasted no time in establishing themselves. Pauline quickly established herself as a central figure in Parisian social life, with the Austrian embassy becoming the place where "everybody" met. She had a very low tolerance for boredom, which resulted in her being wildly outspoken and considered eccentric, at least by the standards of the times. At the same time she was considered, even by her detractors, as intelligent, extremely elegant, and highly fashionable, despite being described by those being generous toward her as "plain." Others, less generous, called her "hideously ugly" or worse.[12] She said of herself, "I may look like a monkey, but at least I'm a fashionable monkey."[13] Her antics, such as smoking cigars, singing show tunes, and deliberately making inappropriate comments at high-society occasions must have struck a chord with Eugénie's youthful mischievousness. The empress needed someone at court who could provide some excitement and energy, and Pauline's powerful political and social background made her a valuable resource and advisor. The Metternichs quickly became close to the Napoleon and Josephine, and Pauline advised Eugénie on all matters regarding fashion, entertainment, and social life in general and more. The larger motive was, of course, the establishing and maintaining of Austrian influence in the French court. One of the empress's biographers writes that the Eugénie saw only and heard only through the princess's eyes and ears and then goes on to say that Pauline Metternich was "the evil genius of the imperial Court."[14] Be that as it may, Metternich involved herself so closely in day-to-day affairs, very likely realizing that the empress needed all the help she could get in the fashion wars and other maneuvering at court. After all, Marie Antoinette had been an Austrian princess, and the Metternichs would have known that history well. She was very probably not, as was implied, a spy for Austria in the strictest sense, but being the ambassador's wife and literally having Austrian ears and eyes at the center of French politics, she could not have been considered anything but a well-placed agent by the Austrian government in a period that closely followed a French-Austrian war. Charles and Marie Worth, following court gossip from their less highly placed clients, must have realized that dressing Metternich would be a step toward dressing the empress. It is difficult not to suspect that Metternich was herself heavily and politically invested in her own decision to bring Worth to the attention of the empress.

Eugénie's Legacy: The Hundred Years' Fashion

In 1860, the Empire was at its peak but Eugénie's fashions were not. Her success at the court of Queen Victoria may have brought on something of a fixation, and she was extremely reluctant to abandon the crinoline. After all, it was *her* fashion. But by 1860, when Europe had become completely obsessed with fashion, both dressmakers and cognoscenti were wishing the crinoline away. Impractical from the beginning, it had ballooned to a size beyond ridiculous, and it was time for a change. The crinoline was on its way out, one way or another. If the change did not come from the empress, this would be a blow to her image and authority.

Under Metternich's guidance, Eugénie's use of fashion as a political tool reflects an instinct for manipulation of public opinion that any seasoned politician would be proud of. Eugénie, who admired Marie Antoinette, took the lessons from her experience and applied them not only to the imperial court but, as the sphere of influence was now outside court circles, to all of high society. One can only guess as to how calculated a move this was, but in anointing Worth as her designer, Eugénie established a system that was much more powerful than Marie Antoinette's or Louis XIV's. It was arguably the most successful endeavor of her reign. In the Second Empire, we can see the beginning of much that has been, for better or for worse, the world of high fashion in the Western hemisphere. The fashion system that grew around Eugénie and Worth was so stable that it is possible to speak, as the French philosopher Gilles Lipovetsky does, of "a hundred years' fashion."[15]

An Englishman in Paris

The history of Charles Worth's youth (Figure 1.4) and first year in Paris is unclear. Most of the information about him comes from himself or from his sons, and much has been mythologized or at least is described largely in romantic hindsight. What is written in later years is also very reverential and often anecdotal, leaving one to read between the lines as well as one can. What is known is that he was born in 1825 and apprenticed in the drapery trade in London from the age of 12. As he developed his early practical knowledge of fabrics and fashion, he would visit the newly opened National Gallery in London, and there he developed an interest in classical painting and the ladies' costumes of bygone eras that would inform his sensibilities throughout his career.

Fashions in London during Worth's apprenticeship were less than exciting, with the ladies going about in poke bonnets and shawls (Figure 1.5). This was the age of Dickens, and the English were going through a transformation of morals that would create what later would be termed the "Victorian" mode. The customers the young Worth would have waited on in his early years in London would have been looking for fabric for a dress that they would wear out, and then the material would be used for lining, or perhaps it would be passed on to a servant or a poor relation. That's not to say that "fashion" as we know it was not pursued, but if Englishwomen wished to do so, London was not the ultimate destination. Paris was the place to go. Lady Margaret (Gardiner) Blessington wrote in 1841:

> The woman who wishes to be a philosopher must avoid Paris! Yesterday I entered it, caring or thinking as little of la mode as if there were no such tyrant; and lo! to-day, I found myself ashamed, as I looked from the Duchess de Guiche, attired in her be-

coming and pretty *peignoir à la neige* and *chapeau du dernier goût,* to my own dress and bonnet, which previously I had considered very wearable, if not very tasteful.

Our first visit was to Herbault's, the high-priest of the Temple of Fashion at Paris; and I confess, the look of astonishment which he bestowed on my bonnet did not help to reassure my confidence as to my appearance.

The Duchesse, too quick-sighted not to observe his surprise, explained that I had been six years absent from Paris, and only arrived the night before from Italy. I saw the words *à la bonne heure* [just in the nick of time] hovering on the lips of Herbault, he was too well-bred to give utterance to them, and immediately ordered to be brought forth the choicest of his hats, caps, and turbans.

Oh, the misery of trying on a new mode for the first time, and before a stranger! . . .

Here Fashion is a despot, and no one dreams of evading its dictates.[16]

FIGURE 1.4. An artistically casual Charles Worth ca. 1864, at the height of the Second Empire.

Worth arrived in Paris in 1845 and was soon employed at Maison Gagelin, one of the "temples of fashion." On the basis of his learning in London, he was put in charge of fabric sales. Worth would have learned the style and manner of the French merchants, so different from the manner in London, and later after setting up his own *maison,* Worth became notorious in the English and French press for his haughty style toward his clients. However, the following text, also from Lady Blessington, shows that Worth's autocratic style was simply a focusing of Parisian tradition to which he had already become accustomed at Gagelin:

In Paris, the tradesman assumes the right of dictating to the taste of his customers; in London, he only administers to it. Enter a Parisian shop, and ask to be shewn velvet, silk, or riband, to assort with a pattern you have brought of some particular colour or

> quality, and the mercer, having glanced at it somewhat contemptuously, places before you six or eight pieces of a different tint and texture.
>
> . . . Similar treatment awaits you in every shop; the owners having, as it appears to me, decided on shewing you only what *they* approve, and not what you seek. The women of high rank in France seldom, if ever, enter any shop except that of Herbault, who is esteemed the *modiste, par excellence*, of Paris, and it is to this habit, probably, that the want of *bienseance* [propriety] so visible in Parisian *boutiquiers*, is to be attributed.[17]

The system at Gagelin was otherwise much the same as Worth had been accustomed to in London. The clients selected their fabrics, which would then be delivered to the couturier or dressmaker to be made into a style of madame's choosing. This system had in fact been established by law. Tailors and dressmakers had not been allowed to stock and sell fabrics and could therefore not produce ready-made models. After the abolition of corporations during the revolution in 1791, this restriction allowed, in effect, the "fashioning" of fabrics into ready-made garments. This was first introduced into mass production for the lower classes. Worth, however, saw the possibility of bringing this system into the trade of luxury goods.[18]

At Maison Gagelin, Worth met a young lady who was to become his wife in 1851, Marie Vernet. They worked as a team; she would wear the gowns he had devised and advise him on their fit and construction. Visiting ladies would order what they saw her wearing, bringing the business into Gagelin, rather than have the store simply supply the fabric. Worth would persuade his most fashionable clients to wear new styles to important social functions, attracting attention to client and designer at the same time. This system of theirs proved so successful that Worth suggested to Mssrs. Gagelin and Opigez that a dressmaking department be set up within their establishment. They were not excited but allowed Worth and Marie to continue as a department within the shop. Marie's involvement in the shop increased, and the year of her marriage to Charles, 1851, was also the year of Napoleon's ascendancy to emperor. However, the couple's relationship with Gagelin deteriorated in the following years. They were overworked, and their contribution to the success of the business was not acknowledged, nor was their family situation accommodated. In 1856 Worth teamed up with a Swede by the name of Otto Bobergh, who, like himself, came from the drapery trade. The partners set up shop in the Rue de la Paix as Worth et Bobergh. A number of customers followed Worth from Gagelin, but as they would not pay Gagelin prices for a dress Worth made under his own label, the business started slowly.

Business continued at a modest pace for three years, and then Princess Pauline von Metternich arrived in Paris with a bang. The collaborators thought that perhaps this could be a break for Maison Worth et Bobergh. And so, early in 1860, Marie Worth set off to see the Princess with an album of designs.

FIGURE 1.5. Evening dress, with extravagant hats, from La Belle Assemblée, 1829.

High Fashion as Ritual

What took place in the 1860s set up a system that is still resonating today. The contradiction that is at the heart of the difficulty experienced by high-fashion design today originated there: A discipline that presents itself as constantly in renewal and constantly forward looking is ever more entrenched in its past. To understand this contradiction, we need to look at how high fashion fits into the creation of human society. Let us step back again from the scene of the Second Empire and observe the formation of its cult of fashion.

{ LOOKING FORWARD LOOKING BACK }

High Fashion: A State of Constant Contradiction?

The course of this history is not always one of linear progress "forward" from some point or another, but rather a journey back and forth across the years. The history of the hundred years' fashion is a panorama: one can look here and there, back and forth, and create

† Each chapter of this book contains a "Looking Forward Looking Back" box like this one. They contain asides that refer to points forward or backward or both on the timeline of the story. In this way they draw attention to how the story of the hundred years' fashion continually loops back on itself.

a big picture where the elements of one period connect to those of another, and these then set up a third. Each generation reacts to the previous one and creates its own version of events, but the creation itself is directed by the same set of human responses, and so history is repeated with new players and new technology but the same themes. High fashion as a historical and cultural entity has in this way a contradiction at its core. The cult of high fashion that came into being in the nineteenth century was so strongly married to the values of that particular aristocratic society that the subsequent history has been continual reevaluation and reaction to that relationship. High fashion is constantly in a state of attempting to come to an agreement with its past that will allow it to move beyond its origins as a service to aristocratic society. But it has been able to do this only by constantly going back to the aristocratic ideals, gender roles, and class distinctions that owned it at the beginning.

Thus is the inherent contradiction of a discipline that proposes to be constantly in a state of creative renewal: it periodically revives itself by looking back and revisiting bygone places and times. Occasional bursts of modernist thinking or revolutionary destruction is answered with a calming reactionary move that, like Worth's original purpose, purports to bring society back into line.

However, to make matters more confusing, these "times gone by," having been filtered through two or three generations, and may never actually have existed except as their own myth describes them. The 1920s through the 1950s have been especially mythologized in this way with the help of film and television programs. Also, more recently, times and places have been so thoroughly mined and mixed up in the search for the "next new thing" that even the idea of cyclical renewal of periods seems to be losing ground as a tactic. For example, the 1980s have attempted to "come back" so frequently in fashion shows that one wonders whether, apart from a brief rest in the 1990s, they can be said ever to have left. Indeed, the linear path of the fashion itself seems to be breaking down as the substructure of its origins is fragmented this way.

Oddly enough, in the rising markets of the newly capitalistic countries of the East, the "times gone by" also tend to reference a national history, culture, and lifestyle that either never existed or were at least completely irrelevant to anyone's experience, the lifestyle of a colonial caste or a supposed capitalist enemy. Yet the cult of high fashion persists and is vibrant in these countries.

High-fashion design lives in a state of constant contradiction, where the headlong rush into the past is its vision of the future, and its reality is only the one it makes for itself—all the while presenting itself as a discipline that is forward-looking and vitally connected to the people on the street. It is worth considering that the opposite state of affairs would probably be out of synch. Personally, our present is continually remade by reference to our individual pasts. This is affirming and secure and grounds us in the world. Meanwhile, our personal reality is just as much the image we present to the world as the inner persona we carry around. This is how civil society operates, and after all, all social conventions are precisely that: conventions. Perhaps the only problem with the contradiction of high fashion is that it cannot sustain itself. It works if there is a relevant past to work with and an agreement on the collective reality of society. However, it would seem that we have arrived at a point where we have neither.

At the heart of human society is ritual behavior. The daily rituals we perform are not ritualistic in the religious sense (although some can be) but are modes of behavior that allow us to navigate society without conflict. We say "good morning" and hold open doors for each other, we sit in assigned places and not in others, we stand in line, we dress according to the customs of place and occasion, and so on. All this allows us to move through our days without continually needing to check our stance against the behavior of the people around us.

A society as a whole also needs such fallbacks to orderly and familiar behavior at times of transition and change. Codes of behavior and dress provide a system of signals that allow for the maintenance of what passes for normalcy during such times. If signals of social status are uncertain or class distinctions are becoming unclear because of new arrivals or economic changes, a rigorously applied dress code and modes of civility can provide security and allow an ordering to take place. The courtly fashions of Europe were precisely a response of this kind to the disorder that continually threatened the old system, as cities and industrialization changed the shape of society. The rigors of clothing oneself to conform were the price to pay for a known place in the world for an individual. Ultimately, the group, the class, the "inner circle" could then be secure in the knowledge that they belonged.

Liminality and Communitas

The two problems of Napoleon's court, the establishment of order and the proof of legitimacy, were addressed admirably by the use of fashion. To fully understand this role of fashionable apparel, one must first understand two concepts: liminality and communitas.

Liminality

Liminality is the situation of being in between, a moment of transition. The word itself derives from the Latin word *limen* or "threshold." An individual may be in a liminal state in a ritual situation when the person is in neither one state nor the other. For example, during a marriage ceremony, the crucial moment is the liminal moment before the words "I now pronounce you married" are spoken. Between the "I do" and this pronouncement, the couple is in a liminal state. It is a state of tension where things could go either way (a plot point in several movies . . .). For societies, liminal moments occur during political or technological transitions. These moments can be equally slippery. For this reason, liminal moments in societies are often times of tension, excitement, and sometimes turmoil. A society that is moving from one state to another, for example in legitimately installing a new government or radically changing its laws, has strict methods for doing so. The new government has a period between elections and taking power in which power is transferred according to customs and laws that ensure a smooth transition. A ceremony is often performed to symbolize the power transfer. Presidents of the United States are sworn in out in the open, in a public show, on the steps of the Capitol Building, and government officials hand over their keys in front of the assembled staff of their agencies. The power transfer is made in public and visibly, with symbolic gestures and words, which allow the public as well as the power groups involved to witness and accept the change. Although the change may already have taken place legally, the acceptance of the fact is not fully recognized. The President-elect is not the President of the United States until the swearing-in is complete. The words, gestures, and comforting ritual transfer the society over the threshold, out of the liminal state.

The Problem of Communitas

In looking at the developments in fashion in society from the Age of Worth onward, one may see a tension between the will to achieve order and structure and the human need for transcending social boundaries. This tendency toward the abolition of class distinction is toward what sociologists and anthropologists call communitas, a state of equality and communion. One sees this in many religious rituals where the individual is subsumed in the group, but also in carnivals and other situations where a group is together in an action outside its normal mode, where class distinction does not matter. The group or society is in a liminal state. This, of course, is a dangerous place for a society to be in, as anything can happen. When there are no rules, the slip into anarchy and chaos can be quick. This is why the liminal moments of society are ordered through rules and rituals.

If the nineteenth-century developments in socialism, anarchism, and the arts are read as a movement toward communitas, one could say that the use of fashion at the French court was a move that went as far as possible in the diametrically opposite direction. The dress code literally mirrored Turner's suggestion that "Those who would maximize communitas often begin by minimizing or even eliminating the outward marks of rank."[19] The dress code of high-society Paris maximized structure by maximizing the outward marks of rank. It also maximized the difference in gender. Men's clothing had been streamlined and stripped of overt decoration half a century before, but the heavily militarized code of the Second Empire resulted in men being bedecked in medals and signals of actual military rank. The women wore their family's wealth as much as possible on wide and enveloping silhouettes, and much is made of the expense of these in the various journals and diaries from the period. But high society had the need "to doff the masks, cloaks, apparel and insignia of status from time to time even if only to don the liberating masks of liminal masquerade."[20] Too much rigidity requires a controlled departure from norms every now and then. Frequent masked balls served the purpose of a carnival-like breakdown of hierarchy at the court of Napoleon. However, the masques themselves were also subverted to the anti-communitas cause. At masquerades, the ostentation was just as extravagant, if not more so. At one ball in 1863, by invitation of the empress, the 300-odd ladies present were dressed by Worth, and the total cost of the gowns was $200,000[21] ($5 million in current purchasing power[22] or approximately $16,000 each, showing that prices for high fashion have at least not changed much[23]). The empress arrived to at least one ball dressed as Marie Antoinette, and the Princess Metternich channeled Marie Antoinette at another masque, wearing a milkmaid's outfit, complete with silver pails slung over her shoulder. The emperor tended always to dress for masked balls in the same costume, a "domino," which was a basic black cloak and Venetian-style masque, and was thus instantly—and very likely deliberately—recognizable although most everyone played along and pretended not to recognize him. To allow the crack in the façade to open by masking the emperor would have been too dangerous, too close to communitas and carnival. The emperor must remain the emperor, even when masked.

That the masques would be used in this way to telegraph a connection to the past, specifically to the recent difficult past of pre-Revolutionary France, shows a degree of calculation that is rather overlooked in biographies of the imperial couple, which, if not completely overly reverential, tend to focus rather heavily on the emperor's lack of sophistication and the impetuousness of the empress. Perhaps it was the Metternichs' influence, but the method in the madness seems too strong to be anything but calculated.

The anthropologist Victor Turner suggests that the basic and perennial human social problem is to discover the balance between belonging to a group and establishing one's individuality at a specific time and place.[24] In the story of the hundred years' fashion, we see this problem played out: At the court of Napoleon III and Eugénie, proper dress subordinated people's need for communitas to that of well-defined structure. Meanwhile, the tendency toward individual expression that was emerging in arts and politics was working to undermine the order of society. Each successive generation would swing the pendulum a little further, leading to the system as it is today, when the high-fashion statement and individualistic expression have nearly met full circle without a societal model in which to fit. The ritual behavior is still there, even though its purpose may be obscured.

Ritual Defined

In order to set up the discussion in the following chapters, we will examine high fashion in the context of ritual before moving ahead. This allows the specifically economic and commercial side of the discussion to be set aside in order that a problem that deals directly with human identity in society can be dealt with in terms of our relationship to and within society. To begin, let us see what we find if we apply the anthropologist Roy A. Rappaport's definition of ritual to high-fashion design. In *Ritual and Religion in the Making of Humanity,* he argues that ritual denotes "the performance of more or less invariant sequences of formal acts and utterances not entirely encoded by the performers" and then goes on to say that this "logically entails the establishment of convention, the sealing of social contract" and that ritual is "the social act basic to humanity."[25]

For Rappaport, there are five features that constitute the ritual form:

1. Encoding by other than performers
2. Formality (as decorum or adherence to form)
3. Invariance (more or less)
4. Performance
5. Formality (vs. physical efficacy)

Let us look at each in turn and determine how high fashion may be read into the ritual form.

The First Feature of Ritual:
The Encoding by Other Than Performers

Rapport suggests that ritual behavior involves actions that are performed in accordance with rules laid down by others. Here is one of the more interesting twists to the development of the designer as an authority during the Second Empire: The authority was separated from the icon.

In earlier centuries, the encoding of a fashion would take place by the example of an iconic figure, usually from royalty or court circles in women's wear and additionally in military circles in men's wear. The example would be noted and copied by the inner circle, and from them, a fashion would propagate outward until it reached the limits of its efficacy, practical, economic, or otherwise. The encoding was therefore more collective and the changes of fashion through individual adaptation much more common.

The Second Empire brought a new more effective power into play with the creation of a separate authority, in the form of the designer. This development created a voice that could issue directives in the form of models and designs that could then in turn be followed "more or less punctiliously"[26] by the fashion icon or muse, and the fashionable community. The icon would then be a safe distance from the decision in case something went wrong.

Politically, this was beneficial. There would be the inevitable detractors of any new fashion, who would wish to make political gain by applying the kind of criticism that was leveled at Marie Antoinette and Eugénie. This now had to be at least shared, if not wholly laid at the feet of the designer. The icon could be seen to be another "fashion victim," and of course be faulted for that, but could not be criticized for the creation of the fashion itself, only its use.

It is worth noting that Worth himself never gave any indication that he was aware of his own political or social significance. He seems to have been unable or very reluctant to discuss any of his inner workings. When pressured to discuss this topic in an interview in 1871, he repeatedly digressed and then brushed it off: "Perhaps I'm too busy to make observations of that sort." His wife, however, interjected with a laugh, "I suspect I know more about all that than my husband does." Worth then rejoined, "Ah, but it is I, and not you, who am being examined, and I mean to keep the answering to myself."[27] And he did. It is a shame that none of Madame Worth's thoughts on the matter were ever recorded.

However, Worth was very aware of his authority. He later said:

> . . . the women who come to me want to ask for my ideas, not to follow their own. They deliver themselves to me in confidence, and I decide for them; that makes them happy. If I tell them they are suited, they need no further evidence. My signature to their gown suffices!

As Worth himself noted, it *really* isn't about the clothes. The authority of the designer, certified by the designer's label, is all that is needed. With his sign, the ladies, upholding all formality, could proceed to enter society with the knowledge that they belonged, and society—whatever it thought of them privately—had to respond by opening the door.

The interviewer Adolphus went on to ask whether there were ever any rebels among the clients who claim the right of personal invention and choice. Worth replied,"Choice? Yes, certainly; but only between my various suggestions. And very few do even that; most of them leave it all to me. But as for invention, no. My business is not only to execute but especially to invent."[28]

The Second Feature of Ritual: Formality (Decorum)

Rappaport's discussion of ritual defines formality as decorum or adherence to form.[29] It goes precisely to the point made previously: The clothes are not just clothes; they are signs. It seems obvious that high-fashion apparel in society is an adherence to formality and decorum, especially in the period under discussion. The late nineteenth century is, after all, the period that provided the modern world with nearly all the dress codes for the events of great formality that Rappaport mentions: inaugurations, coronations, dubbings, and marriages, to which I would add funerals, debutante balls, fine dining, and diplomatic receptions. In these events, the invariant aspects become dominant or, as Rappaport puts it, they themselves become operative. The gown that many young women of the early twenty-first century imagine wearing on their wedding day retains the aesthetics if not the shape of the nineteenth-century gown. Without the dress, the wedding is of a different context. Black tie is still de rigueur code for state events, awards ceremonies, debutante balls, and even senior proms. Early in 2007, for example, President George W. Bush, famous for informality, felt compelled to don full white-tie attire to host a dinner for Queen Elizabeth II.

A point to consider may be that during the Second Empire in France, just as in Victorian England, the codes of decorum in dress and formal behavior were numerous, rigid, and invariable, but also relatively new. Louis XIV had set in place a strict code of court behavior, and the bourgeoisie quickly followed in outdoing the courts all over Europe in adherence to the form of clothing and behavior. By the time of the Second Empire, the English had already become the leaders of "proper" behavior. (Byron called the period the "Age of Cant," meaning pretention or hypocrisy.) Their feeling was that there could be no improvising, no spontaneity in this newly formed urban society if it were to survive. The British had a fear of revolution and invasion from France during the period 1789 to 1835, which added to the urgency that was also felt in France and led to a tightening of morals and delineation of "acceptable" behavior.[30]

The formality of court life in France and its ritual of clothing are so well described in a section from the memoirs of Lillie Moulton (later Lillie de Hegermann-Lindencrone), one of Worth's American clients in Paris, that it is worth quoting wholesale (Figure 1.6). She describes a stay at the Emperor's autumn palace at Compiegne:

FIGURE 1.6. A loyal Worth customer from America: Lillie de Hegermann-Lindencrone (née Moulton) ca. 1870.

I am beginning to learn the ways of the life of Compiegne.

At nine o'clock our tea, coffee, or chocolate (as we choose) is brought to our rooms by a white-stockinged and powdered valet.

If you are very energetic, you can go for a walk in the park, or (as I did to my sorrow) a visit to the town. But you are not energetic more than once, because you do not find it worth your while, as you must hurry back, and change your dress and shoes before appearing in the salon a little before eleven o'clock, the hour for breakfast. You remain in the same dress until you change for dinner or the Empress's tea. You find every morning in your room a programme for the day . . .

So you know what to wear and what to expect; but the invitation to tea is always made by the Empress's private *huissier* [usher], who knocks at your door toward five o'clock and announces, "Her Majesty the Empress desires your presence at five o'clock."

The *toilette de rigueur* [required dress] for this occasion is a high-necked long silk dress, and you generally remain until six o'clock.

If you are not summoned to her Majesty's tea, tea is served in your own salon, where you can invite people to take tea with you, or you are invited to take tea with other people.

If there is a hunt, the ladies wear their green-cloth costumes and the gentlemen wear their hunting gear (a red coat, velvet cap, and top-boots). The gentlemen wear *culottes courtes* [knee breeches] the first evening they arrive, and on such fine occasions as the *curee*, and at the Gala Theater, where outsiders are invited; otherwise they always wear *pantalon collant*, [pantaloons: tight-fitting long pants] which is the most unbecoming thing one can imagine in the way of manly attire.

> At six o'clock you dress for dinner, always in ball dress, and a little before seven you meet in the Grande Salle des Fetes. At dinner the guests are placed according to their rank, but at *dejeuner* [lunch] there is no ceremony, and you engage your partner after your heart's desire.[31]

The Third Feature of Ritual: Invariance (More or Less)

Ritual does not allow much variance. Small details may be altered: You may, for example, light candles during an invocation, but how many is up to you. Lillie Moulton's description of a day at Compiegne illustrates not only the formality but also the invariance of the usage of high-fashion clothing. High fashion operates within extremely invariant boundaries. However, within these boundaries there is variation, and often quite a bit of it. One may wear a variation of fabrics in a variety of colors. There may be a number of possible accessories or a couple of possible variations on a basic theme in style or form, but it is these and *only* these. The system of sanctified designer added the dimension that new fashions would replace old at specific times under a strict regimen of shows and methods. This would be done not by implication and gradual acceptance, but overseen by a governing authority, allowing tradition and market demands to balance. The variance of execution *within* the invariant frame of fashion is necessary to outweigh the uniformity that would otherwise result. If everyone were exactly the same, this would rob the total picture of its richness, thereby diminishing the power of the epideictic display. The power of complete uniformity does not contribute to the strength of society, as complete uniformity in dress is a form of ritualized power from above and therefore the uniform display is a display of the power of a hierarchy or individual leader. It is militarily or politically extreme. The power of a group display of fashion comes from the statement that the group is together, but that each member of the group has it within his or her power to accumulate and display the necessary wealth and power individually. But here also is the necessary balance between adherence to the group and the assertion of individuality that would later explode the system, once the high-society group itself diminished. In the late twentieth century, once fashion became a fully personal statement, there was nowhere to go with that but to extremes.

High fashion is also highly intolerant of imperfection: The fashion *faux pas* ("false step") is deadly. Those who cannot perform the dance leave the floor. Amusing examples of missteps abound, but a tragic revealing example of how the faux pas relates to invariance and how this was used to close ranks in Eugénie's court concerns the Empress Carlota of Mexico, who was born Princess Marie Charlotte Amélie Augustine Victoire Clémentine Léopoldine of Belgium. She and her husband, Maximillian, became Empress and Emperor of Mexico when Napoleon and Eugénie attempted to gain ground in North America by setting up a puppet regime while the United States was busy with its Civil War. Carlota and Maximillian fought an insurgency with too few French troops and were summarily abandoned by Napoleon and Eugénie, who had no more troops to send. As the situation deteriorated in Mexico, Carlota returned to France to beg (quite literally) for help from the imperial couple in Paris. An all too loud and visible reminder of their failed venture, she was considered an embarrassment, especially because in her anguish and distress, she ignored the rules of dress and propriety. Eugénie and Louis-Napoleon avoided her as much as they could, while the court came to their defense, discrediting the "unwelcome visitor" by gossiping critically about her lack of style: "Her dress indeed, had not been made by a Parisian couturier, but hurriedly by some unheard of Mexican dressmaker on the death of her father King Leopold. Her white hat, too, was stiff and heavy, and each day she wore it as the distracted Ophelia might have worn a hat; it appeared to have been dropped on her head and left where it fell without further thought."[32]

There was no help to be had. Carlota went off to Rome to seek help from the Pope. The imperial couple went off to their summer retreat at Biarritz and then to Compiegne for their autumn house parties. Carlota's anxiety caused her to go insane soon after arriving in Rome, and she lived for another 40 years, never knowing that her husband had been executed by the Mexican insurgents under Juarez.

The Fourth Feature of Ritual: Performance

"Unless there is a performance there is no ritual," says Rappaport, who then goes on to explain that the defining relationship of the members of a congregation to the event for which they are present is participation.[33] The passage from Lillie de Hegermann-Lindencrone's memoir above illustrates well the performance aspect of dressing in society. Each event had a prescribe manner of dress, to the degree that a stay at Compiegne must have seemed like a theatrical performance, going from costume change to costume change.

Traveling to and staying at Compiegne was in itself part of a performance. Each of the factions vying for power in France had its autumn house party. While the emperor and Eugénie entertained at Compiegne, the Bourbons would gather at Lucerne around the Count de Chambord "whose house-parties were in such contrast with [those of] the usurper [Napoleon]; here the atmosphere was dignified and somewhat melancholy, and dress counted for very little. At Compiegne, however, dress was of immense importance." A stay at Compiegne gave prestige, and being able to accept the invitation was proof of wealth and social standing, especially for married men.[34] This was in large part due to the enormous cost of the wardrobe required. Lillie Moulton, on her next invitation, went directly to Worth and ordered 18 dresses for her week, to the consternation of her father-in-law, who complained that he bore all the cost and had none of the fun. (In later contrast, Jacqueline Kennedy's father-in-law happily paid the couturier bills during J. F. K.'s run for the presidency, probably better aware of what he was buying.)

The Fifth Feature of Ritual: Formality (versus Physical Efficacy)

Clothing in its basic state operates on a practical level: It covers; it provides shelter and warmth. It operates with matter and energy in accordance with physical laws of cause and effect. This, as Rappaport points out, is *technique*, and quite precisely what ritual does *not* do.[35] Fashionable clothing has, on the other hand, throughout history blatantly ignored practicality, getting its results instead by appealing to the shock-effect of physical hindrance, indulgence, and waste. High fashion has also nearly always been heavily involved with sexual display, operating on a straightforward emotional plane or, if you will, going directly to the central nervous system for its response. High fashion is nearly pure spectacle and, under Rappaport's definition of the fifth feature of ritual, falls squarely into the realm of operating on the physical with the emotional and the emotional with the physical.

Second Empire Fashion: A Religion in Adaptation?

The sanctification of the designer as authority may be seen as an evolutionary change in the fashion system of the eighteenth and early nineteenth centuries. Rappaport maintains that evolutionary changes take place in subsystems in order to maintain more basic aspects of the larger system.[36] To get to the root of the changes, one must answer his question, "What does this change maintain unchanged?" In other words, we must identify the basic aspects of the system and then consider the effect of the change in authority on them.

The basic change in the Second Empire was the relative status of client and couturier–the couturier became "designer" (although this term wasn't used until later), an advisor to an iconic figure, but also accessible to the cognoscenti if so allowed.

The location of the source of authority (apparent and otherwise) had to change in order to maintain the exclusivity of high fashion in an age of mass production. The ultimate authority now is with the designer, but can be fluid between the icon and the designer, where the icon is the designer's muse. However, toward lesser devotees, the designer's authority is absolute.

By separating the fashion arbiter (Worth) from the fashion icon (Eugénie), another layer between the public at large and the authority was placed into the system. When icon and authority were one and the same (Marie Antoinette), all one had to do was look at the icon and imitate the style to the best of one's abilities. A reasonable approximation of the style would allow one to be acceptable. Now, with a designer dictating the "look," one must either go with the designer or be outside the circle. *What* you wore eventually became less important than *who* was on the label. The label in the clothes then became the ticket to society.

Design, therefore, was *reified* (Latin: res = thing, literally "thing-ified") right at its beginning. Fashion became commodity as soon as the market was available for it. However, the system had a clever twist: The fact that fashion was now a commodity in the marketplace did not matter because high prices ensured exclusivity. And in case that did not suffice, Worth would accept clients only by introduction anyway. He would turn clients away if they were somehow crass, not the right sort, or too independent.[37] The social embarrassment of being turned away was a very effective tool for keeping the clients docile to his whims (not to mention Eugénie's and Pauline Metternich's!)

Summing this point up brings us to a most important part of this discussion: By changing the fashion system into a designer-client system, the hierarchy of fashion development–that is, top-down–was maintained, and in maintaining the top-down hierarchy, the control over the self-affirming epideictic displays and the validation of its participants was firmly established in the hands of the iconic figure—Eugénie herself. It was in her hands to sanctify the designer she chose, and once she had done so, his authority gave her legitimacy. Control over fashion became power over society.

The sanctification of the designer, who then in turn invests the icon with visible status, is a closed power-loop. The sanctifying of Worth certified his directives, certified him as an authority, and validated the mythology that was instantly created both of him and of his designs. Sanctity in this way stabilizes the conventions of societies.[38] For this reason, high fashion began by referencing the (idealized if not imagined) past and continued to do so, with the occasional and brief modernist counter-attack, until high fashion ran out of past to reference, when there was no more society to dress, and began referencing itself and its own mythic image in ever tightening circles.

Ritual versus Sincerity

In memoirs dictated to a very sympathetic minister of the Republic who succeeded her, Eugénie de Montijo, Empress of the French, quoted the following lines from Hamlet, before justifying the actions in Mexico that led to the execution of Emperor Maximillian and the tragedy of Empress Carlota. This was her favorite quotation, her "motto":

> This above all: to thine own self be true,
> And it must follow, as the night the day,
> Thou canst not then be false to any man
> (*Hamlet*, Act I, Scene 3)

She quoted these lines, presumably hoping that future readers would be affected in the same way the literary critic Lionel Trilling suggests we should be affected in our opinion of Polonius, the hypocritical, busybody of a character who speaks them. Trilling suggests "that Polonius has had a moment of self-transcendence, of grace and truth. He has conceived of sincerity as an essential condition of virtue and has discovered how it is to be attained."[39]

Be that as it may, it may perhaps have been more appropriate for the empress to begin quoting two paragraphs earlier in Polonius' speech. There she would have captured the full contradiction between ritual and sincerity that her reign left as its legacy in the world of fashion:

Costly thy habit as thy purse can buy,
But not express'd in fancy; rich, not gaudy;
For the apparel oft proclaims the man;
And they in France of the best rank and station
Are of a most select and generous chief in that.

The empress had, whatever other failings may be attributed to her and the emperor, indeed made sure that France was "of the best rank and station" in having apparel proclaim, not just the man, but society as a whole. Building on and adapting traditional court ritual in dress, with the help of her chosen designer, Charles Worth, she set in motion a fashion system that not only outlasted her and the Empire but can still be felt some 150 years later, at the beginning of the twenty-first century.

The game of fashion was familiar enough for it to be included in the platitudes of Polonius in Shakespeare's day (1564–1616). Trilling goes on to say that "it is surely no accident that the idea of sincerity, the own self, and the difficulty of knowing and showing it, should have arisen to vex men's minds in the epoch that saw the sudden efflorescence of the theatre." He then points out that society requires of us to be sincere to the point where we play the role of ourselves in daily life, "we sincerely act the part of the sincere person, with the result that a judgment may be passed upon our sincerity that is not authentic."[40] There is the dilemma of high-fashion design made personal. This game has continued to this day, and although not actually invented in the Second Empire, that is where it was honed and very nearly perfected. The late nineteenth century served to promulgate the practice of fashion awareness and increase the accessibility and availability of both the fashionable clothing and information about it through magazines and events and venues where styles could be observed, such as the balls, cafés, music halls, and Grand Exhibitions. This brought the possibility of *personae* created through clothing to the lower classes. The game today is played whether we are wearing high-fashion items or not, and we adhere to a certain set of garments appropriate to our station, workplace, or neighborhood. We choose clothing to be viewed from the outside more often than to express something from the inside, and more often than not, the clothing serves to mask the inner self. The clothing creates our own imaginary reality of our selves, which in turn becomes the perceived reality. This is so automatic in our day that it is possible many do not give it a second thought: The formation of our identity, the maintenance of it, and often the masking of it are achieved in a large measure through the textiles wrapped draped and fitted on our bodies.

The Spectacle Begins

The social theorist Guy Debord, founder of the Situationist International, in developing the notions of reification and fetishization of commodities, described our current society as "The Society of the Spectacle." He wrote in the mid-1960s that "the first stage of the economy's domination of social life brought about an evident degradation of *being* into *having*—human fulfillment was no longer equated with what one was, but with what one possessed." Following this, he said, Western society progressed to where social life, at the point when he was writing in the mid-1960s, had become so dominated by production that "all *having* must now derive its immediate prestige and its ultimate purpose from *appearances.*"[41]

High fashion came into being in order to serve the spectacle of courtly ritual in a society trying to hold onto its past. A *semblance* of order by the *appearance* of class structure through the selective *having* of the clothing was a method that worked admirably in Worth's day and still works today. However, once the society that called the couturiers into being was no more, the purpose of high fashion became only the maintenance of its own existence as part of the Society of the Spectacle. The high-fashion system managed to survive the disappearance of its initial purpose by virtue of the commercial interests it served, but as time went on, it could not continue to keep up its exclusivity in that its client base was rapidly disappearing. In the early 1960s, the first voices began to be heard declaring *couture* "dead." Despite that, half a century later, high-fashion design continues to be vital. It may not be dead, but it is definitely suffering from a severe existential crisis stemming from a lack of place in the functioning of society.

In keeping with the developments Debord describes, high-fashion design's reality has degenerated from having a vital purpose in defining class structure and being an integral part of society's self-image to being a fully fetishized commodity with no vital connection to the reality of its clientele. In other words, high fashion has fully become its own reality without an exterior reality to support it apart from that of the market for which it exists. The relationship is circular, as the discipline and the market cannot hold unless each continually reaffirms the other. The market must maintain its pressure, which drives the design, and designers must produce "the new thing" at an ever-increasing pace to feed the market. The spectacle is thus maintained, but only for its own sake, and it is this situation that produces the so-called "crisis of design" that intermittently becomes the "death of high fashion."

But observed in today's high-fashion system, the ritualistic elements are obvious if not strong. There are cyclical, repetitive events in the form of seasonal shows of collections. These are attended by initiates and devotees, who are now a mixture of film and rock celebrities and moneyed society. The designers are authorities consecrated by editors and corporate interests, who also designate and demote icons in an ever-quicker procession. There is a strong linkage to tradition and lately an elevation of past designers into a constantly referenced sainthood of sorts. However, the ever-increased speed of the cycle speaks of a problem. The rapid turnaround of styles and talent doesn't allow for the kind of slow development in which creativity thrives and the gradual breakdown of the seasonal show ritual points to a lack of connectivity to the vital currents of our culture.

The Evolving Role of High Fashion in Society

If the fashion system as set up in the mid-nineteenth century may be seen to function and evolve as ritualistic practice, the current crisis may perhaps be understood from within that frame. This may then allow for a discussion of the art and discipline, less in the realm of markets and commerce, but rather in terms that are at the core of the human experience in society. What is the ritual *for*, now that it is removed from its origin? If it is "dead" or "for nothing," then that should not lead to despair or surrender, but to the question, "How do we make it vital again?" One must realize that the question of what high-fashion design represents can be read in a wider context. There is a dilemma facing Western society and the relationships of persons in it. If Trilling's thoughts on ritual and sincerity illuminate the dilemma of high-fashion design, then Debord shines light on the corresponding dilemma of the individual who is shaped by it. Debord turns Trilling's image of us acting our sincere selves inside out, but with much the same conclusion: "At the same time [as all *being* is becoming *having*] all individual reality has become social, in the sense that it is shaped by social forces and is directly dependent on them. Individual reality is allowed to appear only if it is not actually real."[42] That is, we do not play our sincere role, we are played by the role. There is no alternative reality, and the icons and authorities multiply beyond count, appearing and vanishing from one season to the next. By framing our interaction with the illusions of individuality through fashion, the frame of designer authority, set up in 1860 and reinforced for more than 100 years, has pulled us in after it, making the illusion the only reality. The discipline of high-fashion design became so successful at maintaining its image that the image remains despite there not being anything to which the image refers.

The Four Stages of an Image

Jean Baudrillard writes in his essay "The Precession of Simulacra" that an image in society has four stages:

1. It reflects a profound reality.
2. It masks and denatures a profound reality.
3. It masks the absence of a profound reality.
4. It has no relation to any reality whatsoever: it is its own pure simulacrum.[43]

High-fashion design has long gone past his first stage of image: *reflecting profound reality*. If it indeed ever went through this phase, it did so only briefly. Perhaps this was in its transition from a craft into its modern commercial implementation following the brief discrediting of deluxe fashion after the execution of Marie Antoinette. In the early nineteenth century, Western society was attempting to find a style for itself, reflecting the political and practical necessities of the new urban societies, where the new powers were industrial money and the new democracies were creating new hierarchies. However, the discipline's beginnings in the hands of Eugénie, Pauline Metternich, and Charles Worth found it already at the stage of *masking and denaturing a profound reality*. This masking was its largest function in the Second Empire: The balls and summer gatherings all served to mask the true nature of the new urban industrial society and its separation from the old world. Once the Second Empire fell, a critical stage was reached. The high-fashion industry in Western society then served the purpose of *masking an* absence *of a profound reality*, the truth at this point being that the old world of courts and empires was to be no more. But high fashion continued to operate as if the reality were still in place. High fashion has since operated as if there is some profound reality underneath its carefully crafted and elaborate mask. Yet the only reality it had, the reality of the nineteenth century, has faded beneath it. When the image has transitioned into the third stage, it has become a *simulacrum*, an image.

Then once the absence of a profound reality could no longer be denied and while the word "death" began its annual appearance in reviews, the mask and myth *became* the reality. The frame pulled us into the image that has no relation to any reality whatsoever: High fashion points only toward itself. *It is its own pure simulacrum*. Behind the image there is not necessarily anything at all. The important thing to realize is that *it doesn't matter*. The image is everything and does not require anything. This is the road that the Second Empire pointed to. What may actually be the next leg of the journey, given that total simulacra don't seem to allow for anywhere to go, is the exploration we will now pursue by looking at the near century and a half of high fashion that followed the Second Empire.

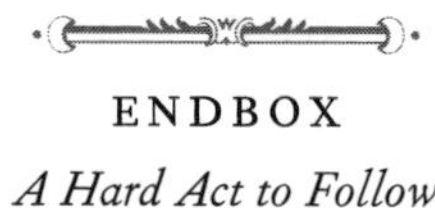

ENDBOX

A Hard Act to Follow

[Being different in order to take the business forward but at the same time staying true to its original appeal] sums up what is becoming a growing problem in the fashion business, one that is particularly evident this season. How do you step into someone else's shoes and keep their customers happy and retain the label's identity, without just churning out pastiches of what came before?

. . . It's a difficult compromise for a company: On the one hand, it wants a new and exciting designer to bring a fresh audience and interest to the label; on the other, it doesn't want some scallywag to trample all over its legacy. Givenchy has a particularly tricky history in this regard. Both Alexander McQueen and Julien Macdonald worked there, and neither seems to have particularly happy memories. The current designer, Riccardo Tisci, has alienated critics with his drop-crotch skinny trousers and gladiator sandals, which don't sit happily with the memories of the ladylike dresses that Hubert de Givenchy created for Audrey Hepburn. The reason that labels such as Givenchy were so exciting when they emerged may have been that their clothes looked so new—but that doesn't necessarily mean customers still want them to be seen as avant-garde. After all, if a designer makes an old label look too modern, it no longer looks like the label.

But if it's so tricky to carry on, why not just shut down the label when a designer leaves?

"The thing with these old houses, particularly the Parisian ones, is you already have the retail in place: the shops, the cosmetics business, the perfumes." . . . "Financially, these are very important sides to the business that no one would just shut down."

Source: Hadley Freeman. *Guardian*. March 14, 2008.

Discussion Points

1. Is it important for a label to maintain tradition?
2. Whose tradition is most likely to be maintained? The labels'? The customers'? Society's? Why?
3. Is high fashion important to today's society? To which is it more important, commercial interests or societal interests?

CHAPTER 2

An Empire of Fashion

Around the time Marie Worth visited Princess Metternich with the volume of sketches in 1860, the crinoline had reached its peak. Its volume, as well as the difficulties it posed for its wearer, was an extremely appropriate metaphor for the Second Empire's excesses and highly differentiated society. The crinoline was facing increasing ridicule in the newspapers (Figure 2.1), and it was becoming a symbol with which to criticize the ostentation and corruption of the imperial court, much in the way fashion had been the point of attack against Marie Antoinette almost a hundred years before. Fashion was, in fact, used as an avenue of criticism, as censorship of newspapers did not allow for political discourse. By discussing fashions, the writers and critics could cloak their opinions in the "frivolous" and could thereby evade the censors. The crinoline was an easy point of attack, as the empress was very attached

FIGURE 2.1. "Again a crinoline!!!!" Caricature for the feminine fashion under the Second Empire, 1852. By the mid-nineteenth century, the crinoline was widely ridiculed and was a favorite of cartoonists.

to the style, having contributed much to its rise, and was firmly indentified with it, having had such success at her first state visit to the court of Queen Victoria.

The ridicule also pointed toward the fact that Parisian society was also quite tired of the fashion. The unwieldiness of the crinoline was simply too much of a problem. This put Eugénie in a difficult position. To maintain the increasing authority she wielded in society, she needed to continue to be the leader of fashion. To initiate another fashion was difficult and could cause a loss of face if it failed, opening her up to ridicule and inviting discussion of irrelevance and illegitimacy. In addition, all the dressmakers were followers of fashion and not innovators, so choices were very limited. To continue with the crinoline was equally difficult, as the fashion would clearly be on the way out, like it or not. Odds were that some other style would appear from someone or somewhere else, with the immediate effect of undercutting the empress's authority over fashion, and with that, a significant measure of the regime's sway over society.

Control of Fashion Leads to Control of the Market

The empress's control of fashion had immediate applications beyond the ritualistic. To be in control of high fashion meant being able to manipulate demand for deluxe goods and influence the market for textiles and luxury apparel. Each dress worn by the empress would influence innumerable copies as well as the production of similar dresses for court ladies, which then again would generate other copies. With all the entertainments and gatherings of the aristocracy requiring many new outfits a day, the icon at the top of this hierarchy wielded immense influence.

Luxury Goods and the Lower Classes

The emperor presided over the industrialization of France and was of the opinion that high-class consumption was beneficial for all, as the increased trade in luxury goods would benefit the lower classes. Like later proponents of "trickle-down" economics, he believed that the increase in the manufacturing of goods, trade in raw materials, transportation, and derived industries led to greater amounts of ready money in the hands of the workers. Perhaps more importantly, the trade in textiles had been a large portion of France's economy for centuries, and the laborers in the textile mills were a large and very vocal portion of the working class. If high-society living resulted in happier workers through increased production, then those workers would be less likely to revolt against the high society and start beheading the aristocrats. For example, with the emperor's input, the empress would later wear a gown created by Worth from a rich Chinese-inspired brocade manufactured exclusively in Lyon,[1] a city where worker unrest and antimonarchic sentiment was endemic. The resulting demand for the textile doubled production in the mills of Lyon, at a time when the city was suffering from poverty due to a lack of work for its weavers.[2] The success of this strategy led to the empress's wardrobe choices becoming part of the politics of the imperial court, investing both Worth and the empress with considerable power over industrial production. The empress would call these her "political wardrobes."[3]

The Demise of the Crinoline

It is not known what sketches Marie Worth showed to the princess, nor is it clear whether they were produced by Worth himself or by his partner, Bobergh,[4] but the white and silver dress Metternich wore was a step in the direction of much needed elegant simplicity. The simplicity may have come partly from Metternich's request that the dresses cost less than 300 francs (the last time she would get a Worth dress at that price), but also from Worth's well-practiced knowledge of fabric and cut. Either way, Worth was the answer to the court's fashion dilemma. By sanctioning the authority of Worth, the empress could continue to dominate fashion without being seen as directly responsible in the way Marie Antoinette had been and Louis XIV had desired to be. Early in 1860, Charles Worth in effect became the minister for imperial fashion.

As soon as the summer arrived, Worth and Metternich agreed to get rid of the crinoline. Metternich's idea was that they would launch their first assault during the summer season. One can assume that with the court and aristocracy away from Paris, being away from the boulevards (and eyes!) of the city allowed for a greater degree of freedom and experimentation. The first change was not extreme but was very significant: The dresses were to be shortened to the point of making the ankles visible. This change could be cloaked in practicality, as the wearing of crinolines was extremely difficult on the mountain walks the empress was fond of. The empress, Metternich, and Worth quietly assembled a group of sympathetic courtiers who would all wear the walking dresses during the summer season when invited to accompany the empress on her cross-country walks (Figure 2.2). The plan was kept secret from those who would voice their disapproval. Worth designed for the empress a short crinoline dress of Scottish tartan (a nod to Queen Victoria), and over it he draped a plain overskirt, which he later said had been inspired by a peasant woman who had tied up her skirt to keep it out of the dust. With this were worn a short jacket and a small brimless hat.

FIGURE 2.2. The new style prompted by Worth and Metternich: a walking dress ca. 1860.

The dresses then appeared all at once in the various locations in which the fashionable women spent the summer. Protests and outrage over the immorality of such dress were heard, but the fashion stayed, and although it could not find its way to the streets immediately, it eventually was accepted as daywear in the cities of Europe. Metternich, Worth, and Eugénie had scored their first fashion victory, but in a revealing moment, Metternich gave away her view of the nature of their status-relationship. When asked how she could be encouraging the empress to be wearing such immoral fashions, and whether she would do the same for her sovereign, the empress of Austria, she replied, "I certainly should not advise the Empress Elisabeth to go out in short skirts; but you must remember that *my* empress is a real princess, a *real* empress, while yours, *ma chère*, is

Mlle de Montijo."[5] That Eugénie let her get away with the comment is probably more revealing than the comment itself. (That being said, it should also be noted, as a measure of her loyalty, Pauline Metternich was the last of the court circle to stay with the empress as the regime collapsed, escorting her in disguise to a carriage as she fled the Tuilleries palace, minutes ahead of a rampaging mob in 1870.)

Worth was more discreet about his relationship with the empress but reveled in his position. He adopted the airs and look of an artist and nourished eccentricities in his relations with his clients. He would behave with complete disdain toward his customers, developed a reputation for haughtiness, and was criticized in the press for being overly familiar with the ladies he was dressing. When Metternich introduced the composer Richard Wagner to Parisian society the following year, she and the composer stepped on too many toes. Parisian society resented the princess's influence, and the opening of the opera *Tannhauser* became heavily politicized. Offenbach was the rage in Paris as far as music was concerned, and Wagner was too advanced for the Parisian musical palate. Because Wagner was German, Metternich's nationality was highlighted, as France and Austria had been at war only a few years before. For the opening night, the Princess urged Worth to excel himself and applauded in her box, superbly dressed and wearing jewelry worth a fortune, as affronted society gentlemen jeered the opera and its composer. This chink in Metternich's armor led to attacks in newspapers, and Worth, as her protégé, was not spared insinuations of impropriety. Resentful competitors claimed to be outraged that a man should be present at fittings, and one article went so far as to accuse him of fondling a client. (None of this came to anything, and the writer of the article actually offered to write a complimentary one for a hefty sum.) Wagner left Paris humiliated,[6] but Metternich and Worth shook it all off and continued their collaboration. In Worth's case, it became an early example of the adage that in fashion, there's no such thing as bad publicity. The scandal only made more people curious to see what the "man-milliner" was producing.

The next change they affected was the abandoning of shawls and mantles. Pauline Metternich and Marie Worth both arrived at the Longchamp race meetings, a traditional display of new fashions, in dresses without any covering. This was, of course, first considered to be quite indecent, but soon Parisian women had ditched the shawls. Small, gradual changes in fashion were affected to create a comparatively less cumbersome style. Marie next initiated a hairstyle cut across the forehead and curled, but getting rid of the crinoline took longer. Manufacturers of the crinoline cage fought back against new fashions, and as the empress herself did not seem to want to abandon the fashion of her youth, the crinoline stayed, but slightly flattened in front. Worth gradually increased that change over the following years until he could introduce the bustle.

Worth and Bobergh, his silent partner, saw their business grow exponentially, with 200 employees in 1861 to more than 1,000 in 1864 in several workshops, creating ball gowns, fancy-dress costumes, traveling dresses, and all the other apparel necessary for a society woman of the empire.

Political Coloring

Worth and Metternich would name new fashion colors after current events, such as Mexican Blue, the favorite color of French high society in 1863, after the French were victorious at Puebla that year. Metternich's part in this game may have been prompted by the fact that the most fashionable color of the past years had been magenta, a synthetic color recently invented and named after the battle at which Napoleon III's armies had defeated her countrymen in 1859. It was after this that she and her husband were sent to Paris on their diplomatic mission. As further proof that Metternich's color games were not just frivolous, a brown fabric that Worth felt was "insipid and uninteresting" and Metternich called "perfectly detestable" earned the name "Bismarck brown" after her countrymen had again met defeat, this time by the Prussians with their far superior rifles, under Count Otto von Bismarck in 1865. This defeat caused Napoleon such anxiety that he became seriously ill, fearing that France would be next to fall to Bismarck. Eugénie contemplated taking over as regent and told Pauline's husband, the Austrian ambassador, "We are moving towards our fall, and the best thing would be if the emperor disappeared for a while."

The Austrian defeat also led to a "Metternich green," as the Princess insisted on making fashionable the Tyrolean green of her homeland after the defeat. Interestingly enough, despite Bismarck being the most hated and feared man in France, Bismarck brown became the most popular color of the time. Different variations developed, women gave up the fashionable blonde—after the empress—and dyed their hair to match the particular Bismarck shade they wore. Paris was conquered in the summer of 1866 by a sea of brown.[7] This odd presaging of the eventual defeat of the empire by Otto von Bismarck five years later was, in hindsight, the first sign from the fashion front that the empire was degenerating. Then the signs lined up, one after the other, in the summer of 1867.

The Beginning of the End of the Empire

Into the middle of the sea of brown came the next sign, in the form of the frantic Empress Carlota of Mexico, unfashionably dressed, badly groomed, and begging for help. Her disregard for fashion, protocol, and deportment brought the reality of what was happening in Mexico, to her husband, and to the empire right to the fore (Figure 2.3). She was like a prophetic ghost, terrorizing the fashionable court by showing them what lay under the polished surface. The empire prided itself on its appearance, and here was one of its beauties, falling apart and raging, not giving a whit for Worth or any of the courtly pleasantries. As she headed deeper into despair and paranoia, comments on her lack of fashion sense became more pointed. Within the ritual of high fashion, Carlotta stepped outside the frame of orthodoxy. Her behavior suggested that fashion didn't matter, that deportment didn't matter, that protocol was a waste of time. Shedding your social identity at a masquerade is one thing, but dismissing it in daily life is another. Unorthodoxy is very dangerous to those in power, as it calls the entire system into question. Coming from someone "on the inside" it is doubly dangerous. Carlota began to claim that she was being poisoned, but this was never proven and was probably unnecessary in any case. The social isolation and cruel dismissal she faced at court was enough to drive her insane, and in losing her mind she provided the rationale for society: It was clear that the woman was insane all along.

FIGURE 2.3. Emperor Maximilian of Mexico (1832–1867) and his wife, the Empress Carlotta (1840–1927). This photo is from ca. 1857 shortly after their marriage.

Ironically, as the empire's Mexican adventure fell apart, the exhibition that had been planned to commemorate the initial Mexican victory at Puebla in 1863 was at its peak. During the summer of 1867, the mood in Paris was frivolous to the extreme. The number of heads of state present on the city's boulevards was unprecedented. More than 80 royal persons visited Paris during the summer, and more and more, the attention was focused on the fact that they were behaving like *ordinary citizens*. Kings were seen strolling about, laughing in the theaters, and eating meals at restaurants (although the illusion of the Prussian king's normalcy was somewhat broken by the fact that he would sit and eat while his retinue stood at attention).

None of the royal heads seem to have been concerned about the danger they faced in opening themselves up to such human interpretation: If royalty is seen to be dressing and behaving like ordinary human beings, the temptation to see them as human *all the time* becomes all too great. Then the concept of their separateness, on which their authority is based, becomes an article of faith and their visible, human imperfections make that faith difficult. Now it was not only that the middle class (to say nothing of the lower classes) was appearing in the guise of aristocracy, but the aristocracy was beginning to appear in the roles and looks of the middle class. The meeting in the middle could not bode well for the Second Empire and would soon prove problematic for high society and high fashion all around.

Worth himself became quite imperial in his realm. Just as Pauline Metternich was comfortable in declaring Eugénie to be a make-believe empress, so could Worth exclaim more explicitly to Metternich after a successful exhibition ball of hers: "To think it was I who invented you!" The princess was taken aback by this statement, thinking it was she who had made Worth, but upon reflection she added to her description of this incident in her memoirs, "Perhaps he was right."[8] Perhaps both were right. Worth, Eugénie, and Metternich had each assisted in the others' invention. The relationship of the fashion authority and the fashion icon is an interdependent ritual relationship. One actor in the relationship cannot exist without the other. Worth would very likely have become a master of design without Eugénie or Pauline Metternich, but he would have needed someone instead of them to serve their purpose in driving up his popularity. The same holds true for the other direction of the relationship. Without Worth, someone else would have needed to be enlisted by Pauline Metternich and be accepted by the empress. The details would have differed and the end result perhaps not the same, but the arc of the story would probably have been similar.

During the exhibition, about a month after the Metternichs' ball, the unraveling of the empire would begin in earnest, attended by fashion in a most macabre way. On July 1, the awards for the exhibition were to be presented. It was meant to be an afternoon event, so the ladies' dresses could be sleeveless and low-cut. Worth had decided to use a yellow *faille*, especially woven for the dress in Lyon and decorated with exquisite lace. Eugénie would never wear the dress, but it would be the second of two dresses abandoned because of violent events in the midst of the harmonious display of the exhibition.

The first dress to be abandoned met its fate after an assassination attempt. The Russian czar had been given the cold shoulder by the populace of Paris, who, in opposition to the court's position, seemed to prefer the King of Prussia, whose "man of the people" act was much appreciated. As the czar rode through the streets, he would be greeted with shouts of "Vive Poland!" protesting the Russian oppression of the Poles. On the day of a grand ball at the Russian embassy, for which Worth and his workshops had been preparing at full clip for weeks, Czar Alexander II rode in an open carriage with Napoleon III. They were returning from a spectacular pageant, where 30,000 troops had paraded before assembled guests and royalty. A Polish exile came through the crowd and took a shot at the Russian emperor. The leader of the mounted escorts saw the man take aim and spurred his horse forward. The bullet hit the horse's head, saving Alexander from certain injury.

FIGURE 2.4. The last moment of grandeur: The handing out of awards at the Paris Exhibition of 1867 in the presence of the emperor Napoleon III and the Empress Eugénie.

Eugénie and Napoleon viewed the assassination attempt as a diplomatic disaster. The czar was the most important guest at the exhibition and had, in addition, spent at least 3 million francs during his stay.[9] Worth received an urgent summons to come to the court. The intended dress, said Eugénie to Worth, was far too beautiful under the circumstances. Worth was to find her a suitable alternative and had two hours to do so. Worth sent for the necessary workers and materials and then looked around the empress's wardrobe. He picked out a white dress, made some alterations, and covered it with three skirts of white and silver tulle. The empress stood pale next to the czar all that evening, looking regal but sufficiently understated and subdued.

The assassination attempt put a chill on the remainder of the exhibition summer. The police were reinforced, and a wariness set in, both in court circles and among the populace. The attempt against the czar seems to have stripped the empire of its final layer of illusion. Worth continued his work on the fabulous yellow dress for the awards ceremony (Figure 2.4). Then the day came and the dress was ready. When Worth arrived at the Tuilleries palace with the dress, the empress looked at it appreciatively and then pushed it away with a sigh. Word of

Maximillian's execution in Mexico had reached the emperor. The ceremony went ahead, but the news had to come out the next day. The court went into mourning; the remainder of the exhibition was conducted in a subdued way, and the royal visitors returned home.

A joke that went around Paris at the end of the exhibition is revealing: Upon taking leave of the emperor, the shah had said, "Sire, your Paris is wonderful, your palaces splendid, and your horses magnificent, but," waving his hand toward the mature but noble ladies of the court with an expression of disapproval, "you must change all that."

The shah needn't have been concerned. It was already changing.

Changing All That

Hostility toward Louis Napoleon's regime had been steadily building. The disaster in Mexico, coupled with the overloaded ostentation of the exhibition, seemed to tip the scales. The emperor had been ailing and was increasingly out of touch because of the pain of kidney stones and the opiates he took to alleviate it. This had allowed the empress to increase her political influence, and she had actually served as regent on several occasions when the emperor was off indulging in his fantasies of being a military commander. This had not endeared her to anyone, and now she was being called "the Spaniard" in the same way that Marie Antoinette had been called "the Austrian." The increasingly alarmed emperor reacted to his critics rather surprisingly by relaxing restrictions on freedoms and making various liberal concessions. Public meetings were allowed, and freedom of the press was mostly restored. He promised a restoration of parliamentary government.

Worth did not approve of any of these new freedoms and the disorder they produced and wished for a return to the previous empire. However, it was in this atmosphere of hostility toward the regime that the crinoline finally disappeared altogether. Eugénie had finally appeared without one in the summer of 1866, but the ladies of France vacillated between the old and new styles into 1868. Worth had created two new styles: a "princess" dress, flat in front and gathered in the back to fall into a train, and the *fourreau*, or sheath dress, which widened out into a train in back. The reasons for Eugénie's acquiescence to the style change are not known. The new, more angular styles may simply have suited her better now that she was no longer young, but there may also have been a conscious effort to move away from the look so firmly associated with the increasingly unpopular regime.

Worth's displeasure at the loosening of the reins may also have been due to a parallel loosening of his fashion dictatorship. There were new voices of authority gaining ground in Parisian fashion. Even though Worth et Bobergh was by now employing over 1,200 people, demand was large enough that there was room for competition, and the competitors had come to the scene prepared for a market that was ready for innovation and had high expectations. The competition, not bound by the rigors of the court with its rigid tradition, had more freedom to experiment. Finally, their clientele was also free of traditions and expectations for court life and looked toward the modern age with excitement rather than the apprehension felt by the courtiers.

In response to the increased competition and the copying of his models, Worth founded, in 1868, an association of couture houses called The Chambre Syndicale de la Confection et de la Couture pour Dames et Fillettes. This association of fashion houses in Paris, which still exists as the Fédération Française de la Couture, du Prêt-á-Porter des Couturiers et des Créateurs de Mode,[10] was founded with the main aim of protecting their designs from piracy and plagiarism. It was also the creation of a guild that would confer legitimacy on the couturiers and, as such, was a necessary counter-move to the dissolution of the system which had begun with Worth.

{ LOOKING FORWARD LOOKING BACK }

The "Fédération" Today

The Fédération Française de la Couture, du Prêt-à-Porter des Couturiers et des Créateurs de Mode is a federation of corporate elements that has approximately 100 members. As the title of the federation shows, this is an umbrella organization, covering haute couture and ready-to-wear, both from couture houses and designer labels. The Fédération organizes and schedules the seasonal shows in Paris and serves as a liaison between the industry and the press.

In conjunction with the French Ministry of Trade, it also maintains standards by sanctioning the use of the appellation "haute couture." This appellation is bandied about in all manner of ways, by fashion labels all over the world, but in France, a designer or label may use the term for its apparel and in advertising only if it includes the following:

- Designs made-to-order for private clients, with one or more fittings.
- Has a workshop/studio in Paris with at least 15 full-time employees.

- Presents, twice a year to the Paris press, a collection of at least 35 models with outfits for both daytime and evening wear.

Membership is not limited to the French. The Fédération also admits associate members from other countries, and will also invite a promising designer or label to exhibit, such as in the autumn/winter shows in 2008 when Ma Ke became the first Chinese designer to exhibit haute couture in Paris, under her label "Wuyong" ("Useless").

The signs that the empire was failing were everywhere, despite the efforts to continue the grand appearances. There were bloody riots in the streets of Paris in 1869, while Eugénie was off in Egypt opening the Suez Canal (a journey for which Worth provided her with 60 dresses). Then the day came early in 1870 when Pauline Metternich's carriage was met with angry cries and insults in the Rue de Rivoli, and she told Worth that "the Empire has had its day."[11]

Indeed it had. Things went from bad to worse. The emperor's health continued to deteriorate, and Eugénie's increased involvement in politics did not help. The long-anticipated war with the Prussians was provoked in the hope that a military victory would rally the populace to the empire again and quiet the dissident voices. However, in September of 1870, the emperor surrendered along with his army at Sedan after a confused and mismanaged campaign.

With the emperor gone, Eugénie made a furtive attempt to cling to power but eventually had to flee her palace, just ahead of an angry mob. Princess Pauline, who had been entrusted with Eugénie's jewels, escorted her to a carriage as the mob came through the front gate. The empress then fled to England to her friend Queen Victoria.

Worth and his family, after contemplating moving the business to Vienna, had stayed in Paris during the war. They turned the showrooms and workshops into a field hospital, accepting the overflow from the overtaxed Paris hospitals. This is probably why Worth et Bobergh escaped being attacked and looted when Paris erupted in revolution and Communards took control of Paris (Figure 2.5).

The Communards had set up an encampment in the Place Vendôme at the end of the Rue de la Paix, where Worth was located, erecting a large barricade and aiming cannons down the street. In March of 1871, a journalist and committed royalist named Henri de Pène thought to lead a large group of Parisians to the barricades in the Place Vendôme, in order to beg the Communards, in the name of the people, to restore order and quiet in the city. The Communards knew they were coming, as he had sent word that they would come unarmed. The crowd bore banners proclaiming their unarmed state, as well as their support of the people of Paris and their support of order.

Lillie Moulton was at Worth's early that afternoon and describes what happened in her memoir:

FIGURE 2.5. A young woman in the hitched-up fashion, celebrating the defenders of Paris at the fall of the Second Empire.

> I wondered why there were so few people in the streets. The Place Vendôme was barricaded with paving-stones, and cannon were pointing down the Rue de la Paix. I walked quietly along to Worth's, and hardly had I reached his salon than we heard distant, confused sounds, and then the shouting in the street below made us all rush to the windows.
>
> What a sight met our eyes!
>
> This handsome young fellow, De Pène, his hat in his outstretched hand, followed by a crowd of men, women, and children, looked the picture of life, health, and enthusiasm.
>
> . . . De Pène, seeing people on Worth's balcony, beckoned to them to join him; but Mr. Worth wisely withdrew inside, and, shaking his Anglo-Saxon head, said, 'Not I.' He, indeed!

Not he, indeed. Worth knew that he did not belong on that street. He represented the fallen regime; he was Eugénie's man. To align himself with the Communards was of course unthinkable, but to fall in step behind a determined royalist like De Pène, no matter for how good a cause, was also impossible. That would be a betrayal of the empress. Turning away may have saved Worth's life, however. Moulton describes what happened next:

> One can't imagine the horror we felt when we heard the roar of a cannon, and looking down saw the street filled with smoke, and frightened screams and terrified groans reached our ears. Someone dragged me inside the window, and shut it to drown the horrible noises outside. De Pène was the first who was killed.[12] The street was filled with dead and wounded. . . . The living members of Les Amis scampered off as fast as their legs could carry them, while the wounded were left to the care of the shopkeepers, and the dead were abandoned where they fell until further aid should come.[13]

More than 300 people sought refuge in Worth's establishment. Lillie Moulton fled through the attic down the back stairs to the street behind, where her carriage was waiting. She fled to Deauville, and shortly thereafter Worth and his family also left Paris. The Communards were putting pressure on Worth's 17-year-old son Gaston to join them, and so the family left, sneaking out of the house one by one to avoid suspicion. They met at the train station and fled to the coast, where they waited out the defeat of the Commune.[14]

The Future Will Be Like the Past, Excepting of Course . . .

Worth's partner had had enough and retired to Sweden, but two months later when the Communards had been defeated, Worth returned to Paris. His business had miraculously survived the looting and burning rampage of the final weeks of the Commune, and he reopened the establishment as Maison Worth. If Lillie Moulton is a fair measure, he was back in business in no time at all. She writes in her memoir for June 18 that she had ordered, for concerts she would be giving in New York, "some fine dresses from Worth, and if my public don't like me they can console themselves with the thought that a look at my clothes is worth a ticket."

Worth survived by keeping his head down but also by not being an integral part of the court. As far as outward appearances were concerned, he was just a merchant, and like Rose Bertin, Marie Antoinette's dressmaker, he could reenter society once everything that had made him was gone. Without Metternich and the empress, he would not be—and never was—viewed as a political force. Although he never spoke or wrote of political matters, Worth's instincts were shrewd. In Worth's gesture on the balcony, we see the apparent turning away from politics that high-fashion design has practiced since: As the guardian of the *status quo*, it resists change, and thereby aligns itself with the ruling class it serves, but outwardly, vocally, is neither for nor against.

Worth himself was optimistic that following August when he claimed:

> Women can't do without new clothes: they may deprive themselves of all sorts of other things, but they won't shut off that one. They can't. I'm quite sure that by the end of the year, we shall be going on as if nothing had happened. Payments will be, for a time, more difficult to get in—French payments I mean; foreign payments are not affected by the war—but trade itself will become as active as ever.[15]

A large part of his trade was from abroad, and therefore things could reasonably be expected to go on as before. His bigger clients were Russian and American rather than French, and rarely did he see an extravagant German or Englishwoman, so unrest in Europe was not going to hit him too badly. He was clearly partial to his American clients:

> Some of them are great spenders; all of them (all of them that I see, I mean) love dress, even if they are not extravagant over it. And I like to dress them, for, as I say occasionally, they have faith, figures and francs,'—faith to believe in me, figures that I can put into shape, francs to pay my bills. Yes, I like to dress Americans.

Worth's weakness was his attachment to the old order of courts and ceremony. He, like so many of that time, thought they were witnessing, at worst, a temporary shift in society's order and that things would go on in much the way they had up until then:

> We have lost a year, and that can never be recovered. But from the nature of things, the war will bring about no permanent change in women's wants. The future will be like the past, excepting of course (unless there is a Restoration of some sort) there will be, from the disappearance of a Court, less brilliancy in Paris itself, and less demand here for extreme elegance. So far as I'm concerned, however, I expect that foreign orders will make up for what I may lose here. That's all.[16]

Worth failed to see the possibility of continuing without a court, and in that failing, set the stage for the problem high fashion is still dealing with today. Without the ritual and the politics of Metternich and the empress, how could Paris high fashion continue? How could "extreme elegance" fit into a French democracy? Yet, at the same time, he was enthusiastic about his Americans. They, from a society without a court, managed to be equaled only by czarist Russia in their extravagance. The shape of the new world was right in front of him, and he didn't quite seem to put his finger on it. But perhaps he did. Perhaps he saw where things were heading. Perhaps he saw that the "foreign orders," his Americans, would be the thrust of the future.

THE TWILIGHT OF THE GODS: CHANGING VALUES AND SOCIETAL NORMS

The unrest of the nineteenth century was the surfacing of tensions that had been brewing in the Old World for generations, if not centuries. Since the Reformation in the sixteenth century, European thinkers had been increasingly at odds with the medieval feudal worldview, and gradually the individual's experience of the world was becoming the central measure of reality. This trend would reach its inevitable destination in the latter part of the twentieth century and is reflected by the trajectory of high fashion from Worth on through the 1960s.

THE NEW RULING CLASS

From observing the entertainments, homes, and fashions of the upper classes in Europe and North America in the last quarter of the nineteenth century, one would be forgiven for thinking that the world of the old European aristocracy was going to continue stronger than ever. The events of 1870 and the shockwave that was felt from the Paris Commune began to seem like a temporary setback to be assigned to history. The new ruling class, the capitalist barons, were investing in their legitimacy and in their bright new cities, creating a lifestyle of conspicuous consumption that, with all the new technologies of travel and manufacturing available, continued to reach new heights. "The Gilded Age" saw more opulence, more entertainments, dinners, balls, concerts, and festivities than the Second Empire ever produced, but now the bourgeoisie was in charge, and their power rested on capital, not lineage or tradition. (See Figure 2.6.) Power in the modern world was power over industrial resources, not hereditary obligations, and this power was spread out, fluid, and growing. In America, the aristocracy of industrial wealth was emulating European society, buying whatever they needed to create a replica of the aristocratic lifestyle in art, architecture, and fashion from all over Europe.

The new ruling class needed structure and legitimacy just as much as Louis Napoleon, if not more so. However, the battle was not yet won. The forces of anarchy that had raised their heads at the end of the Second Empire continued to operate and strengthen. Indeed, they can be seen to have represented an underlying movement in society that had first seriously come to the fore in the first French Revolution and has been in conflict with the established order at any given time since.

FIGURE 2.6. The aristocracy continued to evoke their past at royal occasions and in fancy dress. This portrait from 1905 shows George Charles Spencer Churchill (1871–1934), 9th Duke of Marlborough; his wife Consuela Vanderbilt, Duchess of Marlborough; and sons, John Albert, Marquess of Blandford, and Lord Ivor Spencer Churchill, dressed to evoke the style of Churchill's ancestors of 200 years before.

The Cultural Revolution

Parisian intellectual and artistic circles in the latter half of the nineteenth century were awash in new ideas that were developing at an incredible rate all over Europe. Socialist and anarchist writers were questioning the values of the developing bourgeois society, suggesting that the industrial capitalist culture was degrading and oppressive. Religion was being contested as the answer to humanity's problems. Artists were using their increased autonomy to develop individual voices and challenge accepted artistic practices. Writers and musicians were expanding formal structures and breaking with their own traditions. "Art for art's sake" was a mid-nineteenth-century slogan maintaining that art did not need to have any meaning beyond itself and that art could therefore serve any purpose the artist wanted it to. Science, which had seemed to be on the road to fully and rationally explaining the world and all things in it, was beginning to hint at new disturbing areas of study that questioned all established ideas of nature and human existence itself. Put briefly, there was hardly an area of intellectual or artistic pursuit where authority was not being questioned, if not being completely turned on its head.

Technology Transforms All

One of the catalysts for the explosion of revolutionary and transformative ideas developing in the nineteenth century was the accelerating effect of scientific discovery and technological progress. The increase in knowledge, coupled with improvements in communications and travel, allowed for a rapid dissemination of—and easier access to—new ideas. Meanwhile, the new big cities, with an increased population of artists and university students, allowed for greater proximity to these multiple streams of information (Figure 2.7).

The invention of steamships, trains, and, later, the telegraph, and the speed at which their respective networks were built increased the speed at which ideas could spread. This was, of course, true in all disciplines, but speaking in terms of fashion, the dissemination of new styles now sped up by an order of magnitude. It was now conceivable that infor-

FIGURE 2.7. A Parisian street scene from 1880 by Leon Joseph Voirin: *L'Esplanade des Invalides et Promenade, Paris.*

mation on a new style would make it across the European continent in a day or two and across the Atlantic in less than a week. It is interesting to note that this rate of dissemination would remain until after World War II, when air travel would again change the picture. Travel by rail and news by telegraph contributed to the dissolution of long-standing boundaries that had kept people isolated in their communities. Dissolving these boundaries and bringing in new influences encouraged questioning of age-old ideas and customs. The example of Eugénie and Napoleon serves to illustrate a third case, wherein high society could now in effect be migratory. Their practice of having rotating groups of guests at their autumn house at Compiegne would have been extremely difficult without rail travel, considering the numbers of people and masses of luggage involved. The idea that high society could migrate to fashionable resorts, allowed it to be unbound from the specific locations of royal courts. Eventually the whole aristocratic scene would become internationalized once the courts no longer were the center of gravity, but just one more location in the social round.

Mass Culture, Technology, and Commodification

The modern age can be seen as the age of individualism, but at the same time, it was the age of the emerging masses. Citizens *en masse* as a force in politics, commerce, and culture became something to be reckoned with as the urbanization of culture progressed. Mass politics arguably reached a peak in the West during the years spanning the World Wars of the twentieth century, and Western mass culture and commerce reached their current saturation level at the end of the twentieth century but will continue to grow with new yet unknown communications technology and seem to not be limited by geographical boundaries. Mass-production technology allowed for the creation of luxury goods for these growing markets, and although haute couture is not meant to be associated with mass production in any way, Worth's success was partly due to the fact that he could apply elementary mass-production methods to his manufacturing. Needing to create literally thousands of gowns a season, his workforce of over a thousand people would work from standard patterns that could be mixed and matched and assembled with different fabrics and layering to create unique models. Mass production of textiles allowed the luxury clothing industry to produce the mountains of clothes needed. Maison Worth also kept precise records of what models were sent where in order that no duplication would take place in the various courts and cities where Worth was in demand, a practice that points immediately to the fact that duplicates must have been made but shipped to different parts of the globe and perhaps in different seasons. It must be remembered that the turnaround of fashion was not as swift as it became soon after. Worth considered changing styles every three to five years to be enough to keep everyone happy.

Throughout the nineteenth century, the development of mass-production capabilities and the growth of cities went hand in hand, as this allowed for the creation of a workforce that was not tied to the land and could live in and around the centers of production. This in turn created a demand for more mass-produced goods to furnish the homes, dress the inhabitants, and so on. As the consumer economies were established, more and more of the production was geared toward consumer goods designed for the middle-class homes. With industrialization, the need for specialization grew, and with that, the possibility of turning a talent into a commodity. This is what allowed someone like Charles Worth, for example, who did not construct clothes and could not sketch or even speak French very well to put a large price on garments sold from his maison in Paris. As a youth, he had developed a knowledge of fabrics and their behavior and an eye for fit. These skills, coupled with an ability to conceptualize a "look," to be able to assemble an entire wardrobe, based on some criteria that he may or may not have control over, became something on which a price could be put. The value of this is not objectively measurable by reference to anything but what someone is willing to pay—in other words, "what the market will bear." This talent, later known as the ability to "design," became *commodified*. Once the talent of "design" became a commodity that had a marketplace value, the door opened to what is known as *commodity fetishism*, wherein the "design" becomes an abstraction, separate from the designer and end user, and acquires a value that is again not related to its usefulness or origin. This "fetishization" allows the work to become independent of its origin and a "thing" in itself. Hence, it is reified, which is the final step toward being able to value the name on the label over the garment, the labor of the person who made the garment, or even the labor of the person who designed the garment. (If Charles Worth designed it but the label didn't say "Maison Worth," would one still pay full price?)

The grand exhibitions of the late nineteenth and early twentieth centuries were, from this viewpoint, temples of commodity fetishism. The political nature of the exhibitions, where all the frontline technologies and goods were shown, is perhaps more obvious in that the solidifying nation-states of Europe were displaying what they were capable of. At the same time, the fetishization of consumer goods reduced a national or regional identity to the ownership of specific goods, and the identity of a group became codified into a set of clothing and accessories. For example, the exhibit for which Worth, then working for Gagelin, won a gold medal at the Paris exhibition of 1855, was directed on one level at the consumers of high-fashion gowns as a straightforward advertisment of Gagelin's products. On another level, it served to display to visitors, whether local or from abroad: "This is how we are, here. This is France personified." The official nature of the display, the sanctioning of its message by the award, and the subsequent establishment of its message by the repetition of its content out in the world, reifies the image. It creates its own reality.

Fin de Siècle: Altered States

The view around Paris was very different by the time the *Exposition Universelle* of 1889 opened to commemorate the storming of the Bastille one hundred years before. In the 19 years from the storming of Eugénie's palace, women's fashions had evolved in several new directions.

Worth had continued to narrow the silhouette after removing the most problematic element of the crinoline by flattening the front. The overall style remained very layered and ornamental and was still built on a foundation of corsetry and stiffened skirts (Figure 2.8). Jean Worth, ostensibly in charge of designing, continued his father's vision. In fact, he didn't have any other choice, as Worth required him to submit all his ideas for approval, and the clientele were not very open to innovation in any case. Maison Worth continued in this way to dress all the courts of Europe with all the various local nuances required. Their scope even reached Japan after the imperial court in Tokyo opened up relations with the West and took up Western dress as their official fashion.

FIGURE 2.8. The fashions of the 1890s reflected the relaxation of social norms, as seen in John Singer Sargent's 1892 portrait of the society beauty Lady Agnew of Lochnaw (1865–1932).

In 1889 the scope of the Paris exhibition was beyond

anything that had been seen before. For starters, it featured the Eiffel Tower as its entryway. The exhibition focused heavily on technology, with electricity being the exciting news of the day. There were gramophones, telephones, and Edison's new invention of electric lights, which illuminated a fountain with a synchronized light show. There were also featured colonial and "exotic" themes, along with the usual displays of industrial machinery, manufactured goods, and luxury items. This all aimed to bring the audience of middle-class consumers to a high state of excitement and desire for these status symbols. The industrialization of Europe was now resulting in fantastic advances in consumer goods, and it was not only the Parisians or just the French who came to be amazed. Railway networks carried visitors from all over Europe to see such things as they had never seen before. At the opening of the exhibition, a boy of ten by the name of Paul Poiret was mesmerized by the light show in the fountain. He would later, when he had become the world's most famous designer, wonder whether his taste for color had not been born "amidst the phantasmagoria of pinks, greens, and violets" of the fountain.[17]

ENDBOX

As Couture Shows Open, Some Battles Rage On

What we are seeing is the Balkanization of fashion—a reflection of the wider world. Just as newly independent states are flexing their muscles after years of dictatorship and demanding to control their own destinies, so fashion designers are challenging the autocracy of the Chambre Syndicale de la Couture Parisienne, which has maintained a united front for French fashion.

. . . Whatever adjustments are made, the current situation is really a fashion free-for-all in which the most powerful international designers will pulverize the rest, at least in terms of publicity and attention, which is what the couture shows are now about.

Yet, it is a myth to claim that couture is finished and its clients a dying breed. While high-priced designer ready-to-wear (often confusingly labeled "couture") is a very tough sell, the megarich clients of haute couture have returned since the trauma of the Gulf War. Dior reports business up by 20 percent, with around 200 clients a year, 28 percent of them European...

Hélène de Ludinghausen, haute couture director at Saint Laurent since 1971, believes that fashion is going through a period of transition. She says the Gulf War marked a psychological watershed, bringing about a "malaise" and "panic" among couture clients, 50 percent of them from the United States at YSL.

". . . The truth is that things have been changing for a long time," she says, "when you think that in 1963 Dior had 1,000 couture workers and Balmain 500, and now at Saint Laurent we have 150, which is more than anyone else. Real luxe will never die, but there is a restructuring going on in high fashion, and we and all the other houses are experiencing the growing pains."

Source: Suzy Menkes. *International Herald Tribune*. July 25, 1992.

Discussion Points

1. Since this was written, in 1992, has anything changed?
2. Why is "couture" continually pronounced dead and yet does not die?
3. How does the "Balkanization" of fashion relate to the system as set up in Paris in the late 1800s?

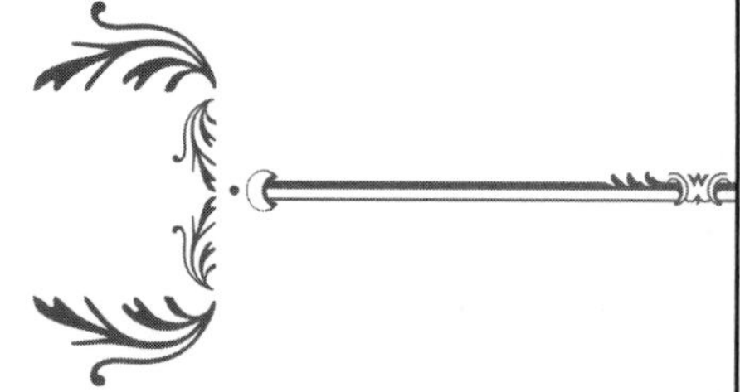

CHAPTER 3

Revolution in the Air

Paris was a center of cultural and political upheaval as the nineteenth century drew to a close. The Third Republic, which had taken the place of Napoleon's Second Empire, was riven by scandal from within, threatened by anarchism and socialism on the left and by royalists on the right. The cracks in the structure of French society became evident in the questioning of all authority: political, spiritual, and artistic.

The fashions and social habits of the Second Empire became symbolic of the old society, and new ideas and practices abounded in responses to the challenges of the new times. Art, music, and fashion all developed a strengthening undercurrent of youthful energy, which meant to sweep away the "old world" of the passing century. This anarchistic bent would be the counterpoint to the reactionary forces of high society well into the twentieth century and high fashion played along. A young Paul Poiret was the first to show the way out of the staid fashions of the old world.

Paris and Poiret: Youth in Revolt

Paul Poiret took high fashion into the twentieth century. His designs broke with the traditions of dress set up in the Second Empire and paved the way for high fashion to become an expressive medium of the individual designer's creativity. If Worth presented the *couturier* as artist, Poiret brought the designer-as-artist approach to *couture*. The environment in which he grew up could not have been better primed for an aspiring artist. In the years leading up to the Exhibition of 1889, the front lines of art and politics had come together in Paris.[1] A new generation of artists, Neo-Impressionists, Post-Impressionists, and Symbolists hadnewly formed. The adherents of these movements were mainly those born during the final years of the Second Empire and soon after. Now in their late teens and early twenties, they were eager to challenge the reigning artistic beliefs. Art had become heavily bound to the emerging middle-class culture and was, as such, lacking in any experimental or revolutionary spirit. The demand for the "modern" became a generational call. The youth of Paris began to form a world for themselves, one that was not modeled on the Second Empire of their parents and grandparents, but on the free-wheeling spirit of the city of the new Republic, which had been formed after the fall of Napoleon in 1871. In the Third Republic, Paris became a magnet for revolutionary spirits in arts, letters, and politics from all over Europe, eager to share in the energy that radiated from the cafés and ateliers. The "café set" (Figure 3.1) became a new urban type: intellectuals, artistic and political, sharing ideas, crossing class boundaries, and questioning all previous structures in society politics and art.

FIGURE 3.1. At the Café, ca. 1879 (oil on canvas) by Edouard Manet.

To understand Poiret as a designer and his contribution to fashion design, it is important to take a close look at the artistic and political situation in Paris during his formative years. His approach not only resonated with the artists and musicians who surrounded him in Paris, but also derived an attitude from the political and philosophical waves in the air.

His instinct to challenge and break down the images set up in the previous decades was as much a product of the times as the impulses of the young painters, musicians, and writers of the day.

Modernism

Art, science, and philosophy had all been accelerating change in the decades leading up to the end of the nineteenth century. The perception of the place and purpose of people in society had moved steadily toward the elevation of the individual. "Art for art's sake" had become a slogan for artists of all kinds, and artists themselves had acquired an autonomy with which they could achieve an individual vision. In fact, a personal vision began to be a requirement to be taken seriously as an artist. With art becoming a commodity for a middle-class market, an artist also needed to be visible in the marketplace. The painter Gustave Courbet began in the mid-century to establish the image of the artist-as-revolutionary through his genuinely radical politics. In addition, realizing that all publicity was good publicity, he was quick off the mark to make use of the enormous number of newspapers and journals that had sprung up. Keeping oneself in the public eye, which Poiret would become extremely good at, became a large part of the artist's task, so that the curiosity of the public for the artist's work would be constantly whetted, thus drawing crowds to shows.

One must be careful in saying about Poiret and others after him that they represented "modernity" against "tradition." Being in the environment creates a spirit but may not necessarily mean that an adherence to a strict theory is also involved. The fashions Poiret and Chanel after him designed, although reacting to the modern age, were not necessarily "modernist," as we shall see when we look more closely at Chanel. Poiret's break from the past was not as radical as that which was taking place in the visual arts. Despite his untraditional approach, he was rooted in the *couture* tradition, while influenced by much of the modern developments in art and architecture and the needs of his new nonaristocratic clientele. But in order to get to the full depth of his connection with both preceding and subsequent history, one must also see Poiret as part of a movement in the dynamic of ritual versus sincerity, as outlined in Chapter 1. His work, like the work of the artists around him, was a reaction to the closed system of the Second Empire. The overemphasis on ritual and contrived tradition required an assertion of individuality in order to establish a new order. Poiret's designs, in tandem with the art world erupting around him, showed that society *could* be different, even as it was connected to past tradition. Poiret provided the bridge that subsequent designers would cross to break fully with the nineteenth century.

SYMBOLISM

The modern idea that each individual's perception of the world is of the utmost importance to that individual's understanding of the world was felt early in the arts. The first stirrings of modernism in the arts can be seen in the works of the Symbolists, who began to appear in Paris during the Second Empire (Figure 3.2). The Symbolist painter Gustave Moreau said:

FIGURE 3.2. A Symbolist painting, *The Wounded Angel* by Hugo Simberg, 1903. The Symbolists took the first steps toward surrealism and the negation of realism in the arts. For them, emotion was all.

> I believe neither in what I touch nor in what I see. I believe only in what I do not see and solely in what I feel; my brain, my reason seem to me ephemeral and of doubtful reality; my inner feelings alone seem to me eternal and incontestably certain.[2]

The central idea of Symbolism in literature and visual art was that sensations and emotions could be evoked through objects and references to objects. Works of art could create a response from their audience through the objects depicted, included, or implied. Even color became removed from its traditional role, stood for itself, and spoke for itself, calling on emotions and reactions. This notion that art was meant to do more than depict and that it had the power and, in some cases, an obligation to speak to emotions became one of the central ideas of the modernism that followed. In literature, visual arts, and music, a work of art now must be emotional. Here is also the beginning of the idea that the arts should all collaborate in a "total artwork," something Richard Wagner had developed with his operas. The Parisian artists of Poiret's day would take this to a new level of excitement: painters collaborating with poets, poets working with musicians, musicians painting and writing poetry, and all of these coming together in theater.

Philosophy and Politics

In the latter half of the nineteenth century, numerous new strains of thought were being examined and appropriated on the Parisian art scene. As it has a more direct bearing on the development of Poiret, we will look at anarchism a little later. First let us clarify quickly two of the contributing thinkers of the age: Marx and Nietzsche.

Karl Marx (1818–1883) provided a frame through which to view the revolutionary struggles of the passing century. In addition to the ideas of workers' rights and class consciousness, Marx's writings had focused young radicals on the notion of a science of history and human progress, wherein progress in human society was shown to be reliant on inherent contradictions that could be resolved only through conflict. Just as in natural systems of growth and decay, human society sets up tensions that maintain and ensure progress. Each resolution sets up new tensions, which, in turn are resolved, and the process is repeated.

As the nineteenth century drew to a close, the artistic movements found themselves trying harder and harder to break from the past (Figure 3.3). But how to leave the past behind

FIGURE 3.3. Rodin's *Danaid* from 1889 shows the tendency to hold on to classical methods and artistic language despite the desire to break barriers of emotionality and expression.

when the past contained the necessary ingredients for the future? This dilemma became the driving question for art and design that continues to our time. Marx was writing about Napoleon III but could have been writing about the dilemma of art and design when he wrote that the tradition of all the dead generations weighs on the brain of the living. People make their own history, not according to their own whims, but according to the circumstances in which history had placed them. The past is in this way always contained in the present. In revolutionizing themselves and creating the new, people will always look to the past right at the liminal moment of crisis in order to legitimize the change that is being affected.[3] The idea of progress therefore became necessary to the approach of a serious artist: Artists were to build upon previous art and expand the boundaries of their work. At the same time, it was necessary to challenge the existing paradigms and, by contradicting and breaking with the past, bring a modern vision into the world. The danger here is, of course, as seen in our time, that history will constantly repeat itself, if the look to the past only repeats previous visions, rather than build on them.

Friedrich Nietzsche's (1844–1900) works were first becoming known in the early 1890s. His most important contribution to the artists and writers of the time was the combination of extreme individualism with his sharp, violent critique of the contemporary way of life. In his most important work, *Thus Spake Zarathustra*, he posited that God was dead and the European society of his youth was over. He challenged his contemporaries to see that they were hopelessly mired in the past and that their present was without any worth or energy: "All periods prate against one another in your spirits; and the dreams and pratings of all periods were even realer than your awakeness!"[4] Another notion that would have a deep resonance was based on the Darwinian thought that our society is merely a bridge between a primitive existence and something greater. Nietzsche's work was read and admired by many Parisian artists and writers and was at the heart of both the Symbolist and anarchist dilemmas. As such, his thinking was one of the strongest linkages between the creative revolutionaries and the revolutionary creators.[5]

FIGURE 3.4. André Gide wrote in 1897 about the "Uprooted" in Montmartre, describing the seeking generation of intellectuals in Paris, who rejected the traditions and faith of previous generations.

A situation was developing that would be very familiar in the 1960s, especially in the United States: The modern state required an educated class to function, and higher education boomed in France under the Third Republic, with university enrollment doubling from 1875 to 1891, then doubling again by 1908. In contrast to the 1960s, employment for all these educated people was unfortunately not readily available. They were described as *Les Déracinés*, or "The Uprooted," in an 1897 novel by that name. André Gide, the writer and one of their numbers, praised them for refusing the desire for faith and certitude that lay in traditional definitions and alliances (Figure 3.4). He likened them to a butterfly on a leaf. These intellectuals, he said, could alight to favor some political cause but could not dwell there for long without sacrificing the freedom and the beauty of their flight.[6] In Paris, creative spirits were going from one experiment to another, pushing at the boundaries of art and human relationships with art.

Young and in Paris

Poiret, growing up in the center of Paris, developed an early interest in art and theater. Already, at the age of 12, he would head off to the galleries after school and attend the "varnishing sessions." These were previews of the exhibitions, where the galleries would be open to the public while the painters were preparing their canvases for exhibition. He admired the revolutionary young painters of the alternative exhibition at the Salon des Indépendants and was especially attracted to those that would later be known as Les Fauves, or "the wild beasts." After these excursions, he would take a ferry along the Seine to get home to the suburb of Billancourt. On the boat, he would listen to the talk of the artists he had been observing, among them the sculptor Rodin (an admirer of Nietzsche) whom Poiret described as "a little thickset god." Paris at the time was crowded with artistic demigods. Apart from Rodin and the Impressionists, Poiret would witness, be among, and be inspired by an amazing concentrations of visual artists, musicians, and writers such as modern cities have ever collected.

Just as high fashion flourished in Paris after the middle of the nineteenth century, so had all creative disciplines. The artists and artisans, with the slogan "art for art's sake," had increased and capitalized on their autonomy and furnished the developing luxuries market that had blossomed with the growth of the middle class. The middle class took up the mantle of luxury left behind by the disappearing aristocracy, and the demand for manufactured "culture" had never been higher.

Poiret had wanted to go to university, and at the age of 16 finished his matriculation exams with enough credit to do so. However, his father, a textile merchant, wouldn't hear of it. The students of Paris had famously and dramatically rioted only two years before, and Poiret's father was probably less than thrilled to see his artistically minded son join that rebellious crowd. He also may have been thinking of his son's employment prospects, not wishing to add young Paul to the swelling ranks of unemployed graduates in Paris, but to have him stay within the traditional merchant class.

Poiret's friends, however, were of the artistic, more rebellious bent. One of them was Francis Picabia, an art student, who would later become one of the driving forces of the modern art movement of the early twentieth century, most notably through his collaboration with the Dada movement. Poiret's parallel journey with Picabia is worth noting, as the latter's artistic development can be read in parallel with Poiret's as a designer.

Picabia studied painting at the École des Arts Décoratifs in 1895, where Georges Braque and Marie Laurencin were fellow students; Vincent Van Gogh and Henri de Toulouse Lautrec were recent graduates. In 1899, Picabia debuted as an artist in the Salon des Artistes Français with the painting, *Une Rue aux Martigues*. After 1902 he went through an Impressionist period, and after 1909, he was associated with all the "isms" that were going through the art world: Fauvism, Futurism, and Cubism. Then, in 1911, Picabia, along with Marcel Duchamp, began to shift away from the Cubist and Symbolist approaches to a much more radical attack on the bourgeois perception and sensibilities. The Dada movement, which they founded, aimed to challenge all traditional values, all criteria for judging the worth of a work of art. Dada tried to shatter the accepted pattern of artistic development and perception by introducing the concept of anti-art. World War I found Picabia in New York, where he had contributed to the famous Armory Show of 1913. We will see more of Picabia in Chapter 4 as we look at the Dada movement and its significance for fashion throughout the twentieth century and into the twenty-first.

Poiret at Doucet

Poiret would paint all his life, but his artistic interests took a different direction. Instead of attending school, he was apprenticed to an umbrella maker, with his father making the express wish to have him cured of his pride. While sweeping floors and gluing holes in silk umbrellas caused Poiret a considerable amount of frustration, he made up for this by making the most of his visits to the new department stores of Paris on delivery runs. He also took leftover scraps of silk from the workshop and in the evenings would create scale garments on a 15-inch mannequin his sisters had given him. The little mannequin became in turn a "piquante Parisienne and an Eastern Queen."[7] Encouraged by a friend, he began sketching his creations and started shopping the sketches around on his umbrella delivery runs. He met with immediate success. Soon he was making enough money by furtively selling sketches that he started taking cabs to deliver umbrellas in order to have more time for designing. Poiret quickly made connections and sold to all the main fashion houses: Doucet (Figure 3.5), Rouff, Redfern, Paquin, and Worth.

Soon after, when Poiret was only 17, Jacques Doucet was impressed enough with the young man's work to invite him to work there exclusively. He quickly made a name for himself, dressing leading actresses and fashionable ladies. Within a year, he was head of Doucet's tailoring shop, living the high life and engaging in affairs. The high living was actually on the

FIGURE 3.5. A tunic dress by Doucet, 1914.

advice of M. Doucet, who counseled him to "establish some small notoriety in Paris." At the same time as he dove into the high life, he was also developing a streak of youthful antagonism toward the high society he was serving. The haughty manners of his clients and the constant stream of orders that he needed to follow stung and he expressed his frustration by developing a wide rebellious streak. His designing began to evidence a deliberate break from the high-society norm. However, he seems to have been eager to conform, at least on the surface. He modeled himself as a bourgeois dandy, after Doucet himself, whom he idolized (Figure 3.6). Poiret made a great effort to emulate his style of high-class well-tailored dress and deportment, and even began collecting art, like M. Doucet.

Doucet's work was characterized by an extreme sense of romance, femininity, and nostalgia for eighteenth-century France. He maintained a major collection of that period's art and objects until in 1912, when he sold all of his old works at auction and began collecting modern art. Among other works, he would acquire Picasso's *Demoiselles d'Avignon*, a milestone in the modern art movement. Poiret would eventually follow in these footsteps as well, amassing an impressive collection of modern art.

Life at Doucet's did not, however, last long for Poiret. Sneaking into a rehearsal of a play for which Poiret was assisting in the creations of costumes for Sarah Bernhardt, Poiret and Francis Picabia were overheard making mocking comments about the proceedings onstage. The rehearsal was stopped and they were evicted from the theater. Bernhardt went to Doucet and insisted that he fire the young upstart. Doucet did so, but with some regret. Thirty years later, Poiret wrote about his time at Doucet's in his autobiography:

> It was a blessed time, when the cares and worries of life, the vexations of tax collectors and the threats of socialists had not yet crushed out the pleasures of thought and all joie de vivre.[8]

The mention of both taxes and socialists is revealing. Despite contributing to the changing face of modern society, Poiret's revolutionary spirit would always be about enjoying and expanding life, not about the seriousness of practical living and modern politics.

FIGURE 3.6. The young Paul Poiret cultivated the look of a bourgeois dandy, backing up his later assertion that he never considered himself a revolutionary of any kind.

Poiret Protests

Poiret next had to fulfill his military service, and it is in writing about this obligation that he reveals the conflicting impulses between traditional service and individual expression that would be so evident in his approach to high fashion. He was, by his own admission, a poor soldier. He was hauled up for insubordination, and faked illness to be allowed back to Paris to return to designing for awhile. On return to the barracks, he convinced his superiors of his loyalty by putting on a patriotic show, faking "up some patriotic couplets which reconciled [him] to the Commandant, and [he] was no longer considered an anarchist."[9] He seems to have feared being branded a revolutionary and was very careful in his autobiography of 1931 to deny all anarchist and socialist sympathies. He loved the high life too much to go completely over to the artistic revolutionary side. But it is also revealing in this context how determined he was to deny all the influences of his beginning years. The Cubists, his wife, the Ballet Russes, his illustration collaborators (Figure 3.7), the café scene—all were dismissed, either directly or through omission. In light of the fact that he would by then have lost everything he created, including the right to his own name on a label, it may not be surprising that he had a desire to claim a larger, more independent authorship of his work. The suspicion is inevitable, however, that he protests too much.

His rebelliousness could not be contained, and he found himself revolutionizing fashion from the inside. He was all for individuality and a break from the stifling mold of the nine-

FIGURE 3.7. A George Lepape illustration of a Poiret headdress, 1911.

teenth century, but he never meant for the break to be destructive in the way later times would have it. Poiret was, in fact, much like a revolutionary college student in the late 1960s who adopted the hippie fashions and lingo but packed the rebelliousness away with the fashions and paraphernalia upon becoming an adult. However, it must be noted that while they persisted, the young rebels had quite an effect.

Poiret's dilemma between revolution and tradition mirrored the tensions in all of Parisian society. From anarchism to the Dreyfus affair, the final decade of the nineteenth century registered the discontent of newly politicized intellectuals, whose numbers were swelled by the ranks of the educated unemployed.[10] Poiret, although well employed, found himself allied with the discontents. For example, he recalls arguing heatedly right across the French generational and political divide about the trial of Alfred Dreyfus. The trial of Dreyfus, a Jewish officer wrongly accused of spying for the Germans, and the subsequent trial of the writer Emile Zola, who supported Dreyfus, became the final settling of the score between the right-wing royalist factions and the left-wing republicans of France. It also became the flashpoint for the political differences between generations. Poiret and his father were, like the generations of many French families, on opposite sides of this debate. The arguments they had would lead on several occasions to him decamping at friends' houses with his paintings and books.

Art and Fashion Join the Revolution

Also in the 1890s, scandals of greed and bribery shook the French government, and an era of violence began soon after the hundredth anniversary of the Revolution of 1792. For two years, bombs exploded in Paris and assassinations by gunshot and dagger took place with alarming frequency. This was not tied only to French politics but was also part of a larger resettling of

FIGURE 3.8. Fashionable socialists of the fin de siècle.

the Western political situation as the monarchies faded in influence and industrial capitalism grew. The same kind of violence erupted in Italy and Spain, as well as in the United States, with King Umberto I of Italy assassinated in 1900 by an anarchist and President McKinley shot and killed by a copycat assassin a year later. The public in general was terrorized into panic as bombs exploded in theaters, in the scandal-ridden French House of Parliament, and even in cafés, randomly injuring people on the street. When reproached by a judge for endangering innocent lives, an anarchist bomber replied: "There are no innocent bourgeois." [11]

In style-conscious Paris, where intellectual fashions were shed as readily as sartorial ones, young artists were not the only ones liable to pick up anarchist ideas as a short-lived vogue (Figure 3.8). Revolution was in the air, the cafés filled with talk of socialism and internationalism, and the atmosphere was saturated with new social ideas. But writers also satirized the student intellectuals whose garbled socialism remained untroubled by sympathy for the suffering poor. The conservative newspaper *Le Figaro* noted the stylish socialism of 1892: "Everyone is unanimous in declaring that something must be done." Furthermore *everyone* was now a socialist, from the Pope to famous can-can dancers: "And the more income one has, the more one dresses at [the fashion boutique] Redfern's, the more one has one's hair done at [the fashionable hair salon] Lentheric, the more one is a socialist!"[12]

Anarchism: The Most Modern of Fashion Statements?

Together with other branches of socialist thought, anarchism was a protest against what was perceived as the evils of the growing industrial society. Anarchists wished for a reaffirmation of the humanitarian principles of freedom, equality, and justice that had been the credo of the Revolution a hundred years before. At a time when the state excluded vast numbers of people from the rights of citizenship, it was easy for many to accept the anarchist criticisms directed against the state. The extreme radicalism of the anarchists was not easy for the essentially middle-class intellectuals of the café set because the anarchists meant to completely reject the social system in which they lived. The artists of Paris therefore furthered the anarchist philosophy indirectly, perceiving in anarchism the justification for the very aesthetic autonomy that had already been expressed as "art for art's sake."

The anarchists, however, in their total opposition to the middle-class system, rejected any sort of fashionable café dandyism. In "An Appeal to the Young," written in 1880, the anarchist Kropotkin wished for his reader "that you are not one of the fops, sad products of a society in decay, who display their well-cut trousers and their monkey faces in the park, and who even at their early age have only an insatiable longing for pleasure at any price . . . "

The idea that a fashionable appearance would be anyone's concern above "loftier" ideals, has pained religious and political writers for centuries, and this, along with the twist, wherein the acceptance or rejection of fashion signified a political stance, continues to our day.

{ LOOKING FORWARD LOOKING BACK }

Youth, Anarchism, and Anti-Fashions

The urban environment breeds youth fashion, and youth fashion is about distinction. Once young people begin to gather in any numbers in colleges, theaters, cafés, and anywhere else they can interact intellectually and visually, a radical desire sets in to differentiate themselves from their elders by their dress. Often this will involve some flamboyance and general weirdness, although there will be conformity within the group. (In Athens of the fifth century BCE, there were complaints of youths dressing outlandishly at the theater.) But the student-artist mix that became part of the scene in Paris in the years following the Second Empire is closer to what became the norm for the century that followed. In the hundred years after the Second Empire, youth fashion tended toward one of two main poles, making two distinct fashion statements: one, a stylish dandyism, such as the zoot suits of the 1940s and the Mods of the 1960s; the other, the development of an anti-fashion, as with the anarchists of the 1880s and the punks of the 1970s. The dandies would pay meticulous attention and heighten the effect of certain details and exaggerate others, while the stylistic elements of anti-fashions set up deliberate opposites (often with just as much attention) in their disregard for society and current fashions, dandyism in particular. For example, ill-fitting clothes and wild or unusual hairstyles are a recurrent theme of protest fashion, guaranteed to irk the older, neater dressers and well-tailored dandies and set clear boundaries. Throughout the hundred years' fashion, the mutual disdain of dandies and anarchists in the 1880s is echoed over and over again, but among ever-younger groups with less and less political significance.

A Nonlinear Story

Accustomed as we are to the notion of the "progress of history," we tend to imagine that ideas progress as well. However, it is more often the case that human society needs to go through cycles of action and reaction and the echoes of developments in one era can be seen in another. Technology may change, but human emotion does not. We will see how the pendulum of fashion swings back and forth from solid establishment to anarchic breakout (Figure 3.9) until the system falls apart a little over 100 years after it began.

FIGURE 3.9. The assassination of Marie François Sadi Carnot, president of the French Republic in 1894, at the hand of Italian anarchist Santo Casario, at Lyon.

A development, also easily recognizable in later times, is how the most radical elements of the nineteenth century shunned the establishment's fashion and created an anti-fashion. Ragged, unpressed, mismatched, bearded, and long-haired, the anarchist image was deliberately opposed to the carefully assembled bourgeois style.[13] By deliberately violating the code, the anarchist sympathizer could make a political statement merely by appearing on the street, just like the hippies and punks of the twentieth century. Also, much like the radicalism of the 1960s and '70s, much of the artistic anarchism bore the traces of a youth movement. Most of those claiming to be anarchists in Paris in the 1890s were of Poiret's age, in their late teens and early twenties, having been born during the Second Empire or shortly thereafter.[14] This age group would then eventually come to be the one on which the development of any fashion would depend.

Ironically, much of the antiestablishmentarian thinking would be set aside by most as they became older. The radical stance seems culturally to be a young person's action. However, the radicalized periods we will look at, the 1890s, 1920s, and 1960s through the 1970s, implemented changes that, even though they were never as sweeping as was hoped, would not be fully reversed, and not all the radicals abandoned their ideals despite entering the "adult world" of business and family. Each generation of radicals opened society to new interpretations, one small glimpse at a time. High fashion would both follow and react.

Serving the Public?

The various artistic and revolutionary movements of the late nineteenth century were somewhat lumped together in popular perception. In the minds of Parisians in the 1890s, the radicals were all "anarchists" or "intellectuals," if not both. The phenomenon of the intellectual frightened many Frenchmen of the 1890s, tainted as it was by revolutionary politics. The intellectuals were considered more dangerous than the workers. The anarchists' theory was that the new anarchist would be found among the class of literate youth and these would bring anarchism to the working class. This combination of college students and workers would create an anarchism that would publicize and serve the political struggle and evolve in the coming years toward a mounting cultural revolution.[15]

Poiret could never—and did not wish to—be classified as an anarchist or a socialist, what with his high living and love of luxury, but his artistic vision, desire for change, and his deliberate turning away from the established order places him in the forward ranks of the artists of the cultural revolution in Paris. His own assessment was that he had been an agent of radical change by presenting his unique vision to the public at large by being more than simply a designer of clothing:

> But it is neither by restoring life to the colour scheme, nor my launching new styles, that I think I rendered the greatest service to my epoch . . . It was in my inspiration of artists, in my dressing of theatrical pieces, in my assimilation of and response to new needs, that I served the public of my day.[16]

This small quotation from Poiret reveals a personal vision that is almost startling. His vision of himself as a force in the culture, opening up new experiences, and making artistic connections is one toward which high-fashion designers in later years have aspired. To consider one's purpose in design to be a service and to consider that service to be showing the public new ways of approaching life places a designer on par with fine art and poetry, to be sure. For a designer to transcend the boundaries of the discipline and bring a vision to theater, textiles, furnishings, and art is a way of serving the needs of society. But Poiret's approach was not that of creating a franchise or of licensing a label, which became the market's answer to this cross-disciplinary approach. He actively resisted this. His vision was to be a part of the artistic redevelopment of the modern age and to create a way for the urban citizens to express themselves in full color and style. In this way he would serve society. Poiret as a model for a designer's approach to the craft is a tempting one, but even Poiret found this to be difficult as he entered a world where commerce and tradition ruled.

Poiret at Worth

On discharge from military service in 1901, Poiret was hired to Maison Worth. Charles Worth had died in 1895, the year before Poiret was hired to Doucet, but Maison Worth was still doing well, even though its customer base was rapidly disappearing. Worth had handed over the reins to his sons by 1880, but he continued to have a presence and an influence until his death. As a result, Jean Worth basically continued his father's methods and traditions as designer. He designed for the remnants of the world his father had known and had become a specialist in the various courtly ceremonial dress of Europe. Gaston Worth, who handled the business side, was more forward-looking. It was Gaston's decision to hire Poiret, as he felt Maison Worth needed to work in the new market. He said Maison Worth was like a restaurant that served only truffles and that they needed to add a department of fried potatoes. He wanted Poiret to design for the new world, where princesses now went on foot in the streets and didn't wear ceremonial dress all the time. "My brother Jean," he said to Poiret, "has always refused to make a certain order of dresses, for which he feels no inclination: simple and practical dresses which, none the less, we are asked for." Poiret was most eager to fry potatoes for such an establishment, but in his stay at Worth, some of the problems that high-fashion design would face for the next hundred years—the conflict between business interests and creativity—quickly came to light.

Business versus Creativity

Gaston, looking after the business, wished to capture a share of the market for streetwear that the new century was turning up. His brother Jean, on the creative side of the company, was horrified by the addition of Poiret, considering this to be a lowering of standards. As Poiret wrote later (in language echoing both Nietzsche and the anarchists of his youth): "He did not like me very much, because in his eyes I represented a new spirit, in which there was a force . . . which was to destroy and sweep away his dreams."[17] Jean Worth, just like his father, did not wish for the world to change. Their vision, relying on a rapidly fading ritualistic framework, could not renew itself any more than the society it represented. Perhaps by holding onto the customs of the Empire, the old society could be maintained.

FIGURE 3.10. Poiret's "Paris" coat, 1919, an evening coat of brown silk velvet with a placket of red and blue wool and couched gilt-silver cording.

Gaston's hiring of Poiret was a direct challenge to his brother, and both Jean Worth and Poiret knew it. The friction created by Poiret's presence extended to the house's clients as well. On one occasion Poiret's designs raised the hackles of an old Russian princess who declared (apparently without any irony): "Ah! What a horror; with us when there are low fellows who run after our sledges and annoy us, we have their heads cut off and we put them in sacks just like that."[18]

Poiret's creative differences with Jean Worth then grew steadily more pronounced while Maison Worth was busy making coronation robes for the coronation of King Edward VII, and the house was taken up with catering to what still remained of nineteenth-century court life. "I confess, to my shame," said Poiret later, "that I have never been able to understand what it was that he found so admirable about it all."[19] The tension between the two designers became impossible, with open insults being delivered in front of the staff. Keeping Poiret's creativity in the house, no matter how good for business, became too difficult. Gaston Worth let Poiret go after politely declining to finance an independent label for him. Poiret's first success in his own house, however, was based on the kimono gown the old Russian princess had derided (Figure 3.10).

Patronage versus the Market

With the end of royal patronage as a guiding principle, the driving force in the fashion market became the needs and desires of the larger middle class. The fashion business was quickly figuring out how to create and manipulate those needs, but there was still a large division between the traditional class of landed aristocracy and the recent arrivals to economic power. The new aristocracy, as it were, had appropriated most of the "traditional" extravagances and had adapted them to urban living and an internationalism resulting from increased ease of travel. This in itself did not really add much new to the market, except that increased demand allowed for an overall increase in business and the maintaining of high prices for haute couture. The liberty gained by the artists and artisans by the ending of dependence on a patron or collector was offset by a dependence on the market as a whole. Instead of the express wishes of a court, the designer would now be at the demand of sales figures in the same way that artists and writers would be under other forms of pressure, exercised by publishers, theatre managers, and art dealers.[20]

The market Gaston Worth was looking at was something new: his "fried potatoes" went to a class of customers who, although adopting the styles based on the previous 20 years, had little or no connection to aristocratic tradition, and perhaps no real desire to go that far in their fashionable pursuits. What was needed were fashions that maintained the quality and craft established in haute couture but were adapted to the practicalities of modern urban living. This they would do by the abandoning of much of the ornament and rigid structure so typical of Worth's heyday. The modern woman wanted to be able to operate freely in the modern city, and the style of the new age was not to be encumbered by ornament and decorative elements. Architecture and interior design had already begun a movement in this direction that would emerge in force over the following decades: the concept that "form follows function" had only recently been voiced as a design principle in architecture by the architect Louis Henri Sullivan in reference to the problem of designing tall buildings.[21] It was becoming clear that skyscrapers, mass production, engines, and machines all required a rethinking of the approach to manufacturing and design, and this thinking would, of course, influence the designing of clothes for the new urban moneyed classes.

The emerging fashions acknowledged the changing dynamics of class and status these new citizens brought into being. With the new status symbols being readily available commodities, social identity could be purchased and assembled. Another important change in the rhythm of fashion and society resulted from the change in how governments operated in the new republics. Power no longer needed to be exhibited in a social context, given that the business of government had been taken over by a professional class of government official and elected politicians. The business of government did not take place at balls and in salons, and, as such, fashion was essentially removed from the operation of the state. As politics became the realm of individuals, so did fashion. In a tumultuous political climate, fashion, now set free from courtly strictures, became politicized. Fashion could either point forward or reestablish the past. Jean Worth wrote in 1914:

> 'Old-fashioned' is accounted a fearsome phrase by the unthinking, by those lacking true genius in dress. Yet, believe me, it would be vastly better for the beauty of the world if women would revert to the spirit of sweet reasonableness that inspired their grandmothers and great-grandmothers, and regard dress in an entirely different light from the garish one of the present day.[22]

Writing in the same volume, Paul Poiret countered:

> The only well-dressed women are those who dare to create original ideas, not those who servilely follow fashions . . . Instead of hiding their individuality, why did not each woman try to bring out her personal type of beauty? . . . But, curiously enough, women fear being called original or individual, but never hesitate to make fools of themselves in following the latest fashion. A woman will submit to any torture, any

ridicule, if she believes she is worshipping the absurd goddess Fashion.[23]

FIGURE 3.11. Poiret's "harem" look on the cover of the review *Les Modes*, from April 1912. Chez Poiret illustration by Georges Barbier (1882–1932).

Maison Paul Poiret

When Poiret opened his own business in 1903, his success was not immediate, but his reputation from Doucet and Worth served him well and there was enough business to keep him afloat. In 1905, deciding that he needed to settle down after what seems to have been much high living, he married the woman who would be his muse. Denise was of a type that was unfashionable at the time, but that most of the twentieth century would instantly recognize as highly fashionable: tall, thin, and angular. She was perfect for the styles Poiret wanted to create and, like Marie Worth, her input was probably more than she ever got credit for. She was not only Poiret's muse but also his stylist, business manager, and model. Poiret would stage the most extravagant themed parties at which Denise would appear in his latest creations, and his success in the United States was helped along enormously by the publicity she generated. At his most famous party "The Thousand and Second Night," themed on "Arabian Nights," Denise lounged in a cage in the center of their courtyard, until set free by Poiret, costumed as the sultan (Figure 3.11). Poiret's parties, like his designs, were full of light, detail, and color.

Poiret put enormous energy into publicizing his work, through staged events like this, through beautiful window displays at his shop, and also by tours around the continent with his models. His fascination with color was right at the crest of the prevailing trend in art and industry. Chemical dyes and a new lithographic printing technique had introduced bright, sharp colors to artwork, posters, and textiles. Gaslight and electricity were lighting up the cities with a previously unseen brilliance. Bright reds and yellows, deep greens and blues, and intense purples took the place of the elegant and gentle if drab colors of previous generations. In 1905 the group of artists known as Les Fauves, whom Poiret had admired growing up, caused a sensation with their exhibition at the new Salon d'Automne for their unorthodox use of unmixed intense color and aggressive compositions. The fascination with the Orient and all things "exotic," which had been stoked by the Grand Exhibitions, reached a fever pitch in 1909 with the arrival in Paris of the modernist ballet company the Ballet Russes under the direction of the impresario Sergei Diaghilev. Diaghilev and the ballet's designer, Leon Bakst, created a new total style for their ballets, and their colorful, orientalist looks influenced the Parisian art world, specifically the Fauves. Poiret himself would, again, deny being influenced by Bakst, saying that he got there first. Be that as it may, Poiret and the Ballet Russes would circle each other for years, each probably inspiring the other as well as drawing inspiration from the same sources.

It was also in 1909 that Poiret's international fame was guaranteed through a minor scandal, when Margot Asquith, the wife of Britain's prime minister, invited him to stage a fashion show at the Prime Minister's official residence at 10 Downing Street in London. This even wound up causing some embarrassment to the Prime Minister, who was, at the time, engaged in a debate on whether to open up to free trade or to protect British industry. The fact that British workers were on strike at the time did not help either. The British press wrote of "Gowning Street" and used the event to criticize the prime minister, noting that the prices of the outfits were many times the annual wages of a chambermaid. This did not stop the ladies of London from continuing to buy Parisian fashion, but they had to do so on the sly for a while. The scandal did, in this way, prevent French high fashion from completely taking over the market.

A New Century in Art

Three years later, in 1912, Debussy´s ballet, *L´Áprés-midi d'un Faune*, with the by-now famous Nijinsky leading, prompted strong reactions in Paris, among them an editorial in the newspaper *Figaro* denouncing "the extraordinary exhibition of erotic bestiality and shameless gesture," referring to an overtly sexual final scene. The scene in question was tamed down, but in the clubs, salons, and cafés nothing else was discussed. The sculptor Rodin wrote a letter the next day in the newspaper *Le Matin* defending Nijinsky in recognizably modern terms, for "restoring the freedom of instinct and human emotion" to the art of dance.

FIGURE 3.12. Mrs. John Rogers and Mrs. Leonard Hand (right) enroll new recruits for a women's suffrage parade through New York City in Madison Square in 1913.

Shortly after, in New York, the excitement of the Parisian art scene arrived, when early in 1913 the *International Exhibition of Modern Art* brought the Impressionists, Fauves, and Cubists to the eyes of America. Three hundred artists showed over 1,200 works, ranging from Monet's gardens to the Cubist "successes by scandal" of the show, Marcel Duchamp's *Nude Descending a Staircase*, and Francis Picabia's *Procession*. The excitement was, of course, mixed with the ridicule that new artistic movements, just like new fashions, would be greeted with on a regular basis. Poiret's friend Picabia acted as the spokesman for the show, and one New York paper offered a prize to anyone who could claim to understand him.

Poiret, in New York later that year, returned the compliment to the New Yorkers, when at the end of his visit in October he could find nothing favorable to say about Americans in an interview for the *New York Times*. His primary complaint was that Americans didn't know how to laugh. He maintained the Americans laughed with their minds not with their hearts and were repressed, with no heart or soul behind their exterior. He also felt that in America there was too little individuality, saying, "One is conscious only of masses, all doing the same things the same way."[24] In describing his impression of American women (Figure 3.12), he goes equally far, saying that there was no such thing as youth in America. The type that stood out to him—her image obliterating everything else in his mind—was an old woman: "She seems very capable and self-sufficient. . . . Black and white—that is what she is. Not a gay ensemble you see."[25]

Not long after returning from New York, Poiret designed both costumes and sets for a play named *Plus Ça Change* or "The More Things Change . . . " His attitude toward the past and future may be seen through his choices in color. For an act taking place during the reign of Louis XIV, he used green and pink, silhouetting a castle with a blue roof against an orange-pink sky. The last act, set in the year 2000, he designed entirely in black and white.[26] This grand colorist had seen the future and it did not conform to his ideal. In his mind, it was not to be the saturated scene of his youth. It was technological and cold. It was his vision of America.

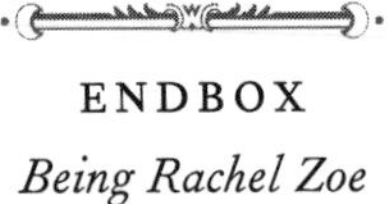

ENDBOX
Being Rachel Zoe

. . . Zoe's phone rang. Her ring tone is the opening notes of "Riders on the Storm," by the Doors. "I'm not sick of it yet," she said as she put the BlackBerry to her ear. "What's up, babe?" It was Taylor Jacobson, one of her two assistants, calling from L.A. "It's bananas here, just bananas. Liv's fitting went great. But she needs some bags. Get some Atwood, Choo and Vivier. And I saw Annie last night. She'll wear the white long for the Hamptons premiere on Monday. You have to get the jewels to her from Cartier. Cavalli is so happy about the premiere. What else? What else? I have lost my short-term memory—I'm just getting blonder by the day."

To translate: Liv Tyler and Anne Hathaway have several events, and clothes are needed. Zoe and her team almost never buy anything new—they borrow or they are given garments from nearly every designer. Some designers say no. A year ago, Zoe contacted

Olivier Theyskens, then the designer of Rochas, about dressing Keira Knightley. He refused. "I was shocked," she said after ending her phone call. "I honestly could not believe that he wouldn't want to dress her. He's a brilliant designer, but he doesn't understand how the business works."

Source: Lynn Hirschberg. The *New York Times.* September 16, 2007.

Discussion Points

1. What is Rachel Zoe talking about? Why is she shocked?
2. Why are actresses important to high fashion? (What is the connection to Poiret's parties?)
3. Where are Jean Worth's "fried potatoes" being served today?

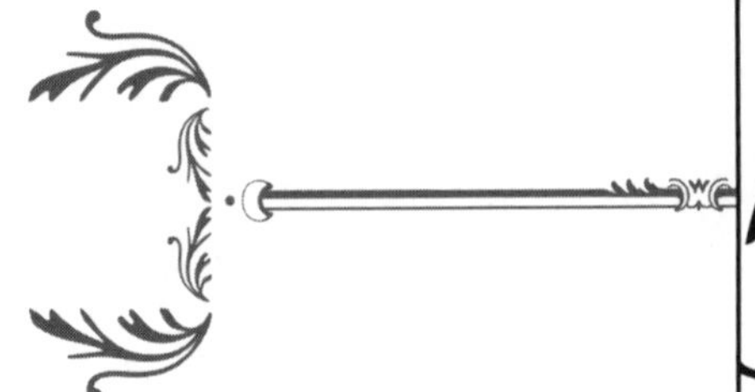

CHAPTER 4

Into a New Century

Backward, Forward, and Sideways

Despite Poiret's break from the fashions of the Second Empire, he cannot be said to have taken high fashion fully into the modern age, as his outlook was essentially still very much in the nineteenth century. In this respect, one might also take the view that the nineteenth century did not really end in 1900, but that the cultural and political century, design included, ended with World War I. Poiret's designs revolutionized the approach to fashion design, but the actual garments continued the tradition of delicacy and decoration that the previous centuries had developed in women's wear. Poiret also continued to design for a woman who was not of the daily grind, as it were. His designs and the illustrations of them portray women as fragile creatures, lounging about, taking part in some Parisian version of an imaginary Orient (Figure 4.1).

Poiret's vision of women seems to have been firmly in this frame. His most cherished image of his parties was of "The Thousand and Second Night" party where he played the sultan and kept his wife in a cage. He did not see himself as freeing women from the confines of dress; he wanted to free them from the confines of conformity. Even though he was credited with freeing women from the corset, he promptly bound them with his "hobble skirt" (Figure 4.2) and was actually quite proud and amused at this himself. He would joke that he had liberated the breasts only to bind the legs.

FIGURE 4.1. An Illustration of Denise Poiret at "The Thousand and Second Night" party, 1911. Gouache by George Lepape (1887–1971).

FIGURE 4.2. A woman wears a black Poiret dress with a tiered, hobble skirt, ca. 1915. Poiret himself joked that he had freed the bust but bound the legs.

It would fall to two female designers to turn the wheel in a different direction by redefining the approach to the look of a twentieth-century woman. This chapter will primarily look at the three designers in question and the forces at play around them. We will continue to follow Poiret but observe as his trajectory crosses with those of Coco Chanel and Elsa Schiaparelli. These three will provide the arc of high-fashion design into the twentieth century, with Poiret looking backward, Chanel looking forward, and Schiaparelli, through her surrealist influences, basically moving sideways, outward from both the others. Each of these three contributed to the total picture and, in doing so, gave fashion design three distinct frameworks in which to grow in the years around the great wars of the twentieth century.

THE GREAT WAR

The poet Sir Osbert Sitwell, himself a soldier on the Western Front, later described how an air of gaiety prevailed in the hot summer of 1914: "Music flowed . . . under the striped awnings and from the balconies; while beyond the open windows in the rooms, the young men about to be slaughtered feasted, unconscious of all but the moment."[1]

The innocent world where all was well, of music and cafés, would be ripped apart with hideous violence for many of those young men, but the horror of what was quickly called "The Great War" would stay away from the striped awnings and gaiety of Paris and London for a while. Even though some of the battlefields were just hours away from Paris, the stories filtered back only slowly. Nineteenth-century notions of "honor" and "dying for your country" remained in full force, and speaking of the horrors and atrocities was initially done only quietly. The twentieth century was meanwhile showing what it could do when its technology was unleashed on a battlefield. The new trains, artillery, machine guns, tanks, and aircraft produced unheard-of carnage. The French lost a million and a half soldiers; Germany, almost 2 million; and Russia, an estimated 20 million. The number of Americans dead was 110,000—twice the number who would die in Vietnam in the 1960s and '70s.

World War I was described as the Great War before it even began. No one had ever before seen a battle of this nature or on this scale, and when the reality of it became apparent, the rejection of the culture that produced such horror would be strong.

Poiret, Chanel, and Schiaparelli

Poiret, by his own account, was not a revolutionary, and observing him from the vantage point of culture and politics 100 years later, it is fairly easy to agree with him. He provided a swing to the pendulum of style that broke the mold of the nineteenth century and opened the door for fashion to be adventurous and experimental. He brought an element of showmanship to the profession and, in his interest in décor and graphic design, widened the scope of a designer's art. His designs however, were rooted in the nineteenth century's vision of the world and women.

Chanel would be the liberator, as she would open the door that would allow fashions to step away from the overload of finery and decoration (Figure 4.3). All the finery had made women's wear into a gorgeous display but at the same time had created a female image that was just that: display. Women were a delicate construction of fine linens, silk, and lace, covered with embroidery, exhibiting on themselves the handicrafts with which they were supposed to be occupying themselves while the men went about in their serious clothes doing serious business.

FIGURE 4.3. Coco Chanel in her signature simplicity in 1935.

One of Chanel's radical moves was to appropriate the ease and comfort of casual menswear. The myths that Chanel perpetrated about the origin of these creations are such that they seem to be almost incidental. She would say things like: "I just cut up a sweater . . . " But put into a larger context, the intent and origin of Chanel's ideas of simplicity and practicality hardly matter. She was right in the center of the theoretical discussions of design, whether she knew it or not. Chanel did not come out of nowhere, any more than did Worth, Poiret, or any of the later influential designers. Tempting as it is to explain them as singular geniuses, one must acknowledge that history creates a place for the right person to step into and that many strands of thought and creativity may come together at that place and time. Chanel was clearly extremely intelligent and driven to succeed. In the atmosphere of Paris at that time she would have been just as informed as anyone in her circles. It is worth remembering that neither Chanel, Poiret, Schiaparelli, nor Worth, for that matter, was a trained designer in the late-twentieth-century sense.

Schiaparelli, although a contemporary of Chanel, came slightly later to the scene. In doing so, she would arrive in an artistic environment that was ready for anything. She would go outward from where Poiret and Chanel were, by bringing a straightforward artistic approach to her creations—sculptural and painterly, collaborating directly with artists (Figure 4.4) in a direct fashion to which we have now become completely accustomed.

It is worth noting that one of the factors that made Paris so spectacularly fertile ground in the arts and humanities at this time was how small it actually was. If one needed to see all the leading artists, designers, philosophers, and writers of the day, one would need only to travel around by bicycle for an afternoon or go to half a dozen cafés in the Montparnasse neighborhood some evening. That's not saying that proximity equals influence, or that everyone talked to everyone (even though reading histories and biographies of the period gives that impression). The point is that the prevailing intellectual and artistic discussions would have been easy to come by for anyone who was listening. Poiret, Chanel, and Schiaparelli were certainly listening and responding, but each had his or her ear turned to a different muse.

FIGURE 4.4. A Schiaparelli design from 1928.

POIRET IN SOCIETY

Poiret had an amazing flair for publicity and began in 1908 to produce illustrated volumes of his designs using young pioneering illustrators, and the latest color-printing techniques. His first volume, illustrated by Paul Iribe, *Les robes Paul Poiret racontées par Paul Iribe* was offered to his major customers and sent to all the royal ladies of Europe. Queen Alexandra of England's copy, however, was returned with the message: "The Queen of England does not read advertising catalogues. Kindly have the courtesy not to send anything of the sort again." Others, less circumspect than the royal court, objected to the "obscenity" of featuring a fully nude Eve on the cover.[2]

Queen Alexandra's rejection of Poiret's album of designs shows that despite the fame and status he had (or believed himself to have), designers, famous or otherwise, were still considered "trade." As such, they had no place consorting with royalty or treating them as equals. Poiret did not accept this at all and, like Worth, made something of a show of arrogance as a way of cultivating an image. After all, Worth had succeeded in making this kind of *hauteur* a signature behavior of the *haute couturier.* Poiret, however, managed to shoot himself in the foot on two occasions with this kind of display. When invited to England, by Margot Asquith, wife of the prime minister and stylish patron of the arts, the resulting "Gowning Street" scandal cost him her open patronage. The fairly innocent event of showing his gowns at Asquith's tea party turned into a major political crisis. The Conservative opposition played up the affair as the British prime minister's support for French industry at a time of economic difficulties and demanded that he explain this "French invasion." Margot Asquith was forced to make a show of buying her clothes from British designers, and any plan of Poiret's becoming the "court designer" for British high society fell through. However, as everyone except Mrs. Asquith continued to buy from Poiret in Paris, the point may have been moot.

What may have been behind the vehemence of the Conservatives' attack was something more personal. A few days before the fateful tea party, Poiret directly ran into the power of aristocracy. Lady Armstrong, a leader of London society and a staunch conservative, came to see his preview at the Curzon Hotel. She laughed at the dresses and called them ridiculous. Poiret's response was to call her an "elderly lady from the provinces" and he invited her to leave. Regrets began to arrive immediately at the prime minister's residence, as the society ladies headed for the hills.

Then, at the end of 1913 at a show in his Paris salon, Poiret took similar revenge on the Baroness de Rothschild[3] for earlier ridiculing his models and designs at a private viewing at her home. He waited until everyone was seated and the hush of anticipation had descended on the crowd. He then entered, declared that he did not consider himself the Baroness's purveyor and asked her in no uncertain terms to leave. When she refused to go, he invited the other audience members to go to the next floor to see the show. The enraged Baroness then left, issuing threats as she went.

That Poiret felt he could eject ladies of such high standing shows what he thought of his own standing in society. But the loss of status in Britain was one thing. What happened in Paris may have been instrumental in costing him the crown. Despite the appearance of power and the abolition of monarchy in France, it would be a while yet before designers would be fully able to dictate the terms of their place in society and move with the high-society crowd they dressed. The illusion of order still had to be maintained. Any challenge to the power of aristocracy had to be met with a counterattack. Charles Worth could order the grand ladies about because he had the protection of the empress. She having anointed him, his authority was then sanctioned by her wearing of his creations until she was no more the icon of Paris fashion. Poiret never had this kind of blessing from anyone anywhere. As a matter of fact, it is doubtful that any designer could claim the kind of sanctification that Worth received. Poiret's authority came from below, as it were, from the fashion-forward café set, which was aligned with the antiestablishment politics of the art world. The fact that the younger aristocrats were wearing his fashions may have caused him to think that he had reached parity with the higher class, but the appropriation of the radical new styles that Poiret represented, along with the wildness of the arts, was an act of generational rebellion, not sanctification.

Chanel in Deauville

The Baroness Rothschild implemented what was visible of her revenge by going to a young milliner who had recently set up a shop in Deauville, a seaside resort by the English Channel, selling radical new fashions. Revenge on Poiret would be inflicted by anointing a new authority. The baroness, who, unlike Margot Asquith, had lost none of her clout in the process of being ostracized from Poiret's maison, brought along to the shop in Deauville a famous actress and clotheshorse of Paris theater. They proceeded to declare the young milliner, Coco Chanel, a talent and personality. In these ladies' wake there arrived a string of princesses and society types. Coco Chanel was in high society's spotlight, just as the continent headed for a war that would show with unprecedented violence that a new world had indeed arrived.

Chanel, bankrolled by her wealthy partner, an Englishman known as "Boy" Capel, had set up shop in Paris in 1909 selling hats. Her hats had been simple and elegant, in contrast to the over-decorated millinery in fashion, and quickly caught on. (See Figure 4.5.) Her

FIGURE 4.5. Coco Chanel brought simplicity and elegance to millinery.

clientele soon included the high-society ladies that frequented the houses of Poiret and Doucet, and these encouraged her to add simple sweaters and blazers. A trend was developing, but Poiret's exoticisms still were the rage. As Chanel's business blossomed, so did her reputation, and she was to be seen around town in the company of Capel and the artists, writers, and aristocrats who were his friends.

By the summer of 1913, Chanel's business in Paris was self-supporting, but with more support from Capel, she opened her shop in Deauville. In the more relaxed atmosphere, she would be seen in clothes she based on Capel's polo outfits. Chanel was a small, thin woman and wore her slightly oversized, mannish outfits well. She took Poiret's removal of the corset to the next stage by creating garments without any stays at all; introduced turtleneck sweaters; and brought knits, flannel, and jersey into style (all influences from Capel's wardrobe, no doubt).

Chanel's early creations seem to have been very much inspired by the moment. She did not sketch; in fact, she couldn't at all. She created all her garments as models, having developed a mastery of fabrics and drape right away, and seems to have had a strong determination to succeed from the very start. The fact that she came from a childhood of poverty may have colored her approach to the work. To her, *couture* was a business, not an art, and she worked hard at it. Not for her the exhibitions of Poiret, but even so, in Deauville with Capel, she became a celebrity for her offbeat fashions and dramatic character. "There too," she said "I started a fashion—couturiers as stars."

The following summer, Chanel's reputation continued to rise, and the uncommon heat brought crowds to her shop for the loose casual clothing she sold. The Baroness Rothschild's blessing brought greater attention still, and the threat of war seemed not to matter a bit to the pleasure-seekers in Deauville.

Modernism and Fashion

From its inception until around the middle of the twentieth century, fashion was shunned by the leading voices in design, the architects and furniture designers that led the Modernist Movement. To the modernists, design needed to strive toward the functional, rational, universal, and permanent. Women's fashion was seen as frivolous, temporary, and

FIGURE 4.6 Men's and women's fashions at the turn of the century: *The Sitwell Family*, 1900, by John Singer Sargent.

irrational. Men's clothing, however, was seen to have evolved into the kind of modernization through design that architecture needed to strive for.[4]

Design was meant to be international, divorced from history, and above all, functional. Men's fashions at the beginning of the twentieth century were models of functionality compared to women (Figure 4.6).

A rejection of "the feminine" was very strong in the early years of modernist design. Anything frivolous or sensual was to be banned, and ornament was the greatest crime. The loaded exoticisms, such as those embraced by Poiret and the Ballet Russes—even their color choices—were antithetical to this thinking, The new age was meant to be robust, strong, and moving at high speeds. In an age of technology, art and design were to be technological and systematic.

The Futurists

The Futurists were a movement that began in Italy in 1909 and took modernist thinking to its logical extreme, fetishizing the technology of the twentieth century. The Futurists embraced the coming war, in that it would lead to the wiping away of the "decaying" old bourgeois world. Their vision of progress is pure Nietzsche and anarchism:

> We want to glorify war—the only cure for the world—militarism, patriotism, the destructive gesture of the anarchists, the beautiful ideas which kill, and contempt for woman.

Notice that not only is there no place for women in this vision of the modern age, but that actual contempt is advocated. Even after World War I, the Futurists' leader, Filippo Thomasso Martinetti, continued in this vein, glorifying the Fascist invasion of Ethiopia by again proclaiming the beauty of war (in decidedly feminine terms!): "War is beautiful because it enriches a flowering meadow with the fiery orchids of machine guns."[5]

It is hard to look at statements like this in light of later developments and not suspect some irony involved, but this was the furthest extreme of the modernist movement that idolized the mechanics of modern living. The adoration of the technologies developing everywhere was so great that the machine became the reigning metaphor for all things. Houses were machines for living in; office buildings were machines for commerce; and the masses on the streets were elements in a great city-machine. This kind of thinking became the basis for much of twentieth-century thinking in politics, economics, and design and is therefore worth noting. It will come into play in shaping the ideologies of the remaining decades of this story, such as when President Herbert Hoover thanked advertising executives, just before the stock market crash of 1929, for having turned his new U.S. citizen-consumers into "constantly moving happiness machines."[6]

Interestingly enough, the Futurists did have ideas of radical fashions, even though those were limited to the masculine, like everything else. The Futurist Giacomo Balla, for instance, wished to do away with the white-collared, dark-suited image and designed asymmetrical outfits for men in the colors of national flags to stir up nationalism and longings for war. Even their fashions were to be utilized for masculine radical destruction. (See Figure 4.7.)

FIGURE 4.7. *Unique Forms of Continuity in Space*, 1913, a sculpture by the Italian Futurist Umberto Boccioni. The Futurists emphasized the beauty and excitement of the speed and power of modern machinery.

It must be noted that the philosophy of tearing down to build up was not limited to the Futurists, but they serve as a clear example of a vocabulary that combined the overthrow of accepted norms with an individualist revolt against bourgeois convention. Their outlook was also shared by the Cubists and others. Picasso himself referred to his work as "a sum of destructions," and the poet Guillaume Apollinaire called on artists to "innovate violently." The artists of the first decade of the twentieth century were steeped in ideas of anarchy and a Nietzschean creation of new social values. Artistic novelty was identified with a new way of thinking and a break from a bourgeois order allied to a derivative and "impotent" academicism.[7] It is no wonder that the insults and comments from Jean Worth to Poiret took on the language of a culture under siege: "Vulgar!" Worth said on one occasion, referring to Poiret's orientalisms, which he found completely unsuitable for the dignity of Parisian society, "Hideous, barbaric!" He said, on another, "They are really only suitable for the women of uncivilized tribes! If we adopt them, let us ride on camels and ostriches! In gray Paris they are impossible, ridiculous!"[8] It is equally understandable that Poiret would ridicule his former employer by describing Worth's coronation gowns as draperies for municipal prize-giving ceremonies.[9] One feared the emotion, the other laughed at the lack of it. Each operated from the position of a firmly held belief in what the world should look like.

It is here, already in the second generation of designers, that a separation begins to appear in the world of high fashion that would continue to widen and solidify for a century. On one hand would be designers who would work within a tradition and look to the past for guidance and inspiration, producing versions of previous fashions for a new audience. On the other hand would be those who would consider their calling to be breaking with the past and bringing new elements into play, seeking inspiration from contemporary trends and arts. Gradually the "past" and "future" would become less clear as a destination, as references began to run again over the same terrain. As the twentieth century progressed, the fabulous future envisioned in the early century would begin to rapidly to lose its luster. We will see how designers eventually began to imbue the past with no specific symbolic meaning other than a reference to some mythical decade or other of media-defined pop culture, as each decade produced its own nostalgic longing.

We will see how fashion design gets caught between the desire for the past and the desire to destroy the past. This turns into the problem that the painter Giorgio de Chirico defined after the war in 1919, when he concluded that "the futurist liberation of painters is like the purification of mankind through war: neither of them exists." The glorification of the modern for its own sake and the drive for destructive change to achieve the new order leads only to empty results, producing a desire to return to a more secure and familiar time. Human beings require in their own identities, personal and societal, a fixed point of reference. In the absence of one, they will appropriate the nearest identity available or invent one. Order will always eventually prevail over the liminal, as human beings reject uncertainty.

Fashion and Dada

Already in 1911, the art world was moving on. Duchamp, Picabia and his wife, along with the aforementioned Apollinaire, attended a theatrical performance involving machines that Duchamp would describe as "the madness of the unexpected."[10]

Duchamp began questioning what it is that "makes" a work of art, and from this questioning produced works that are still confusing to viewers, although perhaps for different reasons. He eventually came up with the concept of the "ready-made"—an ordinary object placed in a viewing situation and designated as a "piece." His ready-mades would include a urinal placed on its side, a snow shovel leaning against a wall, and a bicycle wheel on a stool.

Meanwhile, other Dadaists would create "poetry for fish" and other such writings, in which meaning and understanding were not an objective. The action of placing an object, making a sound, or having a thought was creative in itself. "Art is what you make it." (Figure 4.8).

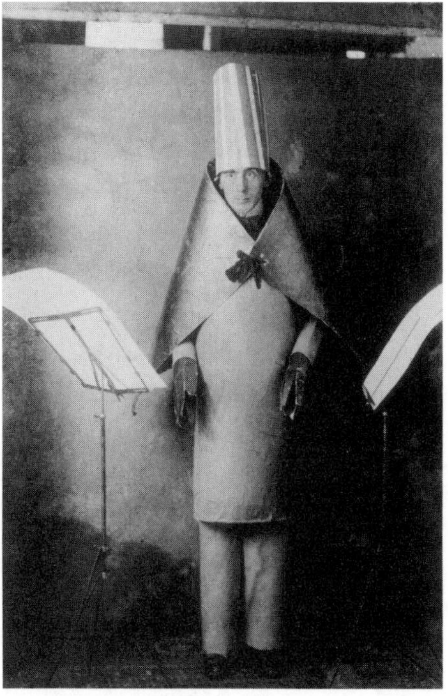

FIGURE 4.8. The Dadaist Hugo Ball, in "Cubist costume," performing his sound poem *Karawane* at the Cabaret Voltaire in 1916.

The grim reality of World War I and the resulting disillusionment with the modern world brought these artists to the realization that art, as they had practiced it up to the point of the Armory Show in 1913, was not capable of speaking to the world in a meaningful way. In fact nothing could. Given the broken future that now was laid in front of them, what could young artists possibly do? The answer was "Dada!" The deliberately meaningless word, evoked a baby babbling, a machinelike repetition of nothing, or as some would have it: A rocking horse. Another leader of Dada, Tristan Tzara, wrote: "The beginnings of Dada were not the beginnings of art, but of disgust."[11]

The significance of Dada became abundantly clear in the 1960s, when that decade's generation of fed-up youth begin to resort to similar tactics. According to this way of thinking, the irrationality of bourgeois society can be met only by irrationality. If one allows that someone else has the right to define whatever he or she likes as meaningful, one has affirmed the other's individuality. In fashion, the adoption of this stance creates a possibility that anything can be done, worn, or not, depending on the designer's say-so. And no one has to explain anything or conform to anything. Fashion, like art, is in that case what you make it.

{ LOOKING FORWARD LOOKING BACK }

The In Joke Is on the In Crowd

The twentieth century produced several waves of surreal nonconformity that fed off disillusionment and dissent. The artists and writers of the Dada movement, reacting to the brutality of modern society after World War I, produced a model for future generations of radicals: the way to change bourgeois society was from within, where one could hold up a mirror showing the "burghers," "squares," or "yuppies" (the clueless establishment du jour) the chinks in their armor. One could "mess with their heads," not with anarchist bombs but by pointing to flaws or absurdities in their commerce-driven, middle-class world. Examples include the "art" of Duchamp's urinal, and the "Death of Hippie/Son of Media" event in San Francisco.

With high-fashion design being the vehicle of self-identification for the establishment, designers could not play this game overtly, even though Poiret had the inclination at first, and Schiaparelli's collaboration with Dali could have headed in this direction. Most high-fashion "Dadaisms" stayed, like Schiaparelli's within the boundary of social acceptability; more of an ironic lark, allowing the upper classes to be in on the joke without scaring anyone.

It wasn't until after Pop Art of the 1960s, as the art and design worlds began to merge in the 1970s and design schools began to adopt an art school approach in the 1980s that young designers picked up the Dada flag. The most high-profile example was Franco Moschino, who, after beginning in a Schiaparelli vein (e.g., hemming a skirt with fried eggs) went further and for example, showed jackets with "Expensive Jacket" or "Stop the Fashion System" embroidered on the back. However, when clients flocked to buy his items anyway, his efforts were dismissed as publicity stunts. The fashionistas of the end of the century were already too versed in anger, absurdity, and irony to not play along, and you can't fight someone who refuses to fight.

Schiaparelli

The end of the war in 1918 found Elsa Schiaparelli and her baby in New York. She had been abandoned by her husband and was one step away from living on the street. She was rescued by Gabrielle Picabia (the estranged wife of Poiret's old friend, the surrealist painter Francis Picabia), who was living in New York during the war. Soon thereafter "Schiap," as she called herself, was ensconced in Greenwich Village, where she seems to have picked up what work she could. Mme. Picabia enlisted her, for example, to sell French underwear she had brought from Paris. The underwear was designed by a sister of Paul Poiret, and according to Schiap, the selling did not go well.[12]

The meeting of Schiaparelli and Picabia produces an circular reference that can illustrate the small world of fashion design in the early decades of the twentieth century: Poiret's two sisters, Germaine Bongard and Nicole Grout, both made names for themselves as designers, and Germaine especially was an active participant in the art circles in Paris. Her business, Jove couturier, doubled as Galerie Thomas, and this was where the first exhibition of the "Purist" art of Le Corbusier and Bongard's close friend Amédée Ozenfant took place. Their 1921 essay on "Purism" underscored their strong opposition to fashion.

Greenwich Village had a large artist community, and it was here that Schiaparelli also met Marcel Duchamp, who, along with Picabia and Man Ray, introduced her to the Dada movement with its anarchic freedom and strange sense of humor. When Schiaparelli went back to Paris in 1922, she stayed again with Gabrielle Picabia. She lived nearby Poiret's maison, and Poiret was immediately charmed by the vivacious Schiap and allowed her free run of his collections, giving her his creations "whether she needed them or not." The near-penniless Schiaparelli was therefore better dressed than most women in Paris.

The Reds

The disintegration of the political scene in Europe during and after World War I made an opening for the political movements that would characterize the following 70 years. Russia's misfortunes in the war opened an opportunity for a Socialist revolution in 1917, and soon after the war, extreme right-wing movements arose all over Europe to combat the "Red Threat." Many embraced socialism as the answer to the crises in European society; others blamed socialism for all the ills.

Fashion after the war began to reflect these politics in that any hint of ostentation could be taken the wrong way in either case. Initially, both extremes of the political world viewed the upper class as "decadent," and well after the dictatorships of Hitler and Stalin showed their true colors, both movements still presented themselves as "peoples'" movements. To be radically political in the years between the wars now meant to shun fashion

FIGURE 4.9. Customers in a Moscow fur shop, ca. March 1939: Soviet Russians emulated the "decadent" fashions of the capitalist West to prove that their system could provide the same standard of living.

altogether. To be a socialist was now to be as anti-fashion as the anarchists had been before. Anarchists were largely marginalized after their tactics at the beginning of the century led nowhere. Fashionable youth were generally to be found outside the realm of politics altogether. A hedonism was setting in; a reaction to the overheated politics of the day. Politics were for serious people; being young was a time for fun. Now instead of Gide's intellectual anarchists who flit about, there would only be flitting about. As one of Hemingway's "Lost Generation" characters says in "Hills Like White Elephants" from 1927: "'That's all we do, isn't it—look at things and try new drinks?"

The Russian Revolution of 1917 led to a five-year civil war, after which the Soviet Union was formed. In the Communist society, any hints of class distinction were meant to be eradicated. Initially this did not preclude competing with the West in luxuries, the theoretical difference being that luxuries such as high-fashion design were supposed to be made available to all in the worker's paradise (Figure 4.9), whereas in the West such things were markers of class distinction and signs of a decadent society. To be able to hold two contradicting beliefs at the same time is often considered a mark of insanity, and it may well be that by now modern society was indeed going insane—or would soon.

In 1936 Schiaparelli was invited to be part of a French trade delegation to Soviet Russia, an invitation that she accepted "because nobody else wanted to go, and that in itself was irresistible."[13] She went with her American publicity manager and Cecil Beaton, the famous fashion photographer. Their trip was a mix of rough living and luxury. Schiap designed a dress for Soviet women, "a plain black dress, high in the neck [that] could be worn both at the office and at the theater. Over it was a loose red coat lined with black which fastened with large simple buttons." The French, British, and American fashion magazines they exhibited proved the most popular item at their exhibit. Most young women in Russia at the time had never seen a fashion magazine. [14]

Schiaparelli was invited to inaugurate the first Soviet fashion boutique and "found a smallish room full of people" where electric mannequins were turning slowly under glass, displaying "bewildering clothes . . . an orgy of chiffon, pleats and furbelows." The scene was too surreal, even for her.

This kind of political showmanship became stock in trade for the strange relations between East and West later, but both before and then some years after World War II, there was a belief all around that the Soviet Union might well overtake Europe and America economically. Progress had been phenomenal in the years since the Revolution, but the cost of this progress in human life and suffering was not witnessed by many outside Russia. In 1936, it was also still a widely held belief that things would calm down and then everyone could "do business." Meanwhile, the Russians could help keep Germany, where Hitler had been in power for three years, in check. Hence, Schiaparelli's exhibition companions were Chanel, Coty, Guerlain, Courvoisier Cognac, and other such "decadent" producers. Perhaps they could do business.

The mass executions, starvations, and forced resettlements would only later come to light. Meanwhile the commissars of the party learned how to foxtrot, and Schiap's dresses were copied and mass produced, no doubt for the party elite.

America Rising

Meanwhile on the other side of the Atlantic, the United States had been steadily growing in size, might, and wealth. From about the time Charles Worth was setting up shop in Paris, Americans, having concluded their Civil War, had been building railroads and cities, mining resources, and forming a unique culture of their own. In the cities on the East Coast, French influences dominated fashions from the start, and just as Worth liked his Americans, so Poiret made great efforts to maintain an American market. He traveled to America, giving lectures and making deals.

FIGURE 4.10. The International Style can be seen in this photo of Helena Rubenstein and her son aboard the SS *Mauretania*, July 18, 1930, in Manhattan.

Americans in Paris

The new aristocracy that began to arrive from America on the Parisian scene at the end of the nineteenth century was an aristocracy based wholly on wealth. The wealth had little connection to any idea of place or birthright and could be spent on anything anywhere. Class and status arose from the display of things bought, worn, and consumed. Money made from shipping or railroads would buy Parisian fashions, Italian artwork, furniture, textiles, and last but not least, invitations to stately houses. The fashions and furnishings would then spark trends "back home," whether in Boston or Kansas City (Figure 4.10). Knockoffs of French fashions became a booming industry, selling great quantities in the department stores that were also booming all across America.

Not everyone in Paris was happy with the Americans. Poiret attempted to revive his famous parties after the war but found that the foreigners who came to Paris in the summer had no understanding of his "revivals." How out of touch he had become by this point can be seen by his displaying of a *tableau* of dancers dressed and seated to reproduce Winterhalter's portrait of the Empress Eugénie and her ladies-in-waiting (Figure 1.1) as the grand finish to the evening's performance. Poiret was greatly insulted that the Americans "went out, as indifferent to the Empress as to Winterhalter, in a hurry to get back to their cosmopolitan palaces, or to kick about in smart dancing places."

On lecture tour in America he was equally bewildered. He was amazed at the size and scale of the cities and the sheer numbers of everything, but he was disappointed at the lack of joy he found in the middle-class Americans he encountered. "And yet America attracts me irresistibly . . . it seems to me that I have need of its atmosphere of activity and of its practical spirit, of its clarity, its intelligence and sense of work." The American woman is the most beautiful in the world, but lacks personality, he says, and warns them of the mass-produced fashions they are buying into:

> Take care! You are being deceived. You imagine you are being provided with the fashions of Paris; but you do not see them! You send to Paris emissaries commissioned to inform you, but they do not tell you what they see. You are women who have won your freedom, cinema, "stars," rich, liberated, independent. Come to Paris![15]

He could not make up his mind regarding the modern-day situation. He agonized over the power of the designer to dictate fashion and then lamented the American woman's "childish" willingness to obey his every whim. Significantly, he lamented the market's takeover of the designer's craft, where "one day, they thought they knew more than their masters. That is what is happening in Parisian dress designing, on which they have sought to impose their taste, and substitute the experience of buyers of the invention of creators." We will see where this phenomenon was heading in the next chapters.

Jazz

But the fascination Americans had with Paris was not limited to the rich. Artists and writers, such as e .e. cummings and Ernest Hemingway, were drawn to Paris, forming an expatriate colony in Montmartre, sometimes referred to as "The Lost Generation." Their politics tended toward the antiestablishment type, and their fashions tended toward a "bohemian" roughness that would actually seem rather tame today.

The reverse was also true. The French had had a fascination with the "Wild Continent," since before the American Revolution in 1776. Now that the continent was developing a style of its own, the flow back and forth created an echoing of cultures in both directions across the Atlantic. The nightlife of Paris began to swing to the sounds of jazz (Figure 4.11).

FIGURE 4.11. As fashions went west across the Atlantic, cultural influences flowed the other way. Bands such as Joe "King" Oliver's Creole Jazz Band, pictured here in 1923, wowed Paris. (Louis Armstrong is to the far left.)

The Americans had no ties to tradition but what they had imported, and anyone could dress anyway he or she wanted, as long as the individual could pay for it. Schiaparelli admired the corset-less women on the streets of New York, and American men felt no need to dress in the rigid fashions of their fathers. The American style was "loose" and fitted the Jazz Age well. The modernist ideal of the stiff white collar was giving way to something less rigid altogether.

Woman Has Got There before Us

In 1925, the changes to women's fashion were such that comparing the silhouettes with those at the beginning of Poiret's career 30 years before, one might imagine that a different species had emerged. Although this would turn back later, the lack of any restrictions or structures in women's clothing was (literally in some cases) breathtaking. Chanel introduced the iconic Chanel suit (Figure 4.12) in her 1925 collection at the Exposition Internationale. A collarless, braid-trimmed cardigan jacket with long tight-fitting sleeves and a simple straight skirt, this design would become the most copied of any *couture* garment in the twentieth century.[16]

FIGURE 4.12. Coco Chanel in a version of her famous suit in 1929.

Even the "Purists" came around. Perhaps through the influence of Poiret's sister, Le Corbusier himself wrote in 1930:

> Woman has got there before us. She has brought about the reform of her dress. She found herself in this dilemma to follow fashion and by doing so gave up what modern technology [and] modern life had to offer. To give up sport and, more materially, the chance of employment which has given her a productive role in modern life and enabled her to earn her living . . . To carry out the daily construction of her dressing and grooming: hairdo, boots, buttoning her dress, she would have had to give up sleeping.
>
> So woman cut off her hair and her skirts and her sleeves. She goes around bareheaded, bare-armed with her legs free, and she can dress in five minutes. Moreover she is beautiful; she enchants us with the grace of her figure . . .
>
> The courage, the enterprise, the inventive spirit with which woman has revolutionized her dress are a miracle of modern times. Thank you![17]

He goes on to attack his own previous fixation with a tailored look and starched collar: "What about us men? A dismal state of affairs! In our clothes, we look like generals of the

FIGURE 4.13. A poster by Robert Bonfils for the Paris Exposition in 1925.

Grand Army and we wear starched collars! We are uncomfortable."[18]

Once again, we come to a Great Exhibition. In 1925, delayed by the war and its aftermath, *L'Exposition des Arts Decoratifs et Industrials Modernes* (Exhibition of Modern Art and Design) opened in Paris. This exhibition brought the Art Deco style to the fore, although because of the delay, the style was already being overtaken by the pure Modernists with their rectilinear machines. For this exhibition, Poiret had rented three barges, with the names *Amours*, *Délices*, and *Orgues*, which he floated on the river Seine. He had converted one into a restaurant, and in the others, the clothes of Worth, Callot, and Lanvin were displayed.[19]

Enter Dior

Entering the story now is a young man who will shadow Poiret for a while before eclipsing him completely. As Poiret's barges lay on the Seine, this young man, whose nanny had also been Poiret's, was only 20 years old. He had just graduated from college and was viewing the Exhibition with his friends in a state of high excitement. Just like Poiret at the color-fountain in 1899, these young men had never seen anything like it (Figure 4.13).

Christian Dior was right there, on the banks of the Seine, among the Cubists, Surrealists, and Dadaists running around in Paris. He was developing his ideas with the most avant-garde modernists of the twentieth century. Yet he would, 20 years later, become the designer who would set women's fashions on a trajectory that headed directly in reverse to everything that was going on around him as a youth: a reversal that is still felt today. Dior's sensibilities in this regard are in keeping with Poiret's, and his ascent will later mark a return to the reactionary view of femininity that Poiret represented at the end. Dior was as inevitable as the rest, but that storyline has to be set aside for a while so that we may explore the trajectory that was interrupted.

Exit Poiret

The three barges were the final party for Poiret. The cost of that venture sank his business. In a move that would become all too typical in later years for the designer, he had sold all his debt-ridden holdings, along with the rights to his name, to a group of investors the year before. Now for the first time, a designer became a "brand." He then essentially became an employee for the group. Never one to be told what to do, the antiauthoritarian in him came to the surface in all his dealings with the conglomerate. They would send him on a lecture tour to the United States, and he would make a point of insulting everyone and turn down all offers for licenses to his name. Meanwhile, his ideas were not renewing themselves, and his dresses were looking decidedly dowdy. After he turned down an offer, in 1929, for $16,000 to license his name for a pair of shoes he didn't like, his board of directors fired him and closed down the house. The crash of the American Stock Market later that year closed off the American market and cut him off from future opportunities. He would come briefly back to designing, but for our story, this could just as well be the last we will see of Paul Poiret.

We will look at the 1930s more closely on the other side of the Atlantic, as Chanel and Schiap went to Hollywood, and the American corporations became the driving force of the fashion business or, rather, created the business as we know it today. One of the developments we will look at more closely is Schiap's collaboration with the Surrealists, but for now, let us leave her and Dior in their respective positions as Europe and the world headed for war.

Fashion and Surrealism

The Surrealists evolved out of the group that began Dada. They used Freud's ideas of dreams delivering the unconscious mind to the surface. To create art, they juxtaposed images and objects or presented shocking subject matter in order to jolt the mind out of its normal frame and into a realization. The Surrealist Manifesto of 1924 stated that from Freud they gathered that the mind was capable of dealing with multiple realities, and so they believed in "the future resolution of these two states—outwardly so contradictory—which are dream and reality, into a sort of absolute reality, a surreality, so to speak."[20]

Schiaparelli, who had been familiar with the Dadaists since her early days in New York, played games with Surrealism in many of her creations. She collaborated with Dali, Man Ray, and the ever-present Jean Cocteau. A year before Hitler's armies invaded Poland, sparking

FIGURE 4.14. Schiaparelli's Tear dress from 1938.

World War II, Schiaparelli created with Dali the "Tear" dress (Figure 4.14). The fabric is painted to look as if the skin of an animal has been flayed to expose raw flesh and a matching veil has matching cuts in three dimensions. Salvador Dali, the most popular of the Surrealists in later years, said that his art was "hand-painted photographs of dreams." In this design, Dali and Schiaparelli brought the coming nightmare of jackbooted brutality into the world, which wasn't really looking. Dali's homeland, Spain, had been engaged in civil war for years, with German planes dive-bombing and strafing civilians. Schiaparelli was in anguish over the devotion her young countrymen in Italy were showing to Mussolini and the Fascists. Hitler had annexed Austria and was clearly heading for Czechoslovakia. Where their previous collaborations had been quite whimsical, involving porkchop hats and lobster dresses, this one was clearly meant to shake their audience.

Paris's Prewar Fling

However, Schiaparelli and Dali may have been alone, as far as fashion designers were concerned. The mood in Paris fashions did not generally reflect the dread of war. In the spring of 1939 Paris society was a whirl of endless balls and crinolines—the Viennese look was all the rage in the salons. In her *New Yorker* column from Paris, correspondent Janet Flanner wrote about the frivolities she witnessed in Paris, as war was once again on the horizon. "It has taken the threat of war," she wrote, "to make the French loosen up and have a really swell and civilized good time."

In June 1938, Robert Piguet offered Dior a full-time position designing creations for his house. For his very first collection, Dior designed a dress called *Café Anglais:* "a

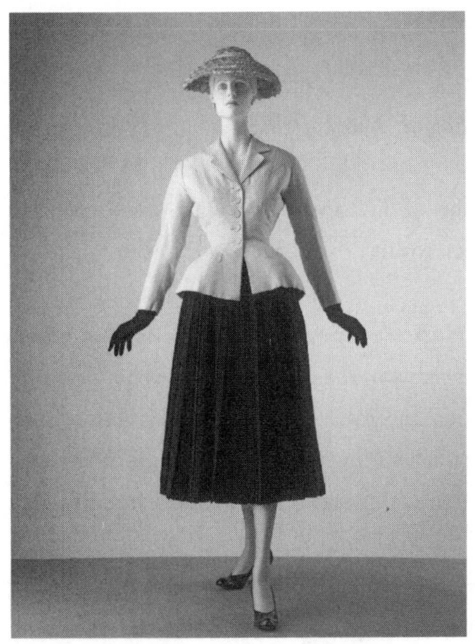

FIGURE 4.15. Dior's inspiration for the *Café Anglais* design would continue to serve him later in his so-called "New Look," as can be seen by comparing Dior's "Bar" Suit from 1947 with . . .

houndstooth dress with a petticoat edging, inspired by *Les Petites Filles Modèles.*" *Les Petites Filles Modèles* was a classic of children's literature, a series of novels in which the child heroines always display the most perfect manners. As illustrated during the Belle Epoque period (Figure 4.15), they wore dresses with rounded collars, little cuffs, and full, rounded skirts in *broderie anglaise*. This was Dior until the end.

And Chanel? Three weeks after Germany invaded Poland on September 2, 1939, she closed the House of Chanel. Unlike Poiret, she will be back. But first, back to America and the Crash of '29.

. . . an illustration from the French children's book *Les Petites Filles Modèles* from 1857.

ENDBOX

Before Models Can Turn Around, Knockoffs Fly

Ms. Anand's company, Simonia Fashions, is one of hundreds that make less-expensive clothes inspired by other designers' runway looks, for trendy stores like Forever 21 and retail behemoths like Macy's and Bloomingdale's.

A debate is raging in the American fashion industry over such designs. Copying, which has always existed in fashion, has become so pervasive in the Internet era it is now the No. 1 priority of the Council of Fashion Designers of America, which is lobbying Congress to extend copyright protection to clothing. Nine senators introduced a bill last month to support the designers. An expert working with the designers' trade group estimates that knockoffs represent a minimum of 5 percent of the $181 billion American apparel market.

Outlawing them is certainly an uphill battle, since many shoppers see nothing wrong with knockoffs, especially as prices for designer goods skyrocket. Critics of the designers' group even argue that copies are good for fashion because they encourage designers to continuously invent new wares to stay ahead.

Designers say that is pre-Internet thinking.

"For me, this is not simply about copying," said Anna Sui, one of more than 20 designers who have filed lawsuits against Forever 21, one of the country's fastest-growing clothing chains, for selling what they claim are copies of their apparel. "The issue is also timing. These copies are hitting the market before the original versions do."

. . . Of several shoppers polled outside a Forever 21 branch in Herald Square in Manhattan recently, none said that knowing a design was copied would stop them from buying it.

"Some people don't want to spend $300 on a pair of jeans just because of the name," said Siovhan McGearey, 16, from London. "They may look nice, but why pay $300 when you can go down the street to Forever 21 and get jeans that are $30 that look exactly the same?"

Designers counter that if the knockoffs continue unabated, their businesses will be in jeopardy.

Ms. Anand maintained that her reproductions of designer styles have been changed enough that they do not violate a designer's intellectual property. "We don't copy anything," she said. "We tweak it. We get inspired before we create it."

She sees her work meeting the needs of the vast majority of consumers who cannot afford designer prices. "Especially the younger girls do not have so much money," Ms. Anand said, "but they want to wear fashionable clothes."

"They want to look fabulous," she said. "It's their right to look fabulous."

Source: Guy Trebay. "Before Models Can Turn Around, Knockoffs Fly."
The *New York Times*. September 4, 2007, p.A1.

Discussion Points

1. Was Poiret right to be alarmed at American women and the American market?
2. What is the relationship of high fashion to politics today?
3. Do women have a right to look fabulous? Do men also have this right? Do they exercise it?

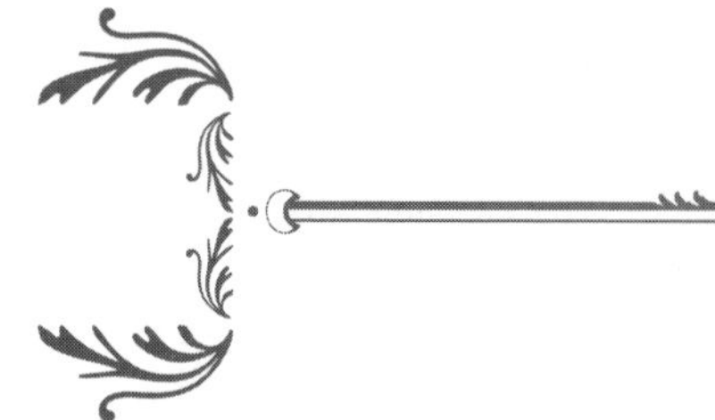

CHAPTER 5

The Fading of Europe

The American Age Begins

The economies of all the nations involved suffered from the effects of the Great War, but not for the same reasons. The United States had loaned money to both Britain and France to finance their war efforts, and the repayments were a heavy burden. Germany was required to make extremely high reparation payments to Britain and France, and when those payments weren't forthcoming and then with a hugely devalued currency, both nations found their debt to the United States an insurmountable obstacle. With the crash of the stock market in 1929, the fragile markets collapsed one after the other. The governments of Britain, France, and the United States, in trying to pick up the pieces, became aware that the international economy may need to take precedence over internal affairs as international trade relations were essential to international peace. Discussions on international trade and tariffs began to open the door for global markets and the resolution of war debt called for a balance of trade.

Meanwhile, in the United States—as elsewhere—a resurgence of nationalism and protectionist policies led to a heightening of political tensions between those who felt that a new world should arise on the ruins of the nineteenth-century world order and those who felt that the social structures of the late nineteenth century should be preserved. The Red Scare in the United States, resulting from the Russian Revolution's capping decades of emerging socialist and anarchist thought, led to a fear of social upheaval, but when the scaremongers' darkest pictures failed to materialize (although bombs did go off on Wall Street), the threat to the new capitalist aristocracy was largely shrugged off.

In Chapter 8, we will examine in detail the activities of our designers, Chanel, Schiaparelli, and Dior, during the war years, but now let's step back and look at the shift away from Paris and the beginning of the emergence of the United States as a force in the development of high fashion.

The Trans-Atlantic Axis

The United States was just at the point of being prepared for war when the World War I ended, but the war preparation created a system that was to serve businesses well. Industries had regulated themselves during the war, and government funds flowed to businesses to keep the economy going. Railroads and roads had been improved and organized to allow for shipping of war products to the East Coast for export to France and Britain. These structures and the organization of American business into a quasi-governmental entity, mobilized and ready to deal with huge tasks, allowed the United States to rapidly outstrip the capabilities of the war-damaged Europeans.

Manufactured goods were not the only American imports to France in the years after World War I. The importation of North American culture to Paris in the form of writers, artists, and musicians was something close to a mass migration and did not go over well in all quarters. The enthusiastic acceptance of jazz in the clubs of Paris was especially thorny to some, seeing this American invasion as a threat to French culture (Figure 5.1).

However, a group of young authors—Ernest Hemingway among them—who had gathered around the writer Gertrude Stein in Paris further emphasized Paris's role as the center of Western culture. The writings of these authors contributed especially to Americans' identification of all things cultural with Paris. The idea of needing to be in Paris in

FIGURE 5.1. The "American Style," a nightclub band at the cosmopolitan Paris nightclub La Boull Blanche, ca. 1930.

order to develop culturally was not new in aristocratic circles, but now this sense of Paris as the center began to appear in popular culture as well.

For fashion, Paris's centrality was unquestionable in the years before World War II, but the changing nature of the fashion business and its five-year disconnect during World War II began a shift that would steadily move the center away from the Rue de la Paix.

France Isolated

When Paris fell to the Germans in 1940, the Nazi regime immediately put into action a plan it had for the fashion industry. The Germans' aim, under orders from Propaganda Minister Goebbels—who was only too knowledgeable of the power of art and design in politics—

FIGURE 5.2. Occupation fashions in Paris: the hats became a focal point because millinery materials were not rationed.

was to transfer the French fashion industry to Berlin and Vienna, which were to be the new cultural capitals of Europe. Seamstresses would be called upon to provide their inimitable skills, and designers were promised "magnificent positions."[1] No longer were the Germans to feel inferior to the French. The *Herrenvolk* were to be leaders in fashion as in all else, according to Goebbels.[2] Paris's centrality in fashion and style had long been a sore point in Germany. The Germans had for decades been the butt of French jokes for what the French saw as their complete lack of fashion sense. Meanwhile, the French fashions had been consistently painted by the Nazis as shameless, frivolous, and amoral. Although the German regime seemed to have a very clear idea of what it wanted, the German fashion industry, such as it was, had mixed feelings about the fall of Paris. On one hand, there was the official line that now the reign of Paris was over and the time had come for the German fashion to take the lead. On the other hand, no one in Germany seemed to know what to do, as they had up until then consistently taken their cues from Paris.[3]

Lucien Lelong, who had been president of the Chamber of Couture since 1937, explained to the Germans:

> You can impose anything on us by force, but Paris couture cannot be uprooted, neither as a whole nor in part. Either it stays in Paris or it does not exist. It is not within the power of any nation to steal fashion creativity, for not only does it function quite spontaneously, but also it is the product of a tradition maintained by a large body of skilled men and women in a variety of crafts and skills.[4]

But in July of 1940, Nazi officers, tired of the Syndicale's evasions and delaying tactics, broke down the doors of the Chambre Syndicale de la Haute Couture and took away its archives, including documents on design, exports, and trade schools; and files on foreign buyers.

The Germans eventually relented, although this may have had more to do with their own mismanagement of the affair and larger war concerns, rather than any resistance from the French. Lelong took the view anyway, that it was better to work with the enemy than to put thousands of people out of work (Figure 5.2). The relationship with the occupiers was rocky, but the industry prevailed (and had to very delicately sidestep accusations of collaboration after the war: Jaques Fath, Marcel Rochas, and Nina Ricci mixed easily with the collaborationist society, while Coco Chanel stayed at the Ritz during the war, living with a German officer[5]). Minor skirmishes took place: Madame Grès' maison was shut down by the Nazis because she had used the French patriotic red, white, and blue tricolor in a collection, and Balenciaga was closed down in early 1944 for exceeding his fabric allowance.

The Germans threatened to close down the entire haute couture operation in Paris in late July 1944, when they felt that Parisian fashions were getting out of hand. Which they may well have been: this was a month after the Allies' invasion at Normandy began the liberation of France, and the French claimed that the exaggerated fashions in Paris had been a way of taunting the Germans. There may have been some truth to that, but there was much chagrin in Britain and the United States when the first images from Paris came back after the war, as fashions had been very practical and pared down there in order to save for the war effort. Besides, women had become used to the more comfortable, straightforward fashions of the war years, and the fashions coming out of Paris seemed cumbersome and overloaded, if not archaic.

Utilitarian Designs in Britain and the United States

Under wartime restrictions, British and American apparel became the best example yet of modernist principles applied to fashion design. The functionalist approach in Britain resulted in clean lines, a nearly total lack of adornment, durability, practical closures, and simple pockets (Figure 5.3). Because British fashions were a patriotic measure and not a sign of protest, the utilitarian code became a sign of pride and of responsibility in the face of an enormous threat to the country.

Before the war, America was French couture's biggest market, but when France was taken out of the picture, American designers had to pick up the reins. Designers like Claire McCardell turned fashions very quickly to an American aesthetic that aligned itself around comfort and practicality while being designed for mass production. This was the decisive

FIGURE 5.3. British utility fashion.

moment for the garment industry, which was quick to seize its chance.

As in Britain, garment production in the United States was limited by laws. The War Production Board, a wartime committee that regulated the production and allocation of materials, limited any new fashions or extreme changes in fashions in order to discourage people from updating their wardrobes too frequently. The board (which included among its members Stanley Marcus, who would later become the CEO of the luxury apparel retailer, Neiman Marcus,) laid down very strict guidelines for the garment industry. Its ruling L-85, for example, banned evening dresses, three-piece suits, pleated skirts, puffed sleeves, and changes in hem lengths (Figure 5.4).

Then in 1942, only months after the United States entered the war, the American garment manufacturers' union invested a million dollars to promote American fashion. With the United States' industrial capabilities, it seemed hard to believe that the French couture industry stood a chance in the postwar world.[6]

FIGURE 5.4. U.S. wartime fashion.

The Theatre de la Mode

When it became clear that the war was coming to an end, Lelong and the Chamber of Couture, in a counteroffensive, recruited more than 50 couturiers to create the *Théâtre de la Fashion*: two thousand miniature mannequins, dressed for all seasons and times of day and placed in little theatrical settings (Figure 5.5) designed by artists like Dior's old friend Christian Bérard and the ubiquitous Jean Cocteau.

The exhibition opened on March 27, 1945, a little more than a month before the war in Europe ended, while the situation in Paris was still dire from rationing—nearly every daily necessity was in short supply. The show attracted huge crowds in Paris and then London,

FIGURE 5.5. Opera Scene by Christian Bérard of the Théâtre de la Mode, 1946.

where it was seen by 120,000 visitors in six weeks. Princess Elizabeth of Britain (later to become queen) had a private viewing, and royalty also viewed the exhibit in Sweden and Denmark. In 1946, an updated version traveled to the United States. It went on display in New York and then in San Francisco, but as no other city in the United States was able to offer a site and funds suitable for the exhibit, and the fashion industry in France was back on its feet, it was packed up and then oddly forgotten about. One hundred sixty of the dolls were kept at the Maryhill Museum of Art in Washington State, where they were rediscovered in the 1980s.

By late 1946 it was clear that haute couture was going to survive in Paris, so the Theatre had served its purpose, even though it perhaps had not received quite the greeting in the United States that had been hoped for. But in the mere year and a half from its opening, the Western world had turned its eye fully to the past as far as high fashion was concerned. The fears that World War I had awakened about the promise of the Western technological society had been brought to a whole new level by the horrors of World War II. The aristocratic world of the previous century did not seem so bad after the concentration camps, mechanized war, and atomic bombs of the 1940s. The world was ready for respite, and the world as exhibited in the Théâtre de la Mode is exactly what the name implies: a theatrical piece; a bit of make-believe put on for show. The Theatre imagines the world as if it had never been interrupted by the Nazis. Now Paris could return to its former glory.

However, Bettina Ballard, the Paris editor of *Vogue*, felt that fashion in Paris was anything but glorious: "not at its most brilliant right after the war and none of the prewar stars were showing great leadership."[7] In a prescient move, she left Paris for New York, becoming chief editor of *Vogue*, where she would continue to make the trip back twice a year for the collections (Figure 5.6).

FIGURE 5.6. Vogue, November 1946.

Ballard's move was a huge shift in fashion authority, officially bringing the seat of power to New York. Once there, for example, she took over editorial control of *Vogue*'s two annual collection editions, which had been in the hands of the Paris office.[8] She felt that the Paris office was too amateurish, and of course New York was by now the hub of world finance and markets, and the buyers from the New York firms had long ago become the most important clients of the Parisian fashion industry anyway (Figure 5.7).

On the other hand, Paris needed to be sustained. Its myth and aura had become too important to the image of the high fashion world. Another editor, Carmel Snow of *Harper's Bazaar*, championed Dior in his 1947 collection, which she called "The New Look" (discussed further in Chapter 7). She had been a fan of Dior since she saw his *Café Anglais* in 1937, but even though her part in Dior's success was significant, her enthusiasm was part of her overall commitment to "do all that was in my power to revive the fashion industry in France . . . I was no more willing to concede the permanent fall of Paris than was General de Gaulle. . . . Since fashion is the second largest industry in France, I felt that my personal contribution to the Allied cause could be to help the revival of that industry."[9]

Myth Created and Sustained

In this way the myth of high-fashion design was re-created for the postwar world. This myth is still presented, with the same key players creating the hierarchy within the system.

FIGURE 5.7. Bettina Ballard looking about at the Dior show in a black Dior suit, 1951.

The editors control the flow of information and anoint the new look, designer, or trend, each hoping to be first in order to reap the reward of status and credit (and increased sales) when their choice proves to be correct.

"It is our role," said Carmel Snow, "to recognize fashions when they are still only seeds of the future. The designers create, but without magazines their creations would never be recognized and accepted."[10]

This astute observation—self-aggrandizing as it is—describes the entire situation of media and creativity in the twentieth century versus earlier times. Newspapers, magazines, films, and then television became, by virtue of the speed and scale of distribution they could provide, the vehicles for a new idea. Without media, modern designers could not be available to the global community that now was their audience. The centrality of Paris called for the reach of media to bring the word to the fashion culture that was now spread over half the world.

Paris had the tradition, the skilled talent, the suppliers, and, of course, the location. After all, Paris was the city for women's high fashion and a label stating anything else would not hold the same magic. The label could not yet say "London" or "New York" even if the names of the designers were the same. The idea of the center of fashion moving from Paris to another city made no more sense in a free market than it did to move it forcibly as a war trophy, regardless of where the fashion editors sat.

A New Look Back

It is interesting to note Christian Dior's approach after the war. In a conversation with the soon-to-be financier of his *maison*, Dior said, "After the long stagnation of fashion as a result of the war, there is a strong desire for something entirely new. To meet this demand, French couture will have to return to its traditions of great luxury." He added that a new couture house that would take on this responsibility would have to be a craftsman's workshop, in order to resist the "age of machines in which we live."[11]

This plan of Dior's—to renew fashion by returning to the past—was perfectly in synch with the wishes of those who could not see a future that did not contain the values of the nineteenth century. To imagine that the "age of machines" could be resisted is a cultural theme that had been underlying the discussions of the modernists, Futurists, and Surrealists since the beginning of the twentieth century. Dior picked up this theme in the early 1950s at the end of his book *Talking about Fashion*. There he outlines his analysis of the success of his New Look (Figure 5.8, left). He says that the woman of 1925 "looked like the machine from which music and decoration of the period took their inspiration" and then adds: "Nowadays we are afraid of the female robot." (See Figure 5.8, right.) Dior felt

FIGURE 5.8. Dior's "New Look" (left) counteracted the dreaded 1920s Robot Women, here in the guise of actress Louise Brooks (right).

FIGURE 5.9. Christian Dior's fame in the United States was unprecedented. Here he is on the cover of Time magazine, March 4, 1957.

that modernism had had its day. Picasso and Matisse had "delivered their message," and fashion was moving away from the kind of exoticism associated with the early part of the century. "Europe," he said, "faced with a hostile and uncivilized society, is becoming more conscious of tradition and culture."[12] (See Figure 5.9.)

If World War I had exhibited the sickness of old European society, World War II rearranged the world order. The old colonial powers had been superseded by the opposing military-industrial giants of the United States and the Soviet Union, and political power had passed from the hands of royalty and aristocrats. However, despite this development, interest in the lives and appearance of the European royal families intensified in the postwar years.

Assorted royalty became the focus of color magazines, which homed in on the fashions and their "humanness." This strange blend of democratization and adulation began with the marriage of Princess Elizabeth and Philip Mountbatten in England, when, in 1947, in the midst of rationing and shortages, the English court used the occasion to inspire the public. They opened the door and set the precedent for press coverage of royalty and celebrities that they might later find cause to regret.

A little later a cruise of royals from all over Europe, heavily publicized in the magazines, was analyzed by the cultural critic Roland Barthes:

> To flaunt the fact that kings are capable of prosaic actions is to recognize that this status is no more natural to them than angelism is to common mortals, is to acknowledge that the king is still king by divine right. King Paul [of Greece] was wearing an open-neck shirt and short sleeves, Queen Frederika a print dress, that is to say one no longer unique but whose pattern can also be seen on the bodies of mere mortals. Formerly, kings dressed up as shepherds; nowadays, to wear for a fortnight clothes from a cheap chain-store is for them a sign of dressing up.[13]

With this kind of pop-culture focus of glossy magazines, the circle drawn around high society by high fashion was becoming porous, and the effects worked both ways. If royalty could play at being human, as Barthes implies, then there should be nothing stopping the lesser mortals from behaving like royalty. High fashion and deluxe goods could now begin to seriously cross the line.

The Corporate Model

One essential difference in the market for high fashion between America and Europe was that in Europe, the closeness of the couturier to the client was built in and essential to the operation of the business. In the fashion houses themselves, business was also localized, with workshops and suppliers in close proximity.

The market on the other side of the Atlantic differed in all aspects. The continent is wide and the cities are spread out. Dealing with clients in Boston, New York, Washington, D.C., Chicago, and Southern California, a designer would find that traveling was all there is. Once the department store model took hold, the enormity of the operation, where each city may have several department stores in which the designer's products were sold, was such that there would be no possible way to pay personal attention to the product in every case. High-fashion design could perhaps have gone into a version of the Parisian system if individual designers had established American fashion houses in the great American cities and served clients in those cities. But the American mission and, along with it, its business model have been expansive and growth-oriented from the beginning, and to keep a business contained seems antithetical. However, the point is moot, as high fashion was sought in Paris, and an American couturier in the old-world style never really emerged.

What is perhaps more important to understand is the attitude toward fashion that very quickly became prevalent in the United States. Despite the attempts to maintain an aristocracy of sorts on the East Coast, the mechanics of high society in the United States were never more than the displays of conspicuous consumption that had framed the aristocracy in Europe. The lack of tradition made American high society need these displays as much as Empress Eugénie's court, if not even more so. The American upper class, being built on wealth, was also porous, in that its membership could not be automatically limited based on ancestry, land ownership, or tradition (although some attempts were made to establish "reigning families"). The fashions of high society could therefore be appropriated at will.

However, the American upper class was generally less ostentatious than European royalty, as the origins of their wealth were from trade or industry, and what sartorial habits existed in the families had been developed in an emerging middle class rather than an upper-class situation. More importantly, as the upper classes began to amass wealth seriously, the ability to observe the upper classes in their display rituals became not only easier, but also with the advent of photojournalism and newsreels, a form of entertainment. With the kind of political unrest that was a steady undercurrent in the interwar years, the conspicuous consumption had to be contained and practiced behind the walls of the grand mansions and town houses, rather than in public promenades. In other words, high fashion in the United States became a societal display within the class, rather than an outward sign of power.

Poiret, for one, could not understand America or that the business of America was purely business. Creativity is good, according to this business orientation, only as long as it sells. This same misunderstanding has cost many designers their position since then. What Poiret expected was simply that the world as he knew it could continue to be what it had been for him, despite changes in the social structure and technology all around him. As we have seen, he also, profoundly and just like Dior later, did not understand that the vision of luxury and elegance they dreamed of belonged to a culture that existed only in its own ever-shrinking circle: an imitation of times gone by, steadily losing its connection to the daily reality of urban living with international styles and global media.

{ LOOKING FORWARD LOOKING BACK }

New Empires, Old Customs?

Paul Poiret could not understand Americans. He could not accept that Americans did not seem to care to live according to the sensibilities of the French. He thought the rising economic power would share the tastes and desires of the empires it was replacing and that its citizenry that came from different cultures, traditions, and customs would care for the same luxuries as the Parisian elites.

The United States was built on a different sensibility, and by the time Poiret was touring the States, mass production had become the characterizing element of the economic juggernaut in the making. Massive technological change, huge new industries, and new industrial wealth that was not bound to land or ancestry defined its ruling class.

We would do well to learn from Poiret's lack of comprehension of the motivation and character of American consumerism. Not only are we heading into a time of unprecedented technological change, but the economic and political power structure of the world is shifting as quickly as it ever has. As the twentieth century drew to a close, the alignment of the post-colonial world of the earlier part of the century began to shift to an alignment for the post-Cold War world. What this alignment is going to be is still not fully apparent in the first decade of the twenty-first century, but the shift is causing political and economic fluctuations that suggest that the mode of Western economic and cultural hegemony is coming to a close. High fashion was already adapting to the shift of the deluxe market away from the North Atlantic axis of New York, Paris, Milan, and London to points east, via Moscow, Dubai, New Delhi, and Beijing when the world's markets went into a tailspin in 2008. At the same time, we see the business model of high-fashion design labels jettison the "star designer" in a final acceleration of the diminishment of the couturier's role after the transition to America in the 1920s and '30s. The individual designer is not central to the global market; the new model is centered on the label. "The Brand" is everything. The question now is whether a new designer can "deliver the brand" and "maintain the vision." What this really means is this: Can the designer deliver what the market has come to expect while tweaking the design just enough to make it different from last year's model? This does not leave much room for radical change or individual vision, and a designer who fails to deliver in the first year is out.

Today's market does not like risks, and if the label is only trying, like Poiret, to bring the old world to the new, with expectation that everything will be taken up as before, there is bound to be a disconnect between the label and the new class of consumers, whoever they may be.

With global economic power decentralized and restructuring and the American Century seemingly on the wane, it may have beeen a mistake to think that the growing deluxe market in Asia and Russia would have the same demands and tastes that have ruled the markets in the West since World War II. However, it is also possible that the marketing methods and economic models of Western capitalist society will simply be layered onto the economies of the East by default and that the newly affluent populations will be sold on the looks and modes of the West in the same way that the fashions of Europe's fading elites became the fashions of the industrial aristocracy of the United States.

Chanel's experience in the United States in the early 1930s was less overtly problematic than Poiret's. But that was because she did not attempt to romanticize the New World or imagine that it in any way could be modeled on the past of Europe. Hollywood left her

FIGURE 5.10. Carmel Snow and Chanel, pictured in early 1953, the year Chanel returned to Paris.

unimpressed. She stayed there to work on only one film and then decided that she could just as well work from Paris. However, on her return trip, she stayed in New York and was fascinated by her visits to the department stores Saks, Macy's, and Klein's. There she saw her designs knocked off in cheap materials. She realized that this was the future of the business, proclaiming that this was "spontaneous publicity" and that it was hopeless to try to fight it.[14]

After the war, Chanel lived in self-imposed exile in Switzerland. After several years of rumors, she came back to Paris in 1953 to reopen her couture house. With anti-collaborationist sentiment waning, she could safely return. She was also prompted by her business partners, as well as her own astute observation, that a countermeasure to the elaborations of Dior would be needed. But she primarily saw an opportunity for her vision to appeal to a new generation of customers. With new mass-production technologies and textiles man-made of fibers, Chanel's knew that her vision of practical, stylish clothes of quality construction was right on the money. Chanel, after all, had always looked at fashion design as a business, not an art. (See Figure 5.10.)

Selling the Sizzle: Accessories and Perfume

When Chanel came back to Paris she sought financing from the brothers Wertheimer, the owners of Les Parfumeries Bourjois, France's largest cosmetic and fragrance company. They had bankrolled and marketed her Chanel No. 5 in the 1920s and had contracted rights to use her name on the perfume as long as they stayed away from fashion, and she, in turn, had to stay away from perfumes and cosmetics (Figure 5.11).

The Wertheimers bankrolled her return in response to a careful ruse by Chanel in which she implied that she would start licensing ready-to-wear and merchandise in America if she could not find financing in France. This would water down the brand and ultimately hurt their business. The perfume company picked up the entire cost of her operation in return for continued ownership of her name as applied to perfumes. They immediately began to lose money on the couture business, while the sales of perfume went up.

The Wertheimers would add immensely to their wealth as a result over the coming

FIGURE 5.11. Chanel No. 5, perhaps Coco's most enduring legacy.

decades, while the couture business would continue to decline. This business model that had been outlined and attempted by Poiret was quickly picked up by other houses and soon became the norm for high fashion. Selling the scent was the new road to riches. After Chanel's comeback show, which was greeted less than enthusiastically by the French press, *Life* magazine described her as "the woman behind the most famous perfume in the world."[15]

However, in a capitalist economy, profits are paramount: once the designer garments stopped being the main product, the designer stopped being central to the company. What the perfume business pointed to was that soon the name on the label, with the label being spread over a multitude of products, would eclipse the reality of the designer to the point where the label on the garment would mean as much or as little as the label on the bottle, bag, gloves, or shoes.

After World War II, the desire for life to return to the tantalizing elegance of the '30s was coupled with the sense—instilled by movies and advertising—that the cocktail-set lifestyle was completely obtainable. If you had the look, as long as you bought the right things, surrounded yourself with the right appliances and furniture, you were there, even thought the venue of your cocktail-set lifestyle was a house in a suburban development. The mass migration of young newly married couples to the suburbs also brought a new lifestyle to the fore. The whole idea of a "life style" now became a selling point for all the consumer goods and clothing being made and marketed in the Western world.

The direction was taken on the nature of the economic engine of the United States. In the decade following World War II, the consumer society that had begun to form in the 1920s became the basis for economic success. The feedback loop between increased consumption and increased production, along with increased international trade in consumer goods, brought the increased possibility of a semblance of luxurious living to the urban middle class. The trend of middle-class consumption that had begun 100 years before was now given extra force with advertising and media coverage of the rich and famous.

The Spectacle Established

Let us consider how fashion design began to answer—and operate within—the myth-making machine of American media culture. In order to market a fashion label in America, the label had to become larger than life—mythological. The designer—as a person of flesh and blood—could not be the authority. The anointing of the designer became instead the anointing of the product, which was the designer's name. The designer was in effect incorporated (in all senses of the word) into the product by the fetishizing of the name. The symbolism of the designer selling her name seems almost too simplistic. Consider, though, the implications of an artist assigning the uncontrolled use of his or her name to a corporation that places it on products. Thereby the product acquires an aura of quality or at least value as a status symbol. The creativity of the work now becomes associated with the appearance of the name rather than the name taking power from the creativity. But as Chanel pointed out, it isn't an art, it's a business. Like the Second Empire, it doesn't matter what underlies the reality, as long as everyone buys into the surface. But, coming back to Baudrillard in Chapter 1, the surface may now no longer be *masking* the underlying reality; it may well *be* the reality. By dissolving the boundaries of use and access to deluxe goods and dissolving the identity of the creative force into a logo and a brand, any driving underlying reality becomes fluid to the point of nonexistence. The creative force can be abstracted only to a certain point before it loses any power it may have over the audiences' emotions and imaginations.

We will revisit this point as we begin to look at Dior along with Chanel and Schiaparelli in more detail in the years during and after World War II. First, though, we will need to explore this notion of the deliberate removal of the creative presence as a development in the arts of the twentieth century. We will have an interlude during which we will look at the relationship of the development in arts over the middle of the twentieth century and the dilemma in which fashion began to find itself.

When we come back to Dior, we will do so by introducing a metaphor that Baudrillard would have had to invent if it weren't already there. We will note that when Dior died in 1957, it was on the eve of the opening in Stanley Marcus's Neiman Marcus store in Dallas, Texas, of an exact reproduction of the Dior boutique in Paris.

ENDBOX

New Word in Couture: Fun

It's odd to see couture, the world of $50,000 dresses, being turned into a populist pursuit. Couturiers aren't making clothes for a matron in the front row. They are designing, as J. D. Salinger wrote in "Franny and Zooey," for the fat lady "sitting on the porch all day, swatting flies, with her radio going full blast from morning till night." Or more aptly, for the lady sitting in front of her television.

No one who tunes in would not understand how the technical outrageousness of Gianni Versace's jeweled, squared-shoulder dresses, Alexander McQueen's jet-beaded jackets or John Galliano's embroidered frock coats and lean skirts might cost $50,000. It is much more difficult to explain why a minimalist suit, with all the technique hidden, could carry such a price.

"I was against it in the beginning, but it is the only way, the only solution, for couture now," said Maria Luisa Pomaillou, the influential Parisian retailer, just after witnessing the fabulous grotesque that was the Givenchy presentation. "It's no longer a private joke for a few people."

So the cloistered days of clients with the attention span, time and desire for the three fittings required to obtain the simplest, most boring suit in the world are over.

. . . Minimalism and sobriety defined the past five years, but couture is now about having a good time because you can afford to. As superficial as that might seem, it is hypocritical to pretend that fashion is anything but that.

Perhaps the most frightening thing to consider about this trend is that where couture goes, ready-to-wear inevitably follows, not only creatively, but from a business perspective. For decades, couture has been a publicity-drawing way to sell licensed products. Now, ready-to-wear is starting to be seen that way.

Fashion may be edging toward a time when going to a runway show has no more to do with what women might wear than going to a performance of "Cats" would. The runway show may soon become like couture: utterly, completely, haplessly divorced from anyone's reality. But everyone sure will have a good time.

Source: Amy M. Spindler. The *New York Times*. July 9, 1997.

Discussion Points

1. Is there any reason why high fashion should reflect any reality but its own?
2. Should high fashion be marketed as spectacle?
3. Should there be a "high" and "less high" fashion in today's culture? Discuss points for and against this.

CHAPTER 6

The Ground Shifts

This chapter is an interlude during which we place Poiret, Chanel, and Schiaparelli into relief against artistic movements of the early twentieth century. Then we take a quick look at the changing nature and influence of modern media. Linking these two topics is an introduction to Jean-François Lyotard's definition of the postmodern condition, which raises questions about the nature and purpose of high-fashion design in our society.

The Fine Art of Fashion

Art trickles down. What begins in the world of high art winds up in the world of high fashion. Maybe not right away, and maybe only as an approach, but eventually what is in the galleries creates an effect on the designer. The art may affect designers directly, but the philosophies, literature, and discussions that influenced the artists will also have had an impact on the designers. Poiret, Chanel, and Schiaparelli were all connected to the artists of their time, both professionally and personally. To clarify where each of them stood in terms of the larger movements of art, let us quickly place them in context.

Vitalism

One of the more potent ideas in the air in Paris in the first decade of the twentieth century was the notion of *élan vital* or the "life force." This was meant to be a "spiritual essence" that endowed inanimate objects with life. In part a reaction to the mechanistic view of nature that had been developing in the sciences for a hundred years, it involved the artistic celebration of the natural condition. The sculptor Rodin was the first to take it up in his art, after Vitalism had reached a literary and scientific peak. Rodin felt that it was the sculptor's job to not imitate life but *convey* it. Vitalism was not a formal movement in art; it was more of a personal ideal for artists, especially in sculpture, where the notion of investing object with a "life" continued well into the middle of the century. The vitalist artist was the creator of life from inanimate materials, and therefore essentially a positive force in the world.[1]

FIGURE 6.1. Denise Poiret in a dress by Paul Poiret, 1919.

In many ways Poiret, who was well tuned toward the Parisian vitalist art circles in his youth, can be seen to belong to the vitalist school of thought. Poiret's vitalist thinking served him well and allowed him to create forceful vibrant fashions, but the *élan* he brought to his work was more of an artist's than a designer's and eventually became too much for his backers to handle.

He freed the female form from corsetry, revealed the body under the garments, draped fabrics directly on the body, rather than constructing heavy architecture, and brought the intense colors of the Fauves into fashion (Figure 6.1). All of this, done with the flamboyant energy with which Poiret approached everything, shows that he had a strong desire to evoke the forces within the human. He wrote in his autobiography that he had awakened the colorists in Lyons, from whose palettes all vitality had been suppressed.[2] Then, in the last page of the same book, he writes: "nothing seems to me better nor more beautiful than to express in colors, as if they were primal cries, all the emotion that is caused in one by the contemplation of nature."[3]

Is Fashion "Modern"?

We have seen how the modernist vision initially denied fashion its place at the table in the 1920s. The men's wear of Corbusier and the Dadaists was meant to be the modern vision, but Chanel showed them what "modern" fashion actually meant by appropriating the men's styles and approach. Although she would subtly slip into old-world décor on occasion, her stripped-down minimalism, functional effect, and disregard for convention mark her as the "modern" that Poiret was not. She approached her work from a very functional point of view as well. In Chanel's view *couture* was a business, not an art.

{ LOOKING FORWARD LOOKING BACK }
Is Fashion "Modern"?

In looking for a definition of true modernist fashion, we would perhaps have to look only to Chanel for her functional redirection of women's fashions. She changed the *approach* to clothing, just as the modernist architects redirected the *thinking of* buildings. Chanel pioneered the approach that allowed Saint Laurent, for example, to rethink the designing of clothes for women. For him, like Chanel, elegance came from the woman; designing was a dialogue between them and the woman. The less the woman was smothered in décor and structure, the more she would shine through. The clothes were vehicles to convey the feminine, not an end in themselves. Through the rise of ready-to-wear as the designer's vehicle, by the time the late 1960s rolled around, the self-established functionalism of late-twentieth-century fashion was already inherently modernist (and mostly without the elitist overtones of modernist design). This renders the question of "modernism" moot, as the revolutionary thing to do in the '60s was something entirely different from following the established modernist methods as the future vision of the prewar years crumbled. The anarchic and antiestablishment styles of the '60's had an agenda that spoke of a different future from that of the streamlined modernisms of the pre-World War II years.

The failure of the modernist program aside, the question of where high-fashion design fit into the modernist program does therefore not really have a clear-cut answer, perhaps through being too obvious or too close to people's daily experience. Or perhaps the question has no meaning. Architecture stands and speaks for generations. Perhaps fashion is too ephemeral to be a political statement when viewed through too narrow a lens. Perhaps it can be seen to be such only if taken into a discussion that is framed by decades or centuries. In this sense, if modernism is essentially a question of stripping away the layers of decoration and construction of the centuries, then high fashion repeatedly fails the test all throughout the twentieth century. However, it also has its victories, notably in Chanel, the futurists of the 1960s, and the minimalists of the 1990s.

It may be possible to state that the true modernism of fashion design came through ready-to-wear (and that this was at the heart of Poiret's disconnect with the American mode). When the mass of customers realized that they didn't have to care about couture but could buy mass-produced designer clothing straight off the rack without losing social or stylistic effect, the functionalism of clothing came to reside not only in construction and wearability but also in the *approach* to it.

The difficulty here is that high-fashion design may actually have no real agenda other than commerce. If it began as a political tool, it lost that job very quickly, and as a tool of any kind of social significance, it remains silent. Architects felt in the early twentieth century that through their modernist program, they would be the agents of social change. This vision failed. It may well be that this blandness of early-twenty-first-century ready-to-wear is the ultimate proof of the modernist nature of fashion in the same way that large housing projects and socialist factory cities became the dismal icons of modernist architecture.

Being the modernist frontrunner is what allowed Chanel to make her comeback in the 1950s, when she saw what Dior and others were doing to the modernist vision. Schiaparelli could not continue as her artistic vision had developed with Dada and the Surrealists, and by the time World War II ended, the energy of these movements had run out. Besides, the retro-romanticism of Dior suited the times better than Schiap's stark vision.

Minimalism

However, Schiaparelli might have found herself at home in the '60s, when artists continued to challenge all classic notions of what "art" actually was. Minimalist artists removed themselves from personal references to their art and began creating art that was stripped down to its absolute minimal elements. Pure forms, white boxes, and rectilinear installations denied any notions of mysterious "artistic" knowledge and forces. What you see is what you see. What you make of it is what you make of it. This then was a short step toward removing "art" from its attachment to objects and opened the door to art that returned some of the Dadaist notions of inspired ridiculousness. From this also, artists like Sol LeWitt arrived, who reduced their art to an almost purely conceptual notion of mathematical systems (Figure 6.2).

FIGURE 6.2. The pendulum would swing as far as possible from the nineteenth-century Symbolists' emotionality to the 1960s minimalist art, such as these Sol LeWitt structures, reducing art to mathematical forms.

Note that apparel, no matter how esoteric the design intends to be, it cannot go to the full extreme of LeWitt. If it did, it would have to become "a Sol LeWitt"—that is, it would be reduced to some mathematical formula or an arrangement of elementary components. True "minimalism" in fashion can therefore exist only as a game of sorts, since the "garmentness" gets removed very quickly when fashion is reduced to nonfunctional abstract systems. (When critics have termed a collection "minimalist," what they generally are referring to is a lack of adornment.) However, designers such as Helmut Lang have explored the stripping down to essentials very successfully. Lang created a look that managed to transcend the seasonal approach and may therefore have come closest to moving the modernism of high fashion into a new paradigm, but he could not sustain his brand long enough to find out.

High fashion in the current day is in full flight from modernism. Chapters 10 and 11 will examine this phenomenon more closely, but for now let us examine how the current fragmented and reactionary fashions align themselves with the late-twentieth-century settling of accounts with modernism.

The Postmodern Condition

In *The Postmodern Condition: A Report on Knowledge,* the philosopher Jean-François Lyotard outlined what he saw as the state of scientific knowledge in the late twentieth century. However, his discussion is also applicable to knowledge outside the scientific sphere, such as art, design, and literature.

His hypothesis is that after World War II, "the status of knowledge is altered as societies enter what is known as the postindustrial age and cultures enter what is known as the postmodern age."[4] In this postmodern age, our culture has changed fundamentally. Transformations throughout the twentieth century in every field of human knowledge have changed how and with what purpose we approach the development of new ideas. Cultural institutions and traditions that used to influence the development of and stance toward ideas no longer have the strength they used to in modern times.

Lyotard uses the term *modern* in his analysis to "designate any science that legitimates itself with reference to a metadiscourse."[5] This means any inquiring discipline that relies on a "grand narrative"—that is, a fixed and accepted philosophy embedded in the tradition of the inquiry itself.

A grand narrative, for example, is the idea that history is a constant journey toward greater and greater worldly or spiritual progress. Another might be the Marxist notion of class struggle as the driving force of history. Lyotard then defines "postmodern" as a questioning of the metanarratives on which our culture has built its systems and wonders "where, after the metanarratives, can legitimacy reside?"[6]

This cuts very close to the heart of the problem underlying our discussion—namely, where does high-fashion design go from here? If high fashion comes into being through a

FIGURE 6.3. At the courts of Europe, fashion was part of the grand narrative that gave legitimacy to the regimes.

society's need for legitimacy and cannot survive without the conferring of authority on its practitioners, then the lack of a grand narrative is a huge problem. (See Figure 6.3.)

The "Ownership" of Culture

Our culture's grand narrative of high fashion, as it has been related for over a century or so, was put into place in the mid-nineteenth century, right in the middle of the construction of the grand cultural vision of European high society. The attempt to maintain this narrative when the supporting social structures have disappeared has resulted in the crisis the discipline is facing today.

Nineteenth-century Europeans had developed a tendency to cast ownership on narratives, claiming as their own both the past and future of their culture as well as that of any of those with whom it connected. This resulted in "interpretations" of the history, art, and literature of other times and cultures, which even when legitimate, were still always viewed through the lens of an educated European culture, with varying degrees of nationalistic and political subtext. It was the age of grand historical and scientific theories and even when cracks began appearing in the façade with Darwin, Marx, Freud, and Nietzsche, it was still a *European* façade, built and upheld with the Enlightenment tradition of scientific progress.

Within this historical tradition, it seemed perfectly normal to assume that fashions should continue to develop according to the man-made systems set in place by this society—in other words, that it would be natural for modern society to assume and change its attire according to the social schedule of the courtly seasons of the nineteenth century. Odd as this sounds when deliberately stated in those terms, the fact is that the system as set in place during Worth's day is still there, although fading and unraveling at an increasing rate.

From our vantage point, it is easy to spot the problem with this view. First of all, we now see the nineteenth-century vision of a constant direction of cultural and historical de-

FIGURE 6.4. Twenty-first-century high society: The "Bal de Debutantes" in Paris 2007. These balls are attended by the daughters and sons of the rich and famous from all over the world. The imagery, visuals, and social signals are straight from the Second Empire with the borrowed gowns from couture houses in Paris.

velopment to have been at least naïve, if not arrogant. Secondly, the rules of high fashion do not apply "naturally" anywhere, nor have they at any time. It is therefore safe to assume that they will be different as the cultural and historical frameworks that required them transform or disappear. Our experience so far shows that this change can take a long time and that, therefore, there may be another couple of decades still before the Second Empire finally lets go and a twenty-first century version of "modern" kicks in.

Is There a Postmodern Fashion?

It is important to note that even though we could say fashion design is in a postmodern *condition*, there is no real postmodern *fashion*. We *have* different styles, but they are more or less variations on the themes of the past 150 years, so they could at best be termed *late-modern* if one needed a classification. (See Figure 6.4.) As in architecture and furniture design, it is not enough to put together a couple of different styles and reference a handful of periods and call it postmodern; this is *pastiche*, which can be used well at times but is not a movement. The referencing of different cultures and periods comes from the desire to anchor the work in a positive, sanctioned past while exploring and illustrating the nonlinearity of the world as presented to us through constant, multiple, and inconsistent media.

There Is No Here Here

In examining whether there *might* be a postmodern fashion, one might find that the question itself is problematic and needs to be rethought. Fashion itself may not be able to be "postmodern" except by virtue of existing within a postmodern cultural structure. That is to say that the postmodern condition precludes a "fashion" by its very nature. The questioning of narratives would immediately preclude the creation of a fashion. On may suggest that the fragmentation of the fashions in general and of high fashion in particular is all that can be said to *be* the postmodern fashion. The fragmentation *is* fashion in the postmodern mode. The individual fashions within the overall fragmented picture are whatever they are, referencing whatever they reference, and can be discussed on their own terms. But they are grounded in their own frame of reference, which can each be discussed as if one were lying on the ground looking at individual clovers, blades of grass, and flowers in an enormous field. But standing up to get the overall view has no meaning, as all that can be seen is the field, which is a composite of each individual plant. The fragmentation of high fashion and the narrowing gap with ready-to-wear is essentially a decentralization. Fashion no longer has a metanarrative. The point to realize is not that there is nowhere to go—it's that there is no definitive *here* to go *from*.

Punk Came Close

The nearest that we may have come to a postmodern fashion may well have been in the first years of punk. As we will explore in more detail in Chapter 9, punk questioned the core notion of fashion as it had been known for a hundred years or more. It was briefly at the start, against the notion of the "done thing," against authority, anti-label, and highly individualized, but—in this contrary stance—lies its ultimate weakness. An "anti" movement carries

FIGURE 6.5. Punk fashions initially were influenced by "Teddy Boy" rocker styles: the Sex Pistols photographed on Oxford Street in London, 1977.

in its nature a contradiction that will force it to negate itself. An anti-fashion fashion is no more possible than an anti-movement movement. But while such a movement lasts, it causes us at a given point to question the fundamental principles upon which we have built things up so far. Movements like punk tear things down to their base to work from the strength that can be found in fundamentals. As such, an anti-movement such as punk provides an energy with which the next state of things can be created. However, two things can be held in mind for the discussion of punk in Chapter 9. First, punk's journey as a fashion, like the hippie fashions of the 1960s, didn't end through this inherent contradiction—that is, by implosion—but rather was appropriated into the commercial world against which it was initially set (Figure 6.5). Second, punk's anti-status could not contain a narrative that would hold. Anarchy of this kind is in the journey, not in the arriving. It is well possible that as a culture we are simply still exploring in preparation for the road ahead.

What punk rockers *did* provide was the realization that *anything* could be done, and so now everything *is* being done. But there is no clear vision of how to approach the future from the point of view of design. It is possible that this revisiting of the entire history of fashion that we have seen in the past years is an exploration in preparation for belated goodbyes to the twentieth century. Cultures may stagnate, but they do not remain in place. History does not end. It may well be that a postmodern condition is absolutely what is needed in order to be pre-what-comes-next.

Media and Messages

Let us now, for a moment, examine the effect of mass communication and information technology on the dissemination of style. In tandem with the dissolution of grand narratives, our society's mode of distributing cultural information to itself changed radically after World War II. Electronic media decentralized, and multiple avenues for experiencing the world became available to the population at large.

Mass Media

Soon after World War II, the capacity for distribution of information to the populace of North America began to increase dramatically. Not only did it increase in volume but also

FIGURE 6.6. A family gathering at the TV in 1956.

in the total informational content itself. Newspapers, magazines, film, and radio had each dramatically changed the connection the average person had with the world around, and now in the 1950s, television was added to the ways in which the world would arrive in people's homes.

Television changed the perspective people could have on the world. Radio and film each had their mode, and both contributed to how the television experience was initially laid out. The experience was static, with the viewer at home entering a metaphor of "theater." (When a new technology strikes a society, a common reaction is to refer it to the immediately preceding period for familiarity. Movie theaters, for example, had curtains in front of the screen that were up before the "show" began.) The metaphor sets us up to be accepting of the message that arrives.

Television separates itself from film in that it establishes a timeless disembodied visual—that is, it is not bound to a time or place other than the TV set (Figure 6.6). Film prepared the ground, but film is seen at a movie theater and is therefore in itself an "event" and a less immediate experience than TV. Like radio, but unlike a movie, one could also change channels and turn it on and off. It had the intimate control of radio but a visual narrative that arrested any movement and tasks. The audience's attention was captured by television in a way it was not by radio. This gives it a participatory element, only further enhanced by the fact that it was in the home, taking the place of the radio and fireplace (and eventually the kitchen table and anything else) as a locus for the family gathering.

Television arrived in homes at an impressive rate. In 1950, 14 million television sets were sold in the United States. By today's standards, this may not seem much, but in that year, this meant a tenfold increase of sets in service. In 1952, things took off when the FCC added 70 UHF channels to the 12 existing VHF channels that were available. This increased the coverage area of existing broadcasts immensely, and television was now a truly national phenomenon. As soon as it reached the point of national coverage, the politicians arrived, of course, and in 1952, presidential campaigns utilized television for the first time with speeches and ads tailored for the television format. Politics in the United States immediately began its journey toward being the overtly stylistic experience it became in later years. Television brought the visual element of news and entertainment to the forefront, and most importantly, it brought *new* visual information of the world into the home on a *daily* basis.

Focusing on Stars and Style

The stars television created, whether in politics or performance, now had a live visual component that was connected to their specific identity. The cultivation of a "look" became an important component. These "looks" would then be transmitted directly into the homes, to be observed and emulated or rejected by whomever happens to be watching a given channel at a given moment. Given the limited number of channels available at the time, there was, well into the 1970s, a funneling effect, in which the impact of each specific musician or performer was made that much greater by being placed in the focusing frame of the TV screen.

In 1956 a young rock 'n' roller named Elvis Presley caused a stir on the popular variety shows, and although much is made of his appearance on *The Ed Sullivan Show,* it was actually the third in a row of competing shows to book him. First, on *The Milton Berle Show,* he caused some outrage with his look and sexy performance style, which was subsequently suppressed and framed out on the second television appearance on the *Steve Allen Show.* The *Ed Sullivan Show* appearance was notable for the fact that, following the controversy over the previous appearances, nearly 60 million people watched the show, which at the time was about 80 percent of the viewing population.

The significance of this event is that the power of television to seriously shape the culture of the nation was immediately evident. With each home generally containing one television set, *The Ed Sullivan Show* was watched by the whole range of ages in a household, and the generation gap was immediately evident in reaction to the broadcast. Presley's appearance brought out the different reactions of the older generation, exemplified by the not-so-veiled cynicism and contempt of the three shows' hosts versus the excited reaction of the younger baby-boomer audience.

A few years later the British pop group the Beatles would take the same route to American mainstream consciousness, appearing on *The Ed Sullivan Show* in 1964 and beating Presley's ratings to become the most-watched program. They would then top themselves in 1967, when they were transmitted worldwide on television, to an audience estimated at 400 million. This was for the first worldwide television satellite hookup, and they appeared with a song titled "All You Need is Love."

Technology Moves

Neither the Beatles nor Presley *became* famous through appearing on television. Radio was still the medium to launch musicians: their records were already selling in the millions when they appeared on the variety shows. What television did was to solidify their audience and create a visual image to go with their music in one appearance, in one evening, for millions of people at a go. The ability of television to disseminate ideas—and thereby spread attitudes, styles, and fashions—was unprecedented and was to be surpassed only by technology that would not go mainstream until 30 years later, but was being theorized and developed throughout the 1960s: computer networks.

In the early 1970s, the Defense Advanced Research Projects Agency (DARPA) developed and presented Internet technology, with the first e-mail application being written in 1972. This was all for military and scientific purposes, but once the technology went to the private sector in 1984, it was only a decade before global communications with the near-instantaneous spread of ideas became commonplace, as the first "personal computers" came on the market in the early 1980s.

Television had its own spate of development in the early '80s, when CNN began broadcasting in 1980, becoming an early model of the 24-hour news cycle and global broadcasting. A year later, MTV began its broadcast of music videos, of which it had 120 to choose from at the time. Television was becoming a much more fragmented cultural force, with nearly 1,400 TV stations in the United States by 1988. In that same year, 98 percent of households owned at least one TV set, with most owning more, so that the number of people and television sets in the United States was nearing parity. The result was that with more stations and more TV screens to look at, the less focused the effect of television's message became. In fact, if one looked closer, one would find a tipping point in the late 1970s, when cable television began 24-hour broadcasting schedules. This would be a moment when television began to lose its overall authority over cultural image-making and became a provider of images to a multitude of desires, supporting rather than forming these desires. In other words, if you had a particular interest or lifestyle, you could probably find programming on television that catered to you and your desires, more or less when you wanted it. You would not have to wait or—as was more often the case—have no other input than what was available on the three or four major networks. Throughout the '80s, the fragmentation continued, and a clear transition had taken place to a cultural system of providers for choice-driven consumers, rather than central authorities and passive audiences.

By 1992 (a year in which a baby boomer was elected President of the United States), the number of Internet servers in the world had gone from a little over a thousand in 1984 to over a million in six years. With the demand produced by user-friendly Web browsers, such as Mosaic and Netscape, this number would rise to nearly 20 million in six more years, and six years later still, the number could only be guessed at and did not really matter. It had no longer any significance beyond statistical curiosity, as if asking about the number of streets in a city when analyzing the interaction of the city's inhabitants.

The Internet has changed the flow of information around the world in ways that no one could foresee, especially in terms of the public and often trivial nature of the traffic involved. The wonderfully democratic and nonelitist nature of the Internet derives directly from its technological base and framework: It has no center and no fully controlling authority. Its impact is well beyond our discussion, but the clear result is that not only can information of any kind go from anywhere to anywhere in practically no time at all, there is also a dizzying amount of information sitting on servers all over the world, waiting to be accessed. Fashions past and present, near and far, mainstream or subculture, all can stream into your consciousness in any order you choose. Your experience of the world is then as linear or nonlinear as you allow it to be.

There Is No Center

The decentralized structure of the Internet serves as a perfect metaphor for the culture in which it is the primary information conduit: no center, no ultimate authority, and no linear ordering of time or information.

High fashion, once it stopped serving the interests of the ruling classes of Europe, became lost in the marketplace. Once it stopped operating within its ritual structure, it lost its power and direction as swiftly as a cult without a leader. It may not have had much of a purpose beyond its value on the market since Chanel closed her doors in 1939.

As ritual provides the glue that holds society together, the hidden danger of doing away with tradition and authority is that we are then completely unpolarized—there is nothing to rebel against when there is no authority.[7] When there is nothing to rebel against, there are no revolutionaries. Without the challenge of revolution, there is stagnation.

ENDBOX

Fashion Sees Its Shadow

Whether the end is nigh is rarely the point. What matters is that, when people fear shifts in the cultural tectonics, they tend to reach for myth and the verities. And, while it may seem like a stretch to extend this observation to a sphere as ostensibly superficial as fashion, it was hard to come away from the season just ended here without thinking that dressmakers are spooked by the cold breath of change.

. . . And there were good reasons for this. Faced with overwhelming shifts in the way clothes are manufactured; with the widespread dispersal and pirating of information on the Internet; with markets broadening to encompass not just familiar consumer elites, but entire swaths of the globe; and with the knowledge that their boldest efforts seem puny compared with the chess moves being enacted by the multinational titans who employ them, a lot of designers are befuddled. What should they do? Change careers?

. . . No one can really blame designers for trying to conserve themselves or to regulate the growing demands on creativity. "People are becoming overwhelmed," the D. J. Michel Gaubert remarked last Thursday, as he stood by an oval portal to a luminous biomorphic tent constructed inside the Grand Palais for the Yves Saint Laurent show.

. . . "Look at the number of outfits people are showing," he said. "Look at how many shows there are a day. Look at how many cities and markets buyers have to think about."

. . . So, perhaps in response to this, designers retrench. They embrace conservative ideas and the clothes that suit them. They look backward. They outfit models as an army of automatons, the way Stefano Pilati, the gifted Saint Laurent designer, did. His pale-faced cadres wore black lipstick, had eyes obscured by black-bowl wigs and bodies encased in clothes of a stark geometry rarely seen outside the Vatican.

"I don't think you want to go out advertising a brand anymore," Mr. Pilati told Style.com after the show.

Mr. Pilati was not alone in balking at the idea of becoming a logo machine. At Balenciaga, Nicolas Ghesquiere produced a collection that was as much about formalist feats as about anything as banal and frivolous as grabbing an after-work cocktail.

Source: Guy Trebay. "Fashion Sees Its Shadow." The *New York Times*. March 6, 2008, p. G1.

Discussion Points

1. What is the main function of a designer of high fashion today?
2. How does the speed of the market and communications change the approach of design?
3. What does "logo machine" mean?

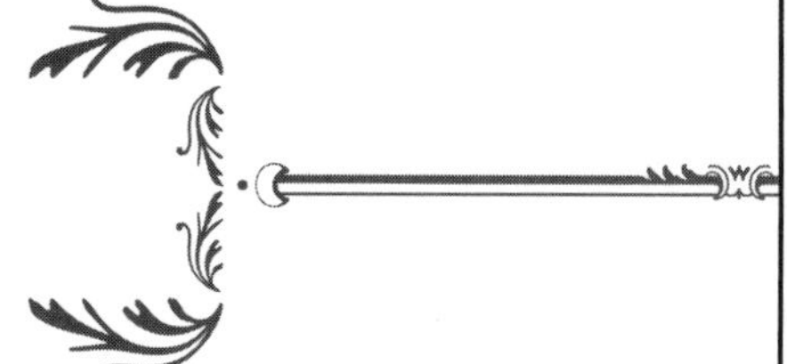

CHAPTER 7

Turning to Youth

In this chapter we will examine the stories and designs of Christian Dior and Yves Saint Laurent, and how the juncture of their stories can be seen to represent high-fashion design's attempt to rescue itself with a turn away from the world of the nineteenth century. This attempt would fail as the control over the image of Western culture slipped from the grasp of the old elite of Europe. While couture stayed where it had been born, a host of young, restless postwar revolutionary thinkers achieved with a restless Dada spirit, something the Dada movement had dreamed of: They took the culture of the West and turned it on its head, removing it from the grasp of the elites who had assumed control for almost 100 years. Questioning everything, the young radicals were not about to adhere to norms and standards of dress handed down from the elites they struggled against. Anyone over 30 years old was suspect, part of the establishment, and "square." However, as the spirit of revolution was realized as a marketable trend, the fashion world found itself with new allegiances, and the revolutionary styles were labeled and sold faster than their message could spread. In this way the high-fashion world became not just "ruled from below," with its primary influences coming from street fashion, but also became obsessed with an image of youth over establishment.

THE REAL FIN DE SIÈCLE: DIOR AND SAINT LAURENT

In a prime example of real life providing all the metaphors one needs, Dior died in France in 1957, on the eve of the opening of the first facsimile reproduction of the Dior boutique. The replica was created for the Neiman Marcus "Quinzaine Française," a French-themed week at the store in Dallas. Dior's business was on the verge of transformation when he died at only 52. He had courted the American businessmen just as much as they had courted him, and although the size and scale of American business was overwhelming to him, he did not look at Americans with the disdain of Poiret and Chanel. America had been good to him from the beginning of his career ten years before. In Paris, Balenciaga commanded more respect, and Balmain had a larger clientele, but it was Dior who had received the blessing of the American editors, and he embraced the attention and licensing agreements that followed.[1]

The irony of the juxtaposition of his death with the opening of a simulated Dior boutique could not have been seen at the time, of course. It is only with hindsight that it becomes visible: The death of high fashion that was heralded soon afterward began at about this time, when the *concept* of French couture became a packaged commodity in America. Divorced from its roots in Paris, the *idea* of couture would be sold only as a representation of a culture that had never authentically existed in the New World, but that the fashion business busily created an image of. The step toward pure simulation, of the kind discussed at the end of Chapter 1, was now to be a short one.

It is entirely fitting that Dior would be the iconic designer to represent the last generation of old-world couture in America, as his own creative vision was firmly focused on the past. Growing up in Paris before World War I, he was 20 years old at the *Exposition Internationale des Arts Decoratifs* in 1925. This was the exhibition where Poiret presented his decorated barges on the Seine, and Chanel her trademark suit. Dior was, according to a friend, incredibly excited about the exhibition that represented the high point of Art Deco and the entrance of modernism into the public vision of design.[2]

Paris, at this time, was an incredible mixture of artistic free-for-all and aristocratic playground. Picasso, Satie, Hemingway, Gertrude Stein, Dali, and Cocteau, to name a few, could be observed taking in the nightlife. The modern art that defines the twentieth century has a number of roots grounded in the late '20s in Paris, but tellingly, Dior was already showing signs of the anti-modernist tendencies that would inspire and drive his postwar designs. Despite being in the thick of things, he and his friends aligned themselves with painters who were reacting against the dominance of Picasso and the Cubists. Dior's nostalgia then bloomed fully some years later, when his mother died in 1931. She was only 51, and Dior, at 26, was devastated. He idolized his mother to the degree that after her death, she became the model of the perfectly elegant woman.[3]

FIGURE 7.1. A Dior dress from 1947, featured in the article "Paris Forgets It's 1947."

This nostalgia and his anti-modernist sentiments would serve him well when, at the end of World War II, the nostalgia that came into fashion found him working alongside Pierre Balmain as a designer at Lucian Lelong. Lelong had kept his studio open during the war, subjecting him to grumblings about collaboration with the Germans, but Dior was not harmed by his association. The fashions of 1946 were looking back, not to pre-World War II years, but to pre-World War I fashions. Dior's romanticized notions of his childhood years would play right in. He had already been noticed by American fashion editor Carmel Snow of *Harper's Bazaar* when he was working for Robert Piuget in the late '30s. In 1946, she reported to the Fashion Group on returning from Paris: "Lelong has a new designer whose collection was sensational—full of ideas. His name is Christian Dior."[4] She would then take up his cause in the fall of 1947, when he showed the line that came to be known as the "New Look" (Figure 7.1). The look was not new at all, of course—just new in terms of what had been seen in the previous six or eight years during the war. Its narrow waists, wide skirts, and extravagances of fabric were direct descendents of the nineteenth century, "a brilliant nostalgia" in the words of Cecil Beaton.[5] The reaction to the "New Look" was incredibly enthusiastic, and the marketing that followed played it to the hilt, brilliantly using the almost shocking ostentation as its main selling point.

Dior and Chanel

Dior had strong views on the ideal feminine image and, like Poiret, his opinion of Chanel's minimalism had been that this had gone too far down the road of simplicity. About his "New Look" he said, "Abundance was still too much of a novelty for us to reinvent an inverted snobbery of poverty."[6] However, he was more generous than Poiret, in that he allowed a little admiration of Chanel to show. He was very admiring of how she used black (something he could not do well), and in 1954, he wrote, "Her personal style was characteristic of her period: by creating a style for the elegant woman rather than the beautiful woman she marked the end of froufrou, feathers, overdressing. When she closed her firm she closed a door on elegance and spirit." Chanel was less generous in her comments about Dior, considering him to be too busy and fussy in comparison to her own minimalist aesthetic.

Chanel, it should be noted, was not the only minimalist designer working at the time. She was following a trend that had begun around 1910 and continued through the 1920s. Women were streamlined and less and less hampered by their fashions. Modernism as a design ideal influenced women's clothing, as we have seen, far more than it did men's wear, and designers had been experimenting and creating minimalist fashions that fit right in with the Bauhaus architectural principles of functionality, nonadornment, and clean lines. The coming war in the late '30s and the subsequent nostalgia for the pre-World War Europe changed all that, and Dior was the right designer at the right time.

Chanel had opted for exile in Switzerland after the war. Because of her affair with a German officer during the occupation, she was viewed as a collaborator, arrested in Paris, and interrogated. The rumor was that only her acquaintance with the Duke and Duchess of Windsor and knowledge that Churchill had paid the Nazis to leave their chalet alone saved her from a trial or worse.[7] After several years of rumors, she came back to Paris in 1953 to reopen her couture house. This move may have been partly prompted by slipping sales of Chanel No. 5, but she was also encouraged by her high-society friends. Primarily, she saw an opportunity for her vision to appeal to a new generation of customers. She also saw there was a need to counterbalance what Dior, Balenciaga, and the other male designers were doing. With new mass-production technologies and man-made textiles, Chanel knew that her vision of practical, stylish clothes of quality construction was right on the money. Chanel, businesswoman that she was, could sense that the world was even more ready for the vision she held of high fashion.

SAINT LAURENT TAKES OVER

When Christian Dior died without warning in 1957, his young apprentice, Yves Saint Laurent, needed to step in quickly in order to keep the House of Dior afloat. Dior had been feeling increasingly overwhelmed by the demands that the market and his own fame put on him. After being crowned the new "King of Fashion" by Carmel Snow, he had been under pressure to continually come up with something new. The media played the game of "what's it going to be this time," and Dior could not get out of the call-and-response mode that his fame dictated. This pressure was now immediately transferred to the 21-year-old Yves, who "saved French fashion" as the media hoopla declared after his collection was shown three months later (Figure 7.2). The line was named the "Trapeze" line and was considered to have upheld the Dior name but also to have added youthfulness to the fashions of the mid-'50s, which were already beginning to look rather dowdy.

FIGURE 7.2. A young Yves Saint Laurent.

Saint Laurent continued to make the fashions younger and more streetwise, but the pressure of being Dior's heir took its toll. His desire to bring the bohemian fashions of Paris's Left Bank to the couture clientele proved too much, and his Beat Look collection of 1960 (Figure 7.3) was not received well. In this collection, Saint Laurent took the amazing step of bringing the radical youth styles, which had begun to appear, into haute couture. The collection showed the little skirts, turtlenecks, and biker-style jackets of the college age crowd in Paris, all immaculately tailored in high-end fabrics. The translation did not go over well. The upper-class customers of Dior were not

FIGURE 7.3. Yves Saint Laurent's Beat Look (left) and the Parisian Beat look that inspired him (right).

ready to be dressed as up-market versions of the radicals and students of the Montparnasse cafés.

To add to his troubles, Saint Laurent was called up for military service and promptly suffered a nervous breakdown in boot camp. While he was recovering, the Dior company used the opportunity and replaced him with Marc Bohan. Saint Laurent had the last word, though. He continued to pursue his vision and, with new financial backing, brought his youthful designs to market, this time to a much better reception. In 1966 he inaugurated his aptly titled "Rive Gauche" (Left Bank) label. This was a watershed moment in fashion. Not only was the celebrated heir to the great Dior designing clothes based on Pop Art and Beat fashions, but he was designing them as ready-to-wear. This was to be a turn that signified the direction that high-fashion was going to go in, turning away from the world of aristocracy and Old Empire sensibilities. This was in full accord with the direction of politics and society, and Yves and his partner, Pierre Bergé, were right on the money.

But outside the world of couture, fashions were evolving on the street without the direction of—and often in opposition to—the editors and high-fashion designers. In London, Mary Quant had recently created the "Chelsea Look" and was popularizing the miniskirt. (See Figure 7.4.) Barbara Hulanicki had also opened a London store two years before and was selling upbeat, relatively low-priced fashions to the newly affluent "hip" crowd, wresting fashion from the privileged few and giving it to the young.

Saint Laurent's move must also be seen in that context. His moving to the Left Bank was certainly leading in the couture world, but in a broader context, he was not leading, but moving in a larger trend that even he was being swept up in.

FIGURE 7.4. Fashion Mackintosh model Jackie Bowyer swings on a lamppost wearing a black oilskin wet-weather outfit from Mary Quant.

BEATS

Even as the World War II ended and the affluent middle-class society that would typify America was rising, voices of dissent were rising with it. The society that was developing was not seen as a positive force by all, and one group of poets and writers who eventually called themselves "Beat" began to publish writings that pointed to other modes of living, as well as severely criticizing the styles and capitalist priorities of postwar America.

Jack Kerouac's novel *On the Road* became one of the seminal writings for this movement, giving directions for a generation that would wish to "drop out" of the rat-race. The term "Beat" referred initially in Kerouac's thinking to the use it had in popular culture of the '40s as "down-and-out." In the *New York Times* from 1952, a writer explained further, "More than mere weariness, it implies the feeling of having been used, of being raw"[8] and went on to note that in an inversion of trends, this was not the "Lost Generation" of the '20s, obsessed with losing their faith, but a new generation that was seeking something to believe in. It was a generation that had large questions to ask of the modern society that seemed to be lacking a place for the individual voice and spiritual fulfillment.

The Beats did not advocate an overthrow of society, but rather a rethinking or even a dropping out. There was no revolutionary intent initially, but very quickly a generation had found a voice. Kerouac's books *On the Road* and *The Dharma Bums* became best sellers, and with that came media attention. The media image of the Beats was generally one of condescending derision, with interviewers focusing on the details of the works and not on their meanings. Their message was taken to be one of style more than content because the content was difficult to take on for those who did not share their vision. For example, in this section of his poem *Howl* from 1955, Allen Ginsberg describes a scene of destruction of the human spirit in the new media age:

> who were burned alive in their innocent flannel suits
> on Madison Avenue amid blasts of leaden verse
> & the tanked-up clatter of the iron regiments
> of fashion & the nitroglycerine shrieks of the
> fairies of advertising & the mustard gas of sinis-
> ter intelligent editors, or were run down by
> drunken taxicabs of Absolute Reality

The media attention had the odd double effect that was repeated again and again in the second half of the twentieth century and now has begun to look quaint: On one hand there was the shocked reaction to the new revolutionary styles and philosophies, and on the other a swift exploitation of the new style in order to sell the looks, books, and music that go with the new cultural wave (Figure 7.5). In the new capitalist culture that had been developing since the '20s, the cultural identification of American society was tied up with the marketplace. We are the children of President Hoover's Happiness Machines and are what we buy. Kerouac himself became increasingly uncomfortable with the effect he was having and felt that his identity had been not only co-opted but also profoundly misunderstood.

The Beat image was, oddly enough, not that of the poets and writers, who wore fairly conventional clothing of the '40s and '50s, to the extent that they are barely distinguishable from anyone else in photographs of the period. The beret, goatee, and horn-rimmed glasses, however, came out of the jazz scene. The primary influence of Beat style came from Kerouac's writing. The clothes and attitude are described as being used by the characters in his novels, traveling around the country with only as much as they can fit in a knapsack. Faded jeans and T-shirts, Army jackets, and a rough outdoors style of shaggy hair and unshaved face would continue to be the college campus and art-café style in America for decades, while the characters in the stories continued to be conflated with Kerouac and the other Beat poets and artists.

FIGURE 7.5. A group of beatniks in Paris in 1955. The Beat look very quickly became the fashion of a new generation of the "Uprooted."

The image took on a life of its own, and while those who adhered to the Beat view of life and the world were experimenting with culture and anticapitalist existence, the media and entertainment industry created the goateed, black-turtle-necked, bongo-playing "beatnik." "Beatnik" combines "beat" with the Slavic suffix "–nik," which indicates someone who belongs to a state or group, and, when used in English, tends to have an ironic connotation. Coined by a columnist in San Francisco, the idea seems to have been to indicate "hangers-on," not "true" Beats.[9] Allen Ginsberg objected to this use of the word and wrote to the *New York Times*, "If beatniks and not illuminated Beat poets overrun this country, they will have been created not by Kerouac but by industries of mass communication which continue to brainwash man."

{ LOOKING FORWARD LOOKING BACK }

Beat by Your Father's Anarchist Pants

The Beats have continued to be a double edged inspiration to the arts and media. They remind later generations of how the American dream had its dissident voices, but in matters of style and politics, their image has blurred to a point at which it has no edge to it at all. The media-fuelled caricature has acquired a life of its own, and the Beats, like Che Guevara and other revolutionary figures of the 1960s, are now simply a choice of T-shirts.

This is especially true of Jack Kerouac, author of the 1951 novel *On the Road*. When it was published in 1957, it quickly made him a celebrity and became a manifesto for the wandering search for America in the '60s. It also became the source for the romanticized image of the Beats that marketers have seized on since. William Burroughs, Kerouac's friend and fellow Beat writer, wrote that Kerouac's book "sold a trillion Levi's, a million espresso coffee machines, and also sent countless kids on the road."*

The marketing of image, divorced from its origin, that we have become so used to in fashion since the 1960s really hit its stride with the appropriation of the "beat" style by Saint Laurent, but the image has been continually repackaged to the point where "beat" as a style has no content beyond the trappings of its clothing or paraphernalia. "Beat" has achieved the perfect state of being its own simulacrum.

A particularly clear example of this total separation of image from meaning was a marketing campaign in the early 1990s for the Gap that used the Beats to play on what the retailer termed the "classic" elements its clothing. A photograph of Kerouac standing in front of a bar's neon sign was altered so the "r" reads like a "P" (implying the Gap logo). The words "Kerouac wore khakis" is superimposed on the image.

The Gap—although definitely not in the arena of high-fashion apparel—became the signifying style for men's wear in the United States in the late '80s and early '90s. The clothes themselves were fairly unremarkable renditions of what was termed "classic" styles, and in this lay their strength. The chinos, oxford shirts, and such followed the gen-

* Hugh Montgomery, "America's First King of the Road," *Sunday Observer*, London, August 5, 2007.

eral development of men's styles from the middle of the twentieth century onward toward nondescript, informal uniformity. Gap clothing became the perfect signature outfit for the casual business atmosphere that developed in the late '80s and '90s, especially around the so-called dot-com bubble, when college styles merged with businesswear. This adoption of the previous generation's leisurewear as business attire conveyed the "seriousness" of the "old school" of business in that it nodded toward neither hippie nor punk, but it allowed men to avoid showing up for work in a bona fide suit.

The connection of a pair of khaki pants to radicals and anarchists in the Gap ad is breathtaking in its audacity, but a perfect example of the total separation of image from content in the Society of the Spectacle. To sell characterless conformity under the guise of radical anarchism requires a mindset in which both marketer and consumer conspire toward complete cluelessness about the origin of their images. The brainwashing is complete. Wearing anarchist pants, the beatniks created by mass media have indeed overrun the country as Allen Ginsberg both feared and predicted.

One could make the case that in this protest, Ginsberg put his finger right on the dilemma of modern counterculture style and fashion: Counterculture cannot survive being picked up by media and marketing campaigns, and even if it does survive in some form, the media creation becomes the perceived reality. The media creation stands in for the original, another creature that lives on as a simulacrum even after the original is gone. Kerouac wrote in 1957:

> In actuality there was only a handful of real hip swinging cats and what there was vanished mightily swiftly during the Korean War when (and after) a sinister new kind of efficiency appeared in America, maybe it was the result of the universalization of Television and nothing else (the Polite Total Police Control of Dragnet's 'peace' officers) but the beat characters after 1950 vanished into jails and madhouses, or were shamed into silent conformity, the generation itself was short-lived and small in number.[10]

The fact that there weren't more "hip cats" is perhaps not the issue. The interesting thought is that there weren't new ones who took the place of those who disappeared into institutions or shame. The universalization of television, as Kerouac observed, is right at the heart of this lack of subversiveness in modern-day fashion. If the image is everywhere, then how can it be nonconformist or revolutionary? What modern technological society cannot confront directly, it envelopes and assimilates by decontextualizing and decentralizing the threat. You cannot be a revolutionary when the revolution has been passed off as entertainment well before anyone has heard of you.

The Recouping of the Working Class Heroes, or "You Say You Want a Revolution . . ."

Yves Saint Laurent seems therefore to have upended the game. He brought Beat fashion to Paris high-fashion and, in doing so, transformed both. The Left Bank fashions became chic and therefore lost their revolutionary cachet. However, high fashion did not become revolutionary; it merely found another market to cater to. But in embracing the antiestablishment fashions, even as ready-to-wear, high fashion demonstrated that it had lost the authority of dictating society's style. It continued to act as if it still had the authority, and the world outside its traditional authority accepted this pretense. However, if an authority has to constantly be taking cues or asking questions outside its domain, it is only a symbolic authority. Such an authority exists only by the mutual agreement of those inside and outside the imaginary circle of influence to continue the established order. In this case, no viable alternative presented itself, and so high fashion continued to play its role, and the society supporting it continued by its own script.

By acknowledging the authority of the street, Saint Laurent legitimized the transfer of authority from the salons to the street. The shrinking market for couture, the political change, the globalization of fashion trends, and the instantaneous distribution of trends and ideas made it inevitable that this transfer would eventually happen, but Saint Laurent provided the model and blessing.

What this resulted in was that now the high-fashion market needed to attune itself to the happenings on the street. The "next new thing" would not come from a royal court by decree or demand. It would have to be picked up from wherever trends were being created. With that, the fashion designer now became trend spotter rather than creator. The designer would now reflect and transform the observed, lift the happening from society, remodel it, and hand it back.

The late twentieth century saw this happen in large movements three times: First, the Beats, as we have already seen. Then the hippies, who were in direct continuation of the Beats, brought William Burrough's fear of marketed counterculture to fruition. Ten years later, the same would happen with punk, although by then the relationship of high fashion and street had broken and high fashion's authority was completely absent.

Hippie

In January 1967, the Haight-Ashbury neighborhood of San Francisco saw an event that changed America's perception of itself and would quickly make itself felt all over Europe. The neighborhood had attracted beatniks and artists for years. By 1967 it had become the "locus and metaphor for a burgeoning national movement."[11] In January of that year, a so-called "Be-In" took place in Golden Gate Park. (See Figure 7.6.) More than 30,000 people gathered to listen to music and take part in the rising sense of power and togetherness of antiestablishment youth who were gathering strength in their disaffection with American society.

FIGURE 7.6. Hippies in the park in San Francisco in 1967.

The Be-In attracted nationwide attention, and the media went into overdrive. *Time* magazine coined the word "hippie" in much the same way as the word "beatnik" had been forged and with the same purpose. The image of the "flower child" went forth, and as the summer approached, Haight-Ashbury was flooded with young people looking to be part of the "scene." The Haight Independent Proprietors (HIP), an association of merchants who sold clothes and paraphernalia in the neighborhood, came up with the idea of a "Summer of Love" and began a publicity campaign to attract even more kids to the area.

The Monterey Pop festival was held in June, and all the kids came up to fill the Haight. The local hipsters were not impressed. The actor Peter Coyote, who at the time was a member of a radical group who called themselves the Diggers, took a harsh view:

> I thought the Summer of Love was horseshit. We thought the Summer of Love, just like Be-In, was basically a campaign by the Haight Independent Proprietors—it was a merchants association—to brand the Haight-Ashbury with a national consciousness. But there are unintended consequences . . . But the genesis, though, was that these guys were trying to create a national consciousness so that people would buy their hash pipes and clothes and what have you. So I just wasn't interested in it. I didn't care. What happened was, the media started hammering this weird stuff going on in San Francisco.[12]

The unintended consequences were, amongst others, the rapid descent of the community into commercialism, legal and illegal: "With [the kids,] the vultures moved in," said Sam Andrew, guitarist for Janis Joplin's band, Big Brother and the Holding Company, who played at both the Be-In and the festival. "What we had done was commercialized. People moved in who wanted to make a buck out of it all, especially the drugs. Hard drugs arrived—speed, meth, cocaine, heroin. The drugs became tiring and boring."[13]

With the increased media attention and the ability for any disaffected kid in some out-of-the-way area to see reports on television and realize that there may be a place for her or him, things got rapidly out of hand in San Francisco. The locals began moving out as the neighborhood was overrun (among them the Grateful Dead and Coyote himself), and on October 10, 1967, a "Death of Hippie" event was held in the Panhandle of Golden Gate Park (Figure 7.7). Janis Joplin and Big Brother and the Holding Company performed, and "people brought bells, bongs and plenty of acid to commemorate the event. A procession

FIGURE 7.7. The "Death of Hippie, Son of Media" event in San Francisco in October of 1967 protested the co-opting of the counterculture by media and market forces.

marched down Haight Street carrying a black coffin with the words "Hippie, Son of Media" painted on the side; at the parade's end the coffin was cremated."[14]

Despite the originators' declaration, "Hippie" did not die and may even still now be seen roaming around. The "hippie" fashions took off that very same summer, with influences from tribal, Indian, and "Eastern" dress. Yves Saint Laurent, among others, began incorporating orientalisms into his designs. He had grown up in Morocco and accessed this inspiration for shapes, colors, and decoration. A veritable explosion of hippie-influenced styles and music spread out over the United States and Western Europe and would become the prevailing baby-boomer fashion, heavily romanticized and infused with instant nostalgia. The explosion would change all notions of youth and fashion, by acknowledging the existence of multiple points of reference and validating the experience of youth. Now "youth culture" existed as a truly independent entity.

Punk

In the next wholesale commodification of a youth culture, things moved equally fast. The hippie image was created from an existing group that had some authentic roots in a political experiment and in the Beat writings. Punk had its roots in disaffected youth as well, but this time the disillusionment was also directed at the previous youth movement, the hippies. Kids were reacting to the overload that had set in to pop music in the late '60s and early '70s by putting together basic, rough bands that played rock 'n' roll with an attitude that mirrored its origin in rough, low-tech individualism.

By the time punk rock came to the fore, those versed in cultural marketing had seen how to operate during the late '60s and understood that one could just as easily *push* a counterculture trend and follow it. Malcolm McLaren, an entrepreneur from London, had by all accounts been trying to get the members of the band the New York Dolls to come to London to start a band called the Sex Pistols. When that didn't pan out, he assembled a group from the customers and hangers-on of the Kings Road store he ran with the designer Vivienne Westwood. The shop was named (among other names) Sex/Seditionaries. Both McLaren and his friend Bernie Rhodes, who became the manager of the band the Clash, professed to an idealism formed by the Situationist Movement in Paris. The Situationists were a group led by Guy Debord, who advocated the revolutionizing of society in opposition to the spectacle with which our capitalistic society holds the citizenry in thrall. The Situationists were heavily involved in the Paris uprisings of 1968, when the students came out in support of a general strike, and once again barricades were rising in the streets of Paris. They were largely responsible for slogans that would appear in Paris, such as

> *"Under the Cobblestones: The beach!"*

and

> *"It's just so awful and boring . . . and then everybody jumped on the bandwagon."*

Malcolm McLaren, in New York in the early '70s, saw the punk musician Richard Hell coming into a venue with his clothes safety pinned together and brought this idea back to London. The idea began to take hold almost immediately:

FIGURE 7.8. Sid Vicious and Johnny Rotten of the Sex Pistols ca. 1977–1978.

> Then in London, we'd see picture of these kids who called themselves "Punks" and they'd have safety pins all over the place. They'd ripped the clothing on purpose, just so they could buy a whole bunch of safety pins and put the safety pins in the rips all over the place. And then we'd have to hear about how they're on the dole and they don't have any money.[15]

Westwood and McLaren saw that the trends could be pushed if the package was the correct one. Music had become essential for any discussion of youth culture, so any fashion worth mentioning needed is music. "The Sex Pistols" as a brand was initially meant to sell clothes, and then the band rode a wave to a sharp success, outgrowing their creators (Figure 7.8). McLaren and Westwood's genius lay in knowing that they were in the right place at the right time and had a good sense of how far they could go (which was considerable). Says Chrissie Hynde of the band the Pretenders, "I don't think punk would have happened without Malcolm and Vivienne, to be honest. Something might have happened and it might have even been called "punk" but it wouldn't have looked the way it did—and the look of it was so important."[16]

Westwood and McLaren essentially grabbed the reins away from the fashionable elites. High-fashion designers like Yves Saint Laurent didn't seem to know what to do with punk at the time and didn't actually seem to even try. It seems odd in hindsight, but at the time punk was considered beyond the pale in civilized society. But the lack of reaction from the high-fashion elite may also have in part been due to how quickly things were happening and how saturated the media coverage of "culture" had become: The Sex Pistols existed as a band only for a little over a year, after releasing their only album. In the '70s, a collection took more time than that to plan and market, and picking up a trend directly from the street was still not a common practice, despite Saint Laurent's efforts. He had picked up the hipsters in Paris and the fashionable hippies in London, but he had smartened them up and recontextualized the influences. But punk is, by its nature, hard to pin down. Its aggressiveness lies completely open on the surface, so its power disappears as soon as it is tidied up for mass consumption. But the marketers learned quickly. Having grabbed with both hands at the street fashions of the '60s, they could now actually create their own countercultures for their own marketing purposes in the '70s. Punk's major contribution to the story was to show that all bets were off. Anything could happen, and from now on it would. But with punk, the fashion that had become a statement of opposition to prevailing culture had been incorporated into the culture. There didn't seem to be anywhere to go next as the circular reference of market—rebellion—new market became the method of the fashion world. The forward-looking designers of the '60s had hung their hopes on a future that wasn't going to exist.

ENDBOX

Paris Show Marks Farewell to Paris

She may have survived prison and she is off to Africa to "bring happiness to the Africans," but the reign of Paris Hilton in the fashion world is over. No other label has been more associated with Hilton and her millions of teenage aspirants this decade than Christian Dior. Any teen starlet worth her Juicy Couture tracksuit owned at least three T-shirts emblazoned with a J'Adore Dior logo.

Although such patronage brought "youth appeal" to the label—and great wealth—the company is seeking to move away from this demographic, as was clear from the Christian Dior show yesterday in Paris. The label's best show for years opened with a sleek, loose and very glamorous pinstripe suit. Trousers all sat on the hipbone, as opposed to slipping down to groin level, the favoured trouser style of the LA teen market. The dresses were midi length and cut for a woman as opposed to an underfed 22-year-old, even if that was who was still modelling them.

In a report in yesterday's Wall Street Journal Dior's chief executive, Ralph Toledano, said, "We needed to move away from the power of the T-shirt." Although these teenage trinkets boosted the company's profile, they were damaging its credibility.

Source: Hadley Freeman. *Guardian*. October 2, 2007.

Discussion Points

1. What is the credibility problem that this article addresses? How does it work?
2. How is this article indicative of a larger cultural shift?
3. What is the extreme of this development, if it continues?

CHAPTER 8

The Flesh Failures

(Let the Sunshine In)

To look at the '60s as a time of hippie counterculture and revolt is to focus on only a small segment of a decade that is a bridge from the fashions of Jackie Kennedy's White House to the chaos of punk rock. The appropriation of the counterculture movements of the Beats and hippies we have seen in Chapter 7 shows how the commercial world had gained control over the development of culture and style. The control was strong, but not entirely complete. The '60s had an arc that led from the last attempt to reinvigorate the old European style of society to the beginnings of punk rock and with it the dissolution of the fashion system. This arc, the beginnings of which we saw outlined by Dior and Yves Saint Laurent along with the appropriation of Beats and hippies, needs to be placed in a political context. The United States was fully establishing itself as the dominant actor on the scene, needing to find an image and, in the wake of its own political turmoil, failing.

With that failure, the idealism of the Beats and hippies, their search for meaning, and their rejection of the consumer society plays out as a counterpoint to the rise of a world power and the establishment of an identity to go with the new order. We must consider the idealistic movements the '60s contained both within the establishment as well as beyond. We must also look at the uplifting politics with which the decade began as well as the disappointment with which it ended. As before, these both reflect and drive the fashions, but it is in the 1960s that the politics of cynicism closed the door to high fashion as the representative fashion of our culture.

As the 1950s progressed, Western Europe became as well functioning a society as it had ever been with the help of the postwar Marshall plan and a strong effort to reestablish strong trade and good relations in the Western hemisphere. London, Paris, Rome, and Milan now reclaimed their centrality to Western culture and identity. Despite New York and Chicago assuming the mantle of capitals of art and architecture, European artists and designers held their own and in many cases created strong new positions for themselves. Danish furniture, Italian film, and, of course, French fashion were innovative and held in high regard. America was still considered "uncultured," in comparison, not in the least by the Americans themselves, who continued to look to Europe for style and inspiration, feeling very much the provincial cousin across the sea. The Kennedy White House attempted to bring the European style back into American high society, with the first lady playing the part of Empress Eugénie and Princess Metternich rolled into one.

The Kennedy White House

When elected in 1960, John F. Kennedy became the second-youngest president in American history (after Theodore Roosevelt) at the age of 43. His wife, Jacqueline Bouvier Kennedy, was only 31, less than half the age of the outgoing first lady, Mamie Eisenhower, whose husband President Eisenhower had recently turned 70. The Kennedys had about them a strong aura of youth and excitement and represented a change in the image of American society (Figure 8.1). Kennedy directed the world's attention to this in his inaugural address: "Let the word go forth from this time and place, to friend and foe alike, that the torch has been passed to a new generation of Americans."

The young couple tapped into what Kennedy's speechwriter Richard Goodwin would later write about as "the desires of a swiftly changing nation . . . some vague and spreading

FIGURE 8.1. President John F. Kennedy and First Lady Jacqueline Kennedy attend the inaugural ball, January 20, 1961, in Washington, D.C.

desire for national renewal."[1] This desire, which found its resonance also in the arts, first with a new expressionistic daring in painting, music, and literature, and then with a whole new "pop" and minimalist approach, came straight out of the new affluence of the postwar years. Americans felt powerful and wealthy, but in the power and wealth there seemed to be a lack of purpose. The rigidity and commercialism of the postwar society that the Beats were reacting against was also a source of discomfort, even though it could not be articulated. The young educated population, living in unprecedented material wealth in orderly suburban life, seemed to want a more fulfilling purpose and belong to a grander scheme than just to shop and be "happiness machines."

With all the mythologizing that has taken place, it is necessary to remember that

FIGURE 8.2. John and Jackie with baby Caroline Kennedy.

Kennedy was not considered a very viable candidate at the beginning of his campaign. What did bring him to the front was his savviness in image-making. He and his circle knew how to use television and print media to connect to the public. There were constant photo ops of Kennedy with his family. Here was the beginning of much that we have become accustomed to in political campaigning in the late twentieth century. This was also the beginning of the kind of multimedia interpretation of current events that would become the norm. Here is where the presence of the camera creates the news. It is quite amazing to compare the number of iconic photographs that are associated with the Kennedy years, with those, for example, of Eisenhower or Truman. Not only are the fashions used to maximum effect to create an aura of "one of us," but also to create an image of the mythical family that Americans were meant to be (Figure 8.2).

The Kennedy family cultivated a style of clothing that became so ingrained in the American psyche that it is still the touchstone today. The impact of their myth-making can still be seen in the iconography of design today, with a "Jackie look" here and "Kennedy look" there. Any young male politician, especially on the Democratic side, is inevitably compared to John F. Kennedy on the basis of charisma and looks alone. Millions of women received their fashion education through following Jacqueline in magazines and on television, and the image of female elegance in politics is still measured against her example.

With cameras for television, magazines, and newspapers on constant watch only what was *seen* to be happening was important. Not only are we closing in on the time when the ultimate measure of real celebrity would be being on TV but also that nothing would be seen as being important unless it was visually represented in the news media. The photogenic candidate with the fashionable, young beauty of a wife became the image Americans wanted to own as the image of their country. Famously, of course, Kennedy was held to have won the debates with his rival, Richard Nixon, on the basis of his superiority in looking good on camera. Whether it is true or not, the fact that it is continually stated makes it worth considering. It is the *belief* in the power of the image that now matters.

But under the surface of the optimism and hope were also fears and dangerous undercurrents. Racial tensions were reaching a breaking point, and the Soviet Union seemed on the road to technological victory over the West and was baring its teeth in Eastern Europe. And other countries were not being reassuring in their stance: European and South American popular politics were increasingly hostile to America. Americans needed to see their country reinvigorated.

In addition to an aura of youth and change, the Kennedys brought a cultured air to the White House, with Jacqueline's French ancestry and schooling influencing her choices in décor and entertaining. It fell to Jacqueline Kennedy to take up the role of arbiter of fashion and style in a society searching for a new identity. She immediately set restoring the White House, which had grown increasingly dowdy with each preceding president. Her aim was for it to be "an emblem of the American Republic." She favored an eighteenth-century style in decorating and proceeded to re-create an elegant White House in a Jeffersonian style. This blending of high European classicism with the most Francophone of American presidents was a masterful compromise in the delicate politics of style that had immediately surrounded her. Her balance of fashion was equally adroit, allowing herself every now and then to be caught "off guard" in sandals and relaxed resort wear, or with her hair stylishly out of order when playing with her children. (A complaint was made that the First Lady should not be going about in sandals, like a beatnik.)

A New Empress

Jacqueline Kennedy's position was very much akin to the Empress Eugénie's in Paris 100 years before. There was a need for a unifying fashion at a time of underlying turmoil, and she provided the perfect icon and model.

She was of French descent, had earned a bachelor's degree in French literature from George Washington University, and had spent a year at Sorbonne in Paris. She was, as a result, very partial to French fashion designers. Jacqueline was an admirer of the fashions of Hubert Givenchy and dressed in the simple, uncluttered style that Givenchy and Audrey Hepburn had begun to popularize through movies like *Breakfast at Tiffany's*. This did not sit well with her husband, who during the campaign was courting the International Ladies

Garment Workers Union, which could—reminiscent of Napoleon III's textile workers in Lyon—make or break his position. The union could deliver almost half a million votes in 40 states. It was Jacqueline's task to not only stay away from foreign fashions, but to create demand for fashions created in the United States. Given the closeness of the election results, it is just as easy to make the case that this is what won the election for Kennedy as it is to say that it was Nixon's sweaty, brooding demeanor on television.

Despite Jackie's care, she would on occasion become frustrated with the media's focus on her clothing and style. Famously, she snapped that she didn't have time to buy a French dress for her daughter Caroline when she was in Paris with JFK and once remarked at the beginning of the presidential campaign, "What does my hairstyle have to do with my husband becoming president?" Also during the campaign's early days, one of her flippant remarks caused a great stir. She was questioned by newswomen on the subject of clothes. She said she had been criticized for spending $30,000 a year on French fashions and retorted, "I couldn't spend that much unless I wore sable underwear." The *New York Times* commented, without indication of jest, that it was feared that this remark might cost her husband votes among women and furriers.[2] Given this kind of scrutiny, she started turning from French designers such as Givenchy to American ones, and once she was first lady, chose Oleg Cassini, a former Hollywood costumer and man-about-town, as her primary designer.

First Ladies

Jacqueline Kennedy was just as astute as the Empress Eugénie in making sure she served her purpose well. She attempted to bring into the White House a sense of style and fashion that had not been there for a while and certainly not in the preceding Eisenhower, Truman, and Roosevelt administrations. Her youth, European background, and cultural leanings gave her quite an edge over her predecessors, who all belonged to the generation that had grown up before World War I. With so many Americans enamored of Europe and Paris in particular after the two world wars, a semi-French ambience to the White House seemed not to be a bad idea.

Eleanor Roosevelt had seen the job of the first lady as being a voice of the people within the government, a guardian of human values, and a fighter for equality. Her ideas of enter-

FIGURE 8.3. Bess Truman, far right, at home in Missouri. She was not one to spend much time socializing in Washington, D.C.

FIGURE 8.4. Mamie Eisenhower greets a young Queen Elizabeth on the White House steps.

tainment in the White House were a far cry from the European elegance of Jacqueline's, offering square dances and informal suppers. (FDR would mix martinis himself.) The dress code was rather dowdy, as it was in the time of Bess Truman, who was not especially interested in the ceremonial role of first lady and kept her social involvement and presence in Washington to the minimum (Figure 8.3). Mamie Eisenhower, on the other hand, maintained a strong domestic image in the White House (she had a famous fudge recipe) but was also well dressed and elegant in her style. She was frequently dressed by Arnold Scaasi but was, of course, a woman in her late 60s in a time when a woman in her 60s was expected to cultivate a dignified, if not matronly, image. The Eisenhowers entertained quite a lot, but their style was very "official" and "presidential," and Mamie, as a mistress of the White House, was apparently rather fearsome (Figure 8.4).

Oleg Cassini

The choice of Oleg Cassini as Jacqueline Kennedy's primary designer raised a number of eyebrows. He was known as a creator of "sexy clothes" and had been generally snubbed by

FIGURE 8.5. Oleg Cassini showing fashion editors sketches of Jacqueline Kennedy's inaugural dress, January 12, 1961.

fashion editors as he was a "wholesaler, a ready-to-wear man." He may have been chosen because he had frequently been critical of French fashions, but he himself told reporters that he was a personal friend of JFK—"we go to the same tailor."[3] Cassini was quite a flamboyant figure, even though he resented the "playboy-designer" label that the media affixed to him (Figure 8.5). It is Mr. Cassini, for example, who has the distinction to have introduced The Twist to the White House at a dinner dance. (The president and First Lady did not join in.) He had numerous affairs and wives and remained something of a ladies' man to the time of his death at the age of 92.

Cassini's background as a Hollywood costume designer was clearly also a good recommendation for the job. With the need to play to the camera now more important than anything, his appointment as "court-couturier" makes perfect sense. His style was well suited to the camera. It was minimalist with clean lines and strong details and was very body-conscious. He hated the sack dress to the point of parody, once sending a model wrapped in burlap, spilling potatoes as she made it down the runway.

Cassini was in a somewhat more subservient role than Charles Worth had been to the empress. This clipping from the *New York Times* shows him performing his courtly duties:

> Mrs. John F. Kennedy was fitted for new clothes here yesterday. One of her visitors at the Carlyle Hotel was Oleg Cassini, the dress designer, who was accompanied by assistants and boxes of new apparel. On his departure, the designer said he was not at liberty to reveal what styles or colors Mrs. Kennedy had chosen.[4]

Of course, letting the cat out of the bag would have meant knockoffs on the streets before the originals appeared, something Worth did not have to worry about.

Talk was that Cassini was just taking orders from the first lady and copying other designers at her request, and many of the garments he designed for her are clearly derivative of French designs of the period. It would seem, though, that she knew what she wanted and asked him to provide it. The relationship was definitely to the advantage of both, just as with Worth and Eugénie's: Jackie received her dresses at no cost, and Cassini achieved fame and recognition as the "court designer."

Cassini began creating the "Jackie look" when he designed the elegantly simple greige wool coat, accented with sable muff and collar, for President Kennedy's inauguration. Apparently she did not like hats, and in tilting her hat for the occasion back on her head to minimize it, she immediately created a signature look. The hat, however, had been created by a young milliner by the name of Roy Halston Frowick and became his first claim to fame. He would eventually become Jackie's designer of choice and become a famous figure in his own right, using only his middle name "Halston" as a label.

It is notable that once again it is the women's fashion that takes the initiative. For his inauguration, President Kennedy, icon of youthfulness, wore a morning suit and—of all things—a top hat, in order to fit into the old-world protocol of Washington of the day. Meanwhile, Jackie wore the most modern of outfits, minimalist, tailored, and elegant, looking every bit the modern woman, beside the outmoded stiff nineteenth-century costume of her husband.

A Style Icon in Black

After John F. Kennedy was assassinated in Dallas in 1963, with the immense media coverage of the funeral, Jacqueline Kennedy became frozen in time as the young widow in black (Figure 8.6) and was therefore removed for a while from a position where she could be an arbiter of fashion. However, in withdrawing from public life, she contributed in an odd, inverse way to her continuing role of fashion icon, as there was really no one to take her place. The new first lady, Lady Bird Johnson, was in her mid-50s and was unwilling or unable to take up the position of fashion icon. It is unlikely that public opinion would have

FIGURE 8.6. First Lady Jacqueline Kennedy holds hands with her daughter, Caroline, at the memorial service for President John Fitzgerald Kennedy, November 24, 1963.

tolerated a replacement of Jackie anyway. Jackie Kennedy's image froze in the public consciousness and the unfinished story of the Kennedy's "Camelot" became for many the image of the '60s' unfulfilled dream.

Shortly after the assassination, pop artist Andy Warhol would create a silkscreen composed of 16 images of Jackie. In six of them she is seen smiling at the crowds, just minutes before the shooting began in Texas. In the others, she is seen just after the event and then at her husband's funeral. It is these three images that have become enduring and fixed in the collective consciousness. It is as if Warhol could sense how the media manipulation had created the image of the woman that would persist. It is, even now, as if she never appeared except in a pink suit or in mourning.

She returned somewhat to fashionable circles in the '70s, with Halston, but her image remained very much that of her first lady role, immortalized in the juxtaposition of Warhol's two Jackies: bright, hopeful, and looking to the future at one instance, and in the next, immobile in grief, inward looking, and fearful, an all-too-apt metaphor for the United States in the '60s.

The Death of Hip

FIGURE 8.7. As "hippie" died, young and hip was high fashion: Saint Laurent's "African Dress" in 1967.

The cynicism that would permeate popular culture in the United States by the end of the twentieth century was largely rooted in the years following John F. Kennedy's assassination in Dallas. The hope for renewal that had accompanied the young Kennedys into the White House was shattered when a bullet tore his head open, further confused by the politics of the Vietnam War and trampled by the murders of Martin Luther King, Jr., and Robert F. Kennedy that bracketed the summer of 1968. The "Death of Hippie" from the year before was further played out (Figure 8.7), and the possibility that the philosophy, style, and fashion of the United States would become young and hopeful again was brought to an end. In that summer, between those assassinations, a couple in, say, the suburbs of New York City could get a baby sitter, head for the city, and spend an evening out watching hippies on stage in the musical *Hair*. The fact that the hippies were being exhibited to the "squares" as entertainment was not a sign of the *imminent* end of "hip" as counterculture; this was a sign that the Death of Hippie march had been right on. "Hippie, son of media" was dead on arrival.

Well-meaning and seemingly radical as it was, the creation of a stage musical of "hippiedom" only showed the separation of the form of the movement from its content (Figure 8.8). Although the final song of *Hair* urges the audience to "let the sunshine in," there is an underlying sense of loss and despair to the show, especially in the way it was filmed ten years later when the end of the Vietnam War and the Watergate scandal had brought the hope of the '60s to nothing.

The creation of the concept of "hippie" was in itself the death of the concept. The "Summer of Love"—named by the merchants of Haight-Asbury—was actually a self-contained narrative, with a beginning at the San Francisco Be-In, a middle at the Monterey Pop festival, and an end in the chaos of July '67 and the Death of Hippie march. What

FIGURE 8.8. A scene from the musical *Hair* on Broadway, on September 25, 1968, nearly a year after the "Death of Hippie" march.

happened afterward was a continuation of the events in San Francisco, to be sure, but it was not of the same world at all. The marketers and producers had taken over faster than the culture could keep up. It was now clear that great profits could be had from counterculture in general and youth culture in particular. The market was established and the lesson learned that a counterculture styles and fashions were profitable if they could be turned into marketable product while they were still perceived to be the "other" and threatening to the social order. Marketing fashion was to be permanently set against the reigning order, rather than represent and solidify the elites' grasp on culture and society.

The articles that first began appearing in 1964 describing the "death of fashion" were equally prescient—and ahead of themselves—in their assessment as the "Death of Hippie" announcements three years later. What was dying was the ability for society to regulate itself by reflecting its image back upon itself. The ritual, so carefully set up in Second Empire Paris, was rendered meaningless by the speed at which the image, cultured or counterculture, was packaged and sold. It would become increasingly difficult for a group, elite or antiestablishment, to be able to define its culture or even base its membership on a shared experience of fashion and style. But, even as "Hippie" was lying in state, new waves were rising.

Tearing It All Down

It became clear that the promises of the early '60s were going to be broken one after another. The disappointment and lack of direction began to produce a reaction that would take the failure of the idealism to produce a new society and revel in it, while attacking any structures that could be found. The Situationist combination of Dada and aggressiveness began to find its way into the counterculture. If the steadiness of European high culture wasn't the answer, and counterculture couldn't be kept out of the hands of the merchants long enough, then styles that were impulsive, aggressive, and bizarre might keep the "squares" away.

{ LOOKING FORWARD LOOKING BACK }
The Problem with Punk

Why couldn't high fashion appropriate punk styles just as it pulled from beat and hippie clothing? The punk look, as it was initially operated on in the late 1970s, was *bricolage*—the creation of something out of whatever happens to be available. This transparent do-it-yourself approach became the defining method and could well have been picked up by high fashion, but the aesthetic and logical contradictions arrive too quickly. There were elements of hippie and Beat styles that transferred easily—with some refinement—to high fashion. But that kind of designing is not *bricolage*. An element of chance is lost: Almost any design is too much design (which is why so much of designed punk looked so tame).

Punk, like hip or Beat, was a state of mind—an approach. The myth of punk rock was that anyone could—and should—pick up an instrument and play. The same went for the graphics of the fanzines and the clothing and hairstyles. Despite this subversive attitude, punk style was certainly *designed* from the start in England, where Vivienne Westwood created a look derived from bondage gear and "Teddy Boy" styles. This, when mixed with elements brought back from the New York punk scene, created the template for the street scene. Westwood's designs were deliberately aggressive and jarring, and the street styles that evolved were deliberately off key. Nothing in punk fashion could be appropriated for high-class socializing, and even if something could, it would lose its vitality.

In March of 1968, a month before *Hair* opened on Broadway, a band called the Psychedelic Stooges played their first show in Detroit's Grande Ballroom (Figure 8.9). Given that punk rock would not be seen on the cultural radar for another eight or ten years, it is often felt that the Detroit scene of the Stooges and a band called MC5 was ahead of its time. To this, Iggy Pop (James Osterberg), the front man of the Stooges, had this to say: "I would have to say that the rest of the world was behind its effin' time, that's what I would say. We were, as far as I was concerned, where things should be."[5] He went on to describe how the aggression and violence of their music and performances was suggested by the "architecture of the times, the ideas of the time, the social quakes of that time."[6]

There was no system in place for incorporating and marketing anger. So while popular music and fashion developed along some imaginary trajectory of "pop," producing sanitized and homogenized "flower power" styles, a deliberately strange and ugly backlash was developing. The styles that began to develop were an anti-fashion, directed anarchically against anything and everything.

Part of the problem, as Iggy notes in the interview previously quoted above, was that the new revolutionaries of the '60s, the musicians, were "talking one thing and living another . . . they all got fat really quickly. It was a visible sign of their incredible corruption." This can be taken to be a metaphor for the entire scheme that lifted the Beats and hippies wholesale out of their context, redesigned and cleaned them up, and sold them as a "lifestyle." That those who were meant to be the leaders of disaffected youth were meanwhile adopting the lifestyles of aristocracy and distancing themselves more and more from their origins was intolerably disappointing to those who came to the party after Hippie was dead. The late boomers who expected to be part of a youth revolution either bought into the myth that they could shop themselves into the Revolution or realized that they were being sold a hollow myth and were appalled at their own gullibility. These—notably

FIGURE 8.9. Iggy Pop at the Grande Ballroom in Detroit in 1968.

fewer—reacted against being a target market for a culture that was meant to be theirs by becoming increasingly distant from the mainstream. The most interesting and provocative fashions therefore appeared outside the system of designers and couture houses. But then, it had to be, as the whole point, until the marketers could figure out the angle, was to be outside. Of course, once the market became about the outside, as well as the inside, there was technically no "outside" to be on.

In their song "Won't Get Fooled Again," the Who put it in these terms: "Meet the new boss, same as the old boss." Iggy and the Stooges had a slightly more straightforward approach: "My band and I came along just a couple of years behind these people and just thought: Gee, do they suck!"[7]

The 1960s had begun with a hopeful vision of young Americans creating a cultured republic of enlightened ideals. The decade wound up with a hollowness at its core that denied all institutions and elevated individual expression above adherence to the community. With high fashion on its deathbed and youth fashion commercialized from the start, inventiveness needed to come to the rescue of high fashion design. The inventiveness that did show up was, however, too alien for mainstream culture, the backlash was too strong, and the distance between the inventors and the high-fashion elite was too great. In Chapter 9, we will see how the split became so great in the 1970s that the fashion system itself, as defined 100 years before at the court of Eugénie, disintegrated and became a marketing free-for-all.

ENDBOX

Summer of Love: 40 Years Later

They flew us in to do the Monterey Pop Festival and that was a lot of fun although I think everybody could see at the time the whole situation in San Francisco was turning. What we saw at Monterey, all the attention it was bringing us, all the attention the press was making about the San Francisco scene . . . I don't [know] who proclaimed it the Summer of Love. But we'd already begun to see people showing up who were basically riff-raff. All the riff-raff and ne'er-do-wells from across the country were headed to San Francisco to see if they could get in on the free love and drugs, which was not really what San Francisco was all about before that. San Francisco was intensely creative place, but the people who were coming starting around June were not creative people so much. They were people working on losing their teeth.

We started getting break-in's and stuff like that. There were a lot of people on the street. Whereas before everybody had a place to go, everybody had something to do. We were in a band. The guys who were running the coffee shops were running the coffee shops, or the clothing shops or the head shops. The Diggers were doing their thing. The poets were writing and poster artists were making posters. Everybody was busy. We would come together for celebrations and stuff like that and it was a lot of fun. But starting around June, the creativity of the scene was starting to be piled over by just having to batten down the hatches, bar your doors and windows 'cause there were speed freaks on the street. I had the front room at 710 Ashbury and people were coming through my front window with fair regularity. They were dressed the part—they were dressed like hippies. But I don't think that they really got it.

Source: Bob Weir. *SFGATE.com*. May 20, 2007.

Discussion Points

1. What was it that they "didn't get?" Who were "they?"
2. What is the relevance of what happened in San Francisco in 1967 to today's fashion?
3. Describe how a "Summer of Love" could—or could not—happen in today's media culture and economic system.

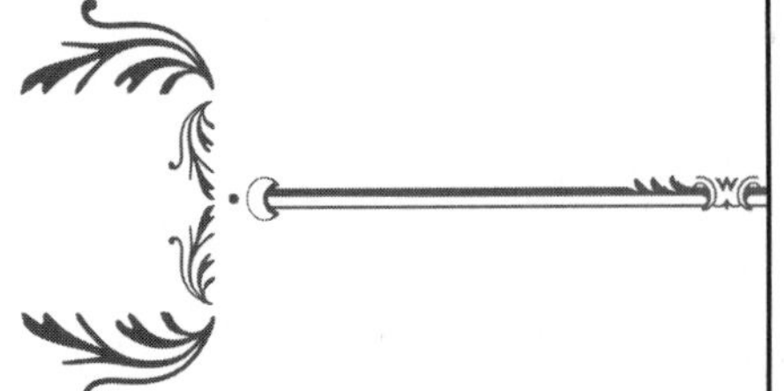

CHAPTER 9

The Great Rock 'n' Roll Swindle

It is tempting to look at the development of style in the late 1960s and '70s as the movement from hippies to disco to punk, and contrast this against the increasingly ineffectual high-fashion labels that were struggling to find an identity in the growing cacophony of cultural voices. However, this is too simplistic a picture, as the styles overlap and dovetail into each other, with each of the dominant styles speaking to a specific segment of the population. Indeed, it is the nonlinearity of the development that needs to be taken into account if one is to get a sense of how the story unfolded.

As the '60s ended, neither the designed high fashion nor the youth fashions, marketed or otherwise, had a clear direction. A nostalgia had already set in during the mid-'60s. Even as designers like Paco Rabanne were bringing out futuristic "space age" fashions using plastics and metals in clean geometric shapes (Figure 9.1), nineteenth-century references were appearing in pop culture and fashions. Whether in the retro-Edwardian styling of the

FIGURE 9.1. The future was still exciting in the 1960s: a mini dress made of lacquered aluminum discs, designed by Paco Rabanne.

album cover of the Beatles' *Sergeant Peppers' Lonely Hearts Club Band*, the Wild West garb of West Coast bands in the United States, or even the typefaces that became associated with "head" culture, the denial of modernist culture being exhibited by the young avant-garde is evident. This denial would carry on into increasingly distanced fashions that primarily sprang from the culture of rock 'n' roll.

Even the fashion world itself seemed at the time to believe in the linearity of its history and the inevitability of its power and purpose. It's hardly surprising that the high-fashion world would behave like a royal court that holds onto its courtly rituals while the mob outside is setting fire to the city, when that is precisely what its rituals trained it to do from the start in the Second Empire. And the blindness exhibited at the court of Marie Antoinette, as well as at the court of Eugénie's Second Empire, was expressed by Coco Chanel, of all people.

She declared in February 1967 that "la mode is now just a question of the length of a skirt—it is idiocy. Fashion cannot come up from the street; it can only go down into the street."[1] In the same interview, however, she saluted Saint Laurent. But this was for having had "the courage to copy Chanel." Saint Laurent, on the other hand, was actually heading in a completely different direction. He would soon introduce his Moroccan and later Cossack-themed fashions, using ethnicities and orientalisms in a way not seen since Poiret. But meanwhile the street was having different ideas that would add to the tug-of-war for influence and unmoor the fashion system completely.

All the Young Dudes

Our story's progress through the '60s and '70s is that of a contradiction involving the continuing increase of distance of high fashion from the reality of daily life, but a continuing increase in the input to high fashion up from the street. As the '60s progressed, Saint Laurent's lead became the model and "young" became the mode. As it became clear that pop culture was becoming the dominant culture of the market, the imagery associated with high-fashion products grew increasingly youthful following the lead of Mary Quant and Biba. Twiggy became the fashion image, giving rise to a vision of girlish femininity that displaced the ladylike Dior figures (Figure 9.2).

FIGURE 9.2. Stylish modern youth: the model Twiggy in March of 1967.

High Fashion after Dior: Establishment Merges with Antiestablishment

High fashion after the Second Empire had been oscillating between a high-class signifier and an avant-garde representation of where the imagination of society was turned. Worth ceded to Poiret, who in turn was succeeded by Chanel and Schiaparelli, who were answered by Dior. The reaction to Dior then in turn produced Saint Laurent, who closed the gap between designer fashion as a tool of the ruling class and street fashion as an expression of antiestablishment.

Each successive swing of the pendulum from action to reaction involved a higher degree of market involvement and removed the high-fashion statement a step away from being a political impulse and a tool of the ruling class. With increased marketing and a culture of saturated media—both of these transcending class and geography—the connection to any kind of class-based or hierarchical system became increasingly tenuous and difficult to implement except through the force of pricing. Even then, with knockoffs and mass-market derivative fashions, price could not maintain an effective barrier between classes.

And as "fashion" became a way of making an antiestablishment statement, even high fashion had to join the forces of revolt. In doing so, both were probably weakened. The case could be made either way to whether the Beats and hippies or the marketers and capitalists came out on top. The class barriers in high fashion certainly came down, and dress codes and modes of fashion have certainly diversified and relaxed. In this way the revolutionaries' influence proved stronger. However, it was the market forces that brought the fashion statements to the fore, and a case can be made that the fashion statements of Beats and hippies have been marketed and sold so thoroughly that to speak of a counterculture in fashion today is nearly impossible. With that in mind, one would have to declare victory for the establishment, if one could define what "victory" actually looks like.

The Summer of Love existed for only a brief moment in San Francisco, but despite the decline that quickly became evident, it continues to echo in all of Western culture. Having created its own myths, "hippie" has become a permanent element in the identity of the late twentieth century well beyond the confines of geography and years. The "look" came afterward, but the tie-dyed, "flower power" was retrofitted to the whole period. However, if one looks beyond the marketed hype of the San Francisco scene, 1967 did not look very loving outside of Haight-Ashbury, and the legacy of what was going down in the industrial cities farther east may, in the end, prove to be the lasting effect. A week after the Monterey Pop festival marked the height of the Summer of Love in San Francisco, for example, a week of racially fuelled violence shook Newark in July. A week later, Detroit exploded in violence that also lasted for a week and required thousands of federal troops who, despite being armed with tanks and machine guns, took 48 hours to pacify the city. Violence spread, with days of firebombing in Toledo and Minneapolis and riots and gunfire in Michigan and New York. In Englewood, New Jersey, snipers engaged police for several nights running.[2] The legacy of the summer of 1967 is as much to be found in these events as in the happenings in San Francisco as the unrest of the industrial cities provided the next shift.

The Vibe of Proto-Punk

Out of Detroit, a year later, a year before the festival at Woodstock that was the high-water mark of hippie culture, the band MC5 and Iggy Pop and the Stooges brought their proto-punk music and aggressive politics into the mix (Figure 9.3). Both appeared on the scene in 1968 and released their first albums in 1969. MC5 were radical in their politics and celebrated the Detroit riots in their performances and songs, while Iggy, as we saw, was reacting to the "Death of Hippie," to what he already saw as the failure of the promise of the '60s. But there was also in this angry and aggressive style something of the industrial cityscape:

> There was this whole culture then into which you were immediately inculcated as a school child; when I was eight we were taken through the plants where they would press the body parts. There was just a whole vibe there, an atmosphere where mechanized things were good.[3]

FIGURE 9.3. With musicians like Iggy Pop leading the way for the punk movement, hippie is truly dead by 1977.

The "vibe" of the mechanized city was an indication of where things were headed. After the seeming failure of the attempt to create a new experience for the youth of America in San Francisco, the industrial heartland found a voice. This voice was not of the old world and not of the model of previous generations except in its denial of authority. In hindsight, one can place it in the continuum of Anarchist-Beat-Hippie, but the punk style had its own agenda:

> Somehow something rubbed off, and the people in the '60s who were trying to make music and culture in Michigan, we just didn't give a flying [expletive deleted] what you thought in London, Paris, New York, L.A. I could get rewarded right there. . . . It was desirable to know about the outside world, but our tastes were direct and honest. Something came up in the air there.[4]

It would not be known as "punk" for another five years or so, and not enter into mainstream consciousness until the heightened aggressiveness of the London punk scene brought it to the attention of mainstream media. Meanwhile, this industrial anarchistic style moved on a parallel track with the music, styles, and fashions of the early '70s, in constant opposition to what it saw as a massive sellout. Ironically, punk would appear on the larger cultural screen only once it was packaged for market.

Britain Goes Glam

Meanwhile in Britain, as the '60s ended, the politics over the Vietnam War were less an issue and were directed toward the United States in any case. Internal politics were more class-oriented, and racial tension had yet to erupt into violence. The youth culture and hippie styles that had developed in the United States were imported as styles rather than as political statements.

It is tempting to connect the arrival of flamboyant and androgynous glam-rock fashions with the repeal of laws criminalizing homosexuality in Britain in 1967, but the British gay scene did not react so quickly after a century of oppression, and the jury is still out on that question. There may be some element of contribution from the increased freedom of gay clubs and cabarets, but more directly, the British performers had already grown up in a culture of strong sartorial statements of class and group identity with Teddy Boy fashions and Mods. The norm was therefore already more flamboyant and open to personal statement than male clothing in the United States had ever been and actually in some opposition to the Beat and hippie image as it developed in the '50s and early '60s. There was also in Britain a tradition of music hall performance, which performers like the Beatles and David Bowie can be seen to have inherited. Others, like the Rolling Stones and the Who were more of the street level and continued the Mod fashions, blending them into the influences from across the Atlantic. (See Figure 9.4.)

In the hands of the British musicians, rock music became theater rather than the club- and ballroom-oriented performance it had been in the United States. This was in part because of a continuation of the strong British music-hall tradition, but also an issue that grew with the venues and technologies and culture of each country. When rock 'n' roll became the official music of the counterculture in San Francisco at the Monterey Pop festival in 1967, it became associated with the ragtag thrift-shop look of Haight-Ashbury. The British had no equivalent, and after the drab postwar '50s a "smart," tailored look that brought back echoes of Edwardian finesse became a look of its own, essentially a stylized version of itself. This Teddy Boy fashion, which was associated with the rock 'n' rollers and skiffle bands of the late '40s and early '50s and the Mods, who came right on their tail in the '60s and identified with the Merseyside music scene in Liverpool, actually upheld a long tradition of British dandyism. The tailored, fitted look of both, the emphasis on stylized hair, and particular footwear choices had a degree of finesse that echoed back from a

FIGURE 9.4. Lead singer Roger Daltrey, drummer Keith Moon, bass player John Entwistle, and guitarist Pete Townshend of The Who in 1965 (left), and rocker Eddie Cochran (right).

century before. However, the "Teds" with their slicked hair and tailored Edwardian jackets, spoke of a harkening back to the days before World War II, and the Mods with their "modern" clothing and new hairstyles had a direction toward the modernist future. It is, of course, worthy of note that in Britain, fashion experimentation was equally adventurous for men and women and on a much wider scale than in the United States. Any flamboyance or elegance that found its way into the mass culture came from outside the white American mainstream. The nature of American society, with its strong Protestant undertones and mythical emphasis on a rugged libertarian frontier spirit, had created a masculine image that could not adorn itself or preen in a way that the continental cultures had allowed for centuries in Europe.

As rock shows became larger and more elaborate, their performance aspect also grew. Light shows and amplification in auditorium shows removed the performer from the audience, and stage costume became part of rock music's method. David Bowie was among the performers of the London rock scene who were experimenting with more dramatic methods, and his involvement with the mime company of the flamboyant and remarkably colorful artist Lindsay Kemp served him as inspiration to create a rock show of a kind that had never before been seen. After several versions of gender-bending styles, he brought out

FIGURE 9.5. David Bowie, in his persona of Ziggy Stardust, at the Radio City Music Hall in New York, 1973.

the character Ziggy Stardust as an alter ego for a theme album and arena shows in 1972 (Figure 9.5). The androgynous otherness of this style gripped the attention of British rock fans and spread quickly. Stateside, the interest in the music was greater than in the styles, but the influence on the performers was perhaps the most important factor. Rock music took to theatricality and large, flamboyant gestures in its presentation.

The slickness of glam rock found its way into high fashion as high fashion found its way onto the rock 'n' roll stage with designers like Halston working off the same impulses with jumpsuits and lurex, platform heels, and sashes. Who influenced whom in the early '70s may be difficult to discern. It seems that in the early '70s, even Saint Laurent was getting in on the rock 'n' roll track by dressing Bianca Jagger in a white pantsuit for her 1970 wedding to Mick Jagger of the Rolling Stones. The scene fully shifted to New York, and Halston and the disco set became the defining fashion royalty of the early '70s. Interestingly enough, Jackie Onassis showed up again, but her iconic status was frozen in her '60s image. Where the converging lines of high fashion and rock might have wound up became anybody's guess, as just when the lines converged, the punks broke the scene wide open.

MOTOR CITY: THE ANTI-PARIS?

While the glam rockers and glitter set of the discos were reveling in their slick tailored outfits, the reaction had already begun. The reaction to the perception of the emptiness of the '60s' promise, the alienation of youth in the industrial centers, and the reaction to what came to be the overblown performance aspect of rock music led to the development of the strain that had already begun to show itself in Detroit. If rock was a counterculture in the '60s, the '70s produced what seemed to be, initially at least, a counter-counterculture. In New York, bands sprang up, rough around the edges, playing in small clubs and bars. Inspired by MC5, Iggy Pop, and the Velvet Underground, they shunned the big arena-style showmanship and stripped the music down to a transparent guitar-based sound. The style of the New York punks, as they began to be known, was tattered and worn, more through necessity than design, but some sense of assembly was there, and the band the New York Dolls managed to inject a bit of glam into the scene (Figure 9.6). America, for the most part, wouldn't have any of it, but the roughness of the New York scene contrasted sharply with the smooth stylized direction fashions and rock were taking together, and in this there was a freshness and sense of adventure for a generation that now felt that the baby boomers had taken all of culture for themselves and weren't letting anyone else play.

FIGURE 9.6. The New York Dolls brought a completely new look to the New York scene. Pictured here in 1974, the Dolls would influence glam rock as well as punk styles.

{ LOOKING FORWARD LOOKING BACK }

Scorecard: Who Is Winning the Fashion Wars?

High fashion design came into existence in a society seeking a new identity, and two polarities emerged: aristocratic high fashion of designers and icons, and anarchic anti-fashion of radicals and youth. As the aristocratic society disappeared in the twentieth century, new fashions attempted to replace the courtly fashions and dominate Western culture.

However, the anti-fashions of the 1960s and 1970s accustomed two generations to the idea that your style was whatever you made it. This crowd did not fall easily into line behind establishmentary fashion icons, who were in short supply anyway. In the late 1970s—at the end of the hundred years' fashion—the game was leaning toward the counterculture.

However, a middle ground developed in ready-to-wear designer labels. The boomers, as they outgrew the '60s, became a generation of unparalleled consumerism, but their ostentation went toward accessories, toys, and real estate, so fashion maintained a minimalist trend in the 1990s. As the century ended, the aristocratic fashion side lost its footing, but new clientele from global markets reestablished the deluxe trade while an investment bubble pushed ostentation in the United States higher than ever. Designer fashions, however, now seemed to be lost, with older periods referenced hither and yon and designers passing through a revolving door of hiring and firing.

Meanwhile, on the counterculture front, voices against the globalization of trade were being heard, and the excesses of the fashion industry came under criticism, but as this was for manufacturing practices rather than the excesses of its clients, it was of little consequence for style. Counterculture fashions at the beginning of the twenty-first century are of several tribes but of little influence, as most of their ideas are recycled from hippie or punk fashions with nothing new or exciting to add. Score: A tie, with both teams exhausted.

The Self-Proclaimed Inventors of Punk

That an astonishing number of people claim or are claimed to have "invented punk" is hardly surprising, given that it is the last of a line of the counterculture movement that began with the Beats. The contradiction involved in claiming ownership of a cultural movement that denies ownership of culture does not seem to be a problem, and it is in this contradiction that the position of punk style in our story can be defined. A sign to note is that among those claiming most loudly to have invented punk are actually people who were in the front line of *marketing* punk, which generally meant marketing a fashion statement. In fact, there was no "punk" until after it had been packaged for popular consumption.

Most of the bands of the New York scene were not self-consciously creating an image, and some—the Ramones, for example—actually objected to the "punk" moniker (just as the Beats had objected to "beatnik" and the San Francisco hipsters had rejected "hippie"). In itself, the term wasn't specific to them at the time, anyway. It had been in use for decades, applying to young slackers, ruffians, and layabouts. Just like the Beats and hippies, punk was over by the time it hit mass consciousness, the difference of development being only in the acceleration of the cycle. If it took five years for the Beats to become mainstream entertainment, and the hippies, two years, then punk can be seen to have been sold even before it was known to be a culture. The Beats knew they had something. Kerouac traveled and wrote. The scene developed and grew into poetics and music. Then "beatnik" fashions were recouped by Saint Laurent and others, and the anti-look had to be radicalized again. The hippies developed a style and knew enough to stage the "Death of Hippie, Son of Media" demonstration as they saw the image being packaged. The marketers were more adept by this time and the designers more in tune to the vibe. Then the retro-nostalgic orientalisms were brought into fashion, again by Saint Laurent and more. Punk, however, which reacted directly to the Death of Hippie, never had time to grow or react. Its anti-fashion aesthetic was sold from the start, and with nowhere to go, became emblematic of the collapse of the whole program of modern design.

Seditionaires and Situationists

In the early '70s, Malcolm McLaren and the designer Vivienne Westwood opened a shop on the Kings Road in London selling Teddy Boy fashions. Scouting around for a new style, McLaren was in New York and became involved with the New York Dolls. He was hugely inspired by the New York scene and found in the glam and thrift shop mash-up the style he was looking for. A story has it that the singer Richard Hell used to walk around with his clothes safety-pinned together out of necessity, but then McLaren formalized this and brought it back to London to be sold as a style in the store that was now named Sex/Seditionaries.

McLaren and his collaborators were admirers of the Situationist movement, which had come to the fore in France around the Paris riots of 1968. The Dada-like anarchism of the Situationists became the method for McLaren's plan. The ripped, safety-pinned, clashing, thrift-store aesthetic was perfect for a new revolutionary style. The "Spectacle" as the

FIGURE 9.7. The Sex Pistols' manager, Malcolm McLaren, created media events such as this one, where the band signed a recording contract outside Buckingham Palace in London, bringing immediate police attention in March 1977.

main Situationist, Guy Debord, termed late capitalist society, needed to be shaken up by something it could not ingest, package, and re-create in its own image. By reconfiguring the idea of fashion to include ugliness, raw edges, and destruction, punk fashion made itself (initially at least) immune to a commercial takeover. The contradiction, of course, is staring us in the face. McLaren merely went one step ahead and recouped the punk style before it even took hold, thereby serving up the revolutionary style from inside the system. A case can be made that this was a way of rescuing punk from being watered down, but the watering down happened nevertheless, so the point is rather moot.

McLaren certainly followed the Situationist ideal in that he created a fashion that could be created by anyone. He took it a step further, and with habitués of his store, created the band the Sex Pistols to be the emblematic band of the style (Figure 9.7). The twist is remarkably clever: Take a street style from bands in New York, formalize it as fashion in London, then create a band that wears the styles to sell it back to more New Yorkers and so on.

Appropriation as art was a possibility that Dada had explored, but this had never been carried out in a commercial sense or on an entire culture. The Dada movement had advocated art for and by everyone; the Situationists included life and politics in their equation. Punk became the gateway for young people to create their own look, their own music, and their own sense of self; the fashion system, like the music industry, looked on in bewilderment. If rock stars had become the new fashion royalty, what was the world to make of this? Being crass and contrary to societal norms of style and beauty was problematic enough, but given the do-it-yourself attitude of the clothing as well as the music, the styles could always stay one step ahead of the "mugs." By the time the marketers were ready, punk had usually moved on, at least in the first couple of years. Regardless of the motives or methods of Malcolm McLaren, what happened changed everything.

Punk Fashion

The high point of punk was probably in 1977, the year in which the Sex Pistols scandalized England and then the world with their manner, look, and lyrics. For a band that released only one album, the influence of their arrival on the scene has been remarkable. The horror of the establishment at these "punks" was too good to be true for the angry youth of England, and punk was taken up with great glee and creativity, while politicians and community leaders denounced and decried what they saw as a complete breakdown of society. The sheer aggression and lack of deference shown by the punks was such that there was no way for the establishment to envelope them at the start.

While established designers had a hard time getting a grip on things, young designers began coming out of school with a punk aesthetic built in. With Vivienne Westwood leading the charge, these were the years that saw John Galliano (Figure 9.8) and Alexander McQueen graduate from Central St. Martin's in London, starting a steady stream of talent to arrive from the school's program.

But now that the fashion that had become a statement of opposition to prevailing culture had been incorporated into the culture, there didn't seem to be anywhere to go after the hippies and punks. The forward-looking designers had hung their hopes on a future that didn't seem like it was going to exist.

Punk did, of course, have its day, and then it was recouped, just like the Beats and hippies before. Being "punk" became as easy as buying a T-shirt, and that's where things

FIGURE 9.8. John Galliano, once fashion's "bad boy," hobnobbing with royalty in New York in 1996 at the Metropolitan Museum of Art's retrospective of 50 years of Dior.

stood as the '80s began: Punk became a hairstyle and a studded belt. The effect of punk is lasting; however, it is lacking in authenticity. Punk showed that in fashion, anything and everything is possible, and, perhaps most importantly, that the power over fashion can be wrested away from the upper class and the market in such a way that things become very uncomfortable. Finally—and perhaps most effectively—it showed that the cutting edge of fashion was no longer in high fashion at all.

What ended punk was not a recouping in the manner of Saint Laurent's Beats, but simply that there was nowhere else to go for now. The alienation that punk grew from and then produced in amplified form has also been tempered. Like the hippies, punk has become a cultural icon, and fashion designers who grew up with punk have no problem with navigating alienation.

The question is this: Was punk actually ever recouped into the system, or did it render the system obsolete by showing it to be powerless? If punk could come along and by merely taking what was lying there in true Dadaist fashion, scare everyone into confusion, where did that leave fashion? The music industry was slow to respond, but eventually it did, and punk became "New Wave" and is now just another genre. Fashion design, however, never quite got there.

Punk fashion, as it started out, was the perfect anti-fashion and remains so today, despite the fact that punks from the '70s are now becoming grandparents. The game was over, whether anyone knew it or not (or even cared).

It seems doubtful that the rest of the fashion world got the message though, and the reason for this lies in the fact that the punks (without knowing what they had) had it right. The reality of fashion, as it had become in the early 1970s, as the famed houses of Europe all began to fade (Figure 9.9), was that it had become such a hollow image of itself that nothing could save it but a total breakdown and reordering.

Punk was the final sign of the breakdown of the system of the 100 years of high fashion that began with Worth. What has yet to come to pass is the reordering that follows a breakdown of a social system. However, a reordering is difficult while the system operates the

FIGURE 9.9. By the mid-1970s, high-fashion designers had become celebrities on par with actors and rock stars, with the same media attention: a New Year's Eve party at Studio 54 in New York. Left to right: Halston, Bianca Jagger, Jack Haley, Jr. and wife Liza Minnelli, and Andy Warhol.

way it does. So much is at stake that the markets must continue with the current model, even if it is broken. With the markets firmly in charge of the creative aspect (of all aspects), there is no way out until the need becomes so intense that we can only go to the extremes to get out of the cycle. Beat, hippie, punk, and then . . . ? What experiment will finally lead to a paradigm of high fashion that belongs to the world as it is, not as it was decades in the past?

The model of "King of Fashion" is still so tempting that a lot of energy and activity goes into promoting and selling new young designers' work before they can really prove themselves. Saint Laurent retired in 2002, a shell of himself when he left. Galliano and McQueen, the bad boys of the '80s and '90s, have quietly become the establishment. But like the punks: "Every culture, every century has a handful of these dudes, guys and girls who just go: 'Oh no you don't.'"[5]

And so it goes. With the Situationists, we can still say, as did graffiti in Paris during the protests of 1968, "Under the cobblestones: The beach!"

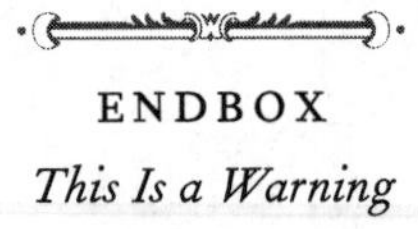

ENDBOX

This Is a Warning

Twenty years have passed since Andy Warhol died during what was expected to be a routine gallbladder operation. He was 58, and his sudden end was neither a bang nor a whimper, but meaningless. Every year since, his art has become more perversely alive. Twenty years ago, most people probably pictured a soup can when they heard he had died. A measure of how much richer our taste in Warhol has become is the fact that the National Galleries of Scotland is about to open an ambitious retrospective of him without a single soup can among its silver floating pillows, stitched Polaroids, skulls, toys and films—and those electrically charged paintings. It is a tremendous exhibition in a beautiful venue: a spacious neoclassical hall on the Mound, where Warhol's art has air and light. American art of his era demands elbow room and gets it in a show that is nothing less than a passionate essay on why Warhol is a great artist.

. . . If you want to know why Warhol is so enduring an artist, look at his gravest images. Look at his blue-and-black portraits of Jackie Kennedy before and after the assassination in Dallas: as she takes the salute at JFK's funeral, the violence of Warhol's time is refuted in an elegy to a woman he sees as maintaining dignity in a world gone mad. In the biggest gallery, the one work of art that triumphs over the cow wallpaper is his doubled, colossal 1981 painting of a handgun. Warhol lived in a world becoming more randomly and coldly violent—and was himself shot and nearly killed in 1968. The literal and metaphorical violence of modern life has intensified this decade. Artists of the earlier 20th century joined the communist party, supported world revolution and thought utopia was coming. [Andy Warhol] described our world when it was only half-formed. He saw it all coming. He's the prophet of our crisis.

Source: Jonathan Jones. *Guardian*. July 31, 2007.

Discussion Points

1. What is our "crisis"? Is it specific to our time?
2. Why is this a fashion problem?
3. Why is Andy Warhol's imagery so powerful?

CHAPTER 10

High Fashion Becomes Art

Chanel said that couture is not an art—it's a craft, and a business[1]—but approached her work with all the intensity of a driven fine artist. Poiret and Worth presented themselves as artists, and Schiaparelli, like Poiret, may well have been more of an artist than a designer. Saint Laurent was the quintessential modern designer, but wrote in 1983 that "playing with fashion is an art." (He added: "The first rule is don't burn your own wings.")[2] While generally being run by their business interests, all the designers we have had in view have established their visions so strongly that each of their names is now definitive of a look adopted by an entire culture at some point over the last one hundred years. Despite how fashion is still downplayed in the manner of the early modernists as something frivolous and inconsequential, the creativity and influence of high fashion over the past 120 years are without question. At the core of a high-fashion business there is still the underlying drive—and need—to create clothing within an artistic vision. Despite the nearly complete takeover by the business interests, there is at the core a designer, or team of designers, developing a vision. The vision, enabled by the idea that the designing of fashion is an art, bends to market forces but is also a product of prevailing artistic trends.

Young designers come into the high-fashion business less out of the business itself than out of an art- or design-school environment, or are attracted from other design disciplines to the business for the artistic flair (and the possibility of becoming the "next big thing"). The business of fashion, of course, also requires a skill set different from the young designers' artistic skills, for which the hands-on approach of the early-twentieth-century couturier no longer really applies. Less and less, because of the prevailing mass-market approach, are the young designers well trained in the practical application of tailoring or dressmaking *before* an artistic vision is encouraged. The gradual eradication of the couture system has indeed removed the designer from the practical aspects of production for individual customers, so the high-fashion designer as couturier is now a very separate type within the discipline. The job of the designer has become more and more that of one creating a "vision" or "image." The increasing role of designer as "stylist" has, in fact, allowed for a widening of the distance between the actual creation of the clothing and the vision of the "designer." Indeed, the title of "designer" has itself changed in its meaning, as it has now become descriptive of any conceptual work involved in the production of a line of clothing or accessories; regardless of whatever dint of personality, business interests, or celebrity, the name on the label has come to be responsible for the creation. As a result, the impulses and inspirations of new designers are just as connected to trends and developments in art and design as any notion of construction or the Paris-based couture tradition.

High-fashion design was always in a relationship of tension with the art and design world around it. Poiret, Chanel, and Schiaparelli had been heavily involved with the arts scene in Paris and New York. They developed their fashions in the same atmosphere and all together the designers, artists, and architects were creating a style for the times. This does not mean that all were traveling hand in hand. On the contrary, Worth, Poiret, and Dior all worked—with varying degrees of determination—in opposition to the modernist artistic influences of their day. Saint Laurent, however, dove deeply into the zeitgeist of the '60s, being just as much a progenitor as a participant in the definition of the styles of the decade. Toward the end of the twentieth century, the connection of the high-fashion world to the world of art, architecture, and design was stronger than ever. However, the connection can be seen to be twofold. The influence of art and design on fashion was certainly there, but the influences of postmodern theory felt in both spheres was perhaps an experience shared by the disciplines rather than a direct influence by one on the other.

Art Trickles Down

To understand how this relationship may work and how, in the current state of the discipline, we may be looking at a new paradigm, let's investigate the "trickle-down" theory of design influence that was mentioned briefly in Chapter 6. It is true of fashion in general and high fashion in particular that a new style arrives from centers of prestige and creativity, and its instigators include both creative entrepreneurs and fashion-conscious consumers.[3] The creativity of the community within which both groups are operating may be overtly influencing their choices or not, but even if they are not aware (or, like Poiret, refuse to acknowledge their influences), they are never operating in a vacuum. In our days of rapid connectivity and media saturation, a designer's philosophical and creative isolation from the influences of the surrounding world is even less possible than before.

Forces of fashion and style move at different rates of speed in different disciplines and communities. In the Western, modernist milieu that we are examining, one can see several basic forces operating within the world of art and design, each at a different rate, but even so, in tandem. The shortening of the professional distance between the disciplines, with designers crossing from one to the other and the subsequent blurring of lines between them, has changed the strict hierarchy that used to exist.

Up to the end of the Worth era, the disciplines as they changed and related, ranging from the slowest to the fastest moving, are presented in Figure 10.1. The so-called fine arts led the way, but even the fine artists were often led by and reflected trends in politics, literature, and philosophy. Trends in fine art would also be mirrored by, and might even have a reciprocal influence on, architecture through the application of decorative elements and the periodic resurgence of "classical" styles. One could say that fine art and architecture, as practiced in the post-Renaissance West, set the stage on which craftspeople that would become "designers" could develop their visions. The trickling down of the influence of fine art and architecture would then begin to affect high-concept design (such as jewelry or high-end furniture) as the students were schooled in history, styles, and traditions. From

FIGURE 10.1. The relationship of trend cycles in art and design.

there, the theories and concepts would trickle down to interior design and, when the time came, to industrial design. From industry, the sphere of influence would expand to graphic design and decorative arts and finally to apparel design. High fashion then influenced ready-to-wear, accessories, and all the attendant trends that follow.

This progression was more or less true until after the middle of the twentieth century, when developments in the worlds of art, architecture, and design began to blur the distinction between the disciplines, and designers and architects began to receive the same kind of adulation and critique as artists. Meanwhile, the artists came to be seen as designers and architects, creating installations and environments.

Artists as Celebrities

As both the fine arts and architecture began to produce a different breed of superstars akin to the kings and queens of fashion. The disciplines now had a new "star," if not every season, then at least every few years. Then, various awards and prizes were developed to kindle the public's interest and to indicate whom the establishment in the field (or business) had consecrated. (For example, architects were awarded the Pritzker Prize beginning in 1979, the Council of Fashion Designers of America began awarding prizes in 1981, and so on.) The increased focus on individual artist's characters and personalities through new media and magazines devoted to arts contributed to a dissolution of the progression of influence. But it was the art itself that turned everything inside out by completely redefining the nature of the discussion of what was "art."

Ready-Mades and Concepts as Art

The beginnings of the new definition of art can be traced back to the Dadaists in New York and Paris in the years around World War I. Marcel Duchamp, for one, subverted the nineteenth-century notions of art so thoroughly that it took a good part of the twentieth century for the art world to come to terms with his actions, and even now, popular opinion has still not fully accepted—much less appreciated—what he set in motion.

Duchamp conceived of the notion of "ready-mades" at this time. These were industrial objects that he picked up in stores—for example, a snow shovel and a bottle rack—that he chose to call "art," and by doing so, literally caused them to become art. The most famous of Duchamp's ready-mades is probably one that was actually never exhibited. The Society of Independent Artists had a show in New York in 1917. The show was open to all artists, and Marcel Duchamp, Dadaist and one of the society's directors, submitted a piece he called *Fountain* under the pseudonym "R. Mutt" (Figure 10.2). The piece was a standard porcelain urinal set on its back and signed with the name of its "contributor." The show's organizers hid it away in embarrassment, not knowing that Duchamp was its "creator." He promptly quit the organization, having made his point that the Independents were not nearly as open to "anything" as they thought.

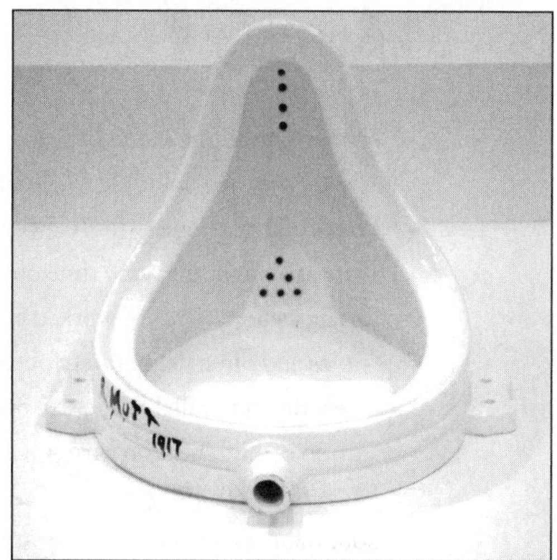

FIGURE 10.2. *Fountain* by Marcel Duchamp (signed R. Mutt), 1917. Marcel Duchamp's "ready-mades" questioned the commitment of the arts to radical change and foreshadowed the opening up of the definition of "art" that would take place in the twentieth century.

The ready-mades resurfaced in the '60s, when the

FIGURE 10.3. Andy Warhol at work in The Factory, 1965.

questioning of capitalist consumer society that had prompted the Dadaists to start tearing away the artifice of the art world continued with a heightened intensity. Duchamp reproduced his ready-mades in the '50s and '60s, adding to the irony of their creation, given that he had now "created" replicas of works that were industrial objects that had become icons of revolutionary art. In becoming icons, the redesigned ready-mades even negated their original purpose—this irony making the statement of the pieces all the more poignant. As modernism presented contradictions like this with increasing frequency, the increased numbers of artists and designers in the market sped up the experimentation of Western art through increased demands for "originality" from the schools, artists, and designers, putting art on nearly equal footing with fashion in terms of the need for the "next new thing" every season.

Then the pop artists of the '60s picked up the flag (Figure 10.3). The artist Andy Warhol added a new dimension to the game by mass-producing art at his workshop, which he called "The Factory," creating multiple "originals" using silkscreen techniques. The distancing effect of work like this opens the viewers' eyes to the artificiality of the designation of "art" and "artist," but at the same time opens up the possibility that the viewers' perception can create art anywhere. Warhol worked against the notion of "original" by creating his works in multiples and often deliberately obscuring his own involvement in the creative process. Here we see a direct parallel to the disappearance of the couturiers' visibility as well as to the redefinition of high fashion through branding.

As the '60s progressed, other philosophies added to this chorus, with minimalist artists stripping art down to systems and geometry, and conceptual artists removing the object from art altogether, suggesting instead concepts through statements or, with performance art, by placing their audience into a situation that would prompt a reaction from them or shock them into a realization of some kind. The work of art became the experience of the audience, the moment of perception itself.

Such art seems at first glance perhaps well beyond the realm of fashion design, but the streams of thought that swirl around a culture do so for reasons that are larger than what may be represented by a single artistic movement. The questioning of art and ownership of culture that Dada and the art of the '60s represent finds its way into fashion, or rather fashion finds it. The avant-garde politics of the '60s questioned all authority and asked for the representation of the individual as a way to break out of the deadening conformity that the postwar society had insisted on. This was the same cultural discomfort felt after World War I, but now it had a direction that was, initially at least, forward-looking. If one could understand art as a relationship of a person with the world, and a work of art could be created purely through the arrangement of found objects or individuals' thoughts, then creative works could no longer be held to be the sacred domain of artists, just as music did not have to come from superstars or fashion from "big name" designers.

FIGURE 10.4. Modern women of the late '20s posed with the height of modern technology.

However, we must keep in mind that artists continue to create art and designers continue to design and the public continues to buy the creations without engaging in heavy theoretical speech. But what the artists created was reflected in the designer's work and on a level of cultural understanding taken in by the public without much discourse. Once an understanding of this approach became common enough among an increasingly educated and media-savvy public, it didn't matter whether the public agreed with or even fully understood the implications of the shift that was taking place. The idea that art and design were not sacred had entered into the background of the cultural discourse. For example, most architects of the early 1960s were still fully enamored of the ideals of modernism. One can see that effect of this thinking reflected in the fashions of the early '60s. The stripped-down minimalism reflected the technical industrial look of mass-produced products, with its solid colors and clean lines (Figure 10.4).

MODERNISTS BEGIN TO FALL

"Less is more." This, one of the chief modernist designers, Mies van der Rohe (1886–1969) had declared to be one of the main guiding principles of modern architecture and design. The principle that "form follows function" had become a mantra that found its way into all fields of industrial design. However, already in the mid-1950s, a critical response to modernism had begun to appear. The elation of the Futurists in the 1930s and the visions of gleaming cities with organized technical solutions to urban dwelling dimmed after World War II as the modernist program did not produce hoped-for results.

In 1966, in *Complexity and Contradiction in Modern Architecture*,[4] the architect Robert Venturi attacked the precepts of modernism, setting the stage for what became known as postmodern architecture. Venturi countered Corbusier's philosophy of buildings as machines, and answered Mies van der Rohe by summing up his opinion of modernism's rejection of decoration and complexity as "less is a bore." He pushed this agenda further still in *Learning from Las Vegas*[5] in 1972, where the commercial, garish architecture of the Las Vegas Strip is discussed and analyzed. That same year is sometimes referred to as "the year

FIGURE 10.5. When the massive Pruitt Igoe public housing complex was demolished by dynamite in 1972, many took this to be emblematic of the failure of the modernist ideal. The model of progress through design and technology was definitely looking tarnished.

Fashioning Society

Empress Eugénie, 1862. By Winterhalter.

1912 AVRIL N° 136

LES MODES

G. BARBIER

Paul Poiret, April 1912.

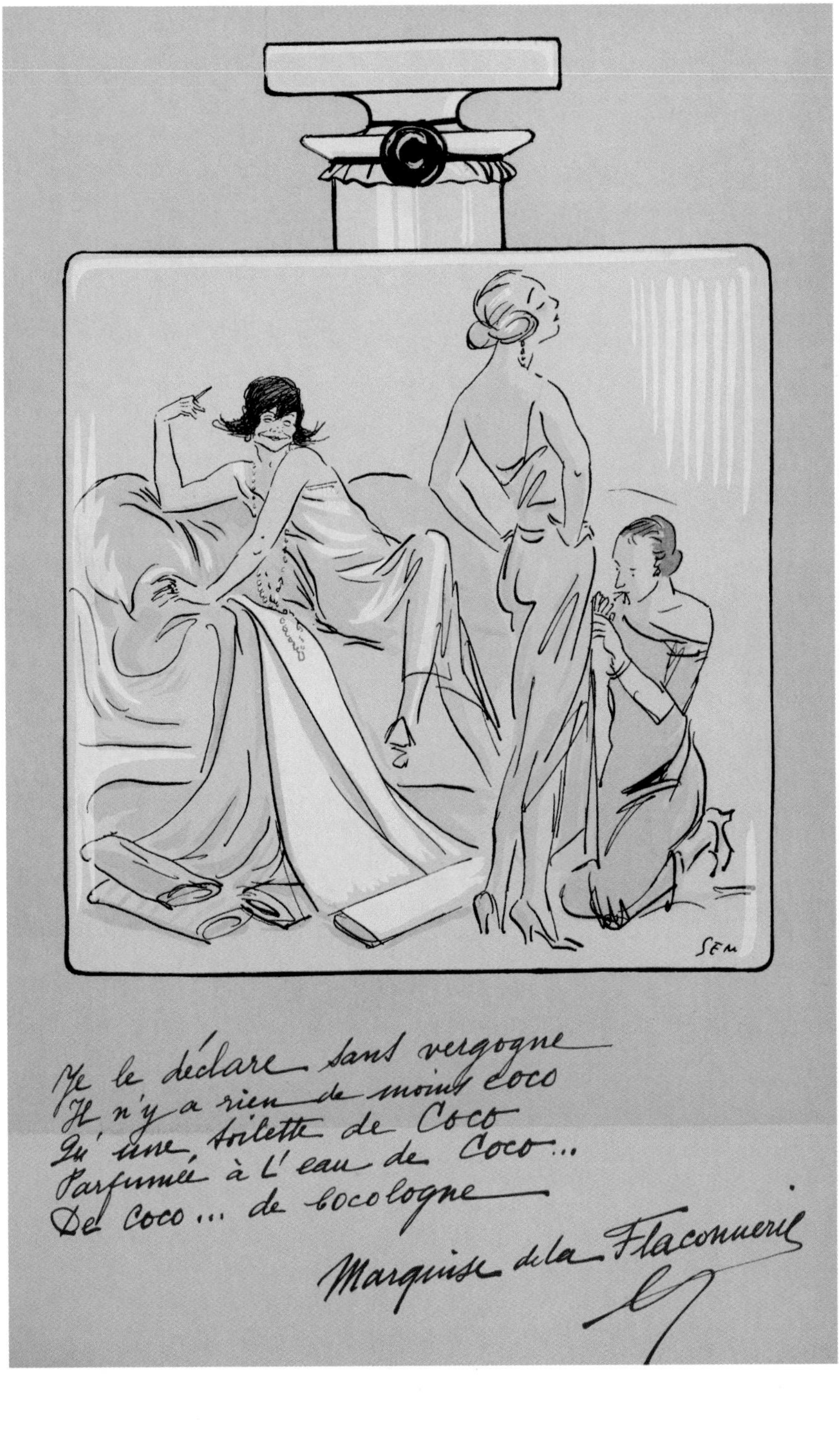

Caricature of Coco Chanel, 1921.

SEM

Je le déclare sans vergogne
Il n'y a rien de moins coco
Qu'une toilette de Coco
Parfumée à l'eau de Coco...
De coco... de cocologne

Marquise de la Flaconnerie

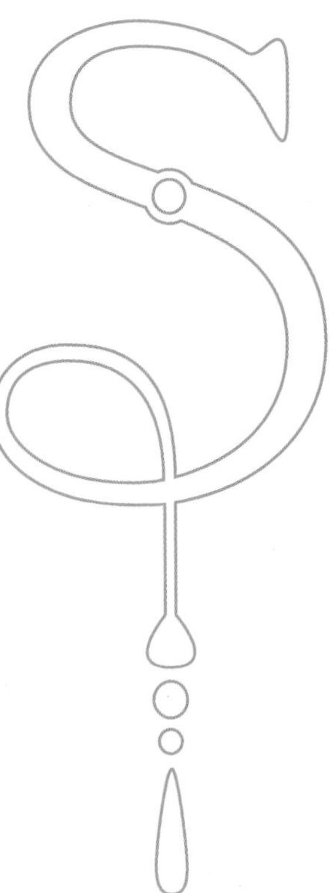

Veil, by Elsa Schiaparelli, 1938.

American fashions, 1941.

Christian Dior, assistants, and models preparing for show, 1957.

The First Lady Jacqueline Kennedy at an event in Washington, 1963.

Merry Pranksters in San Francisco, 1966. Gretchin Fetchin, the Slime Queen, is seated with baby Mouse, and Intrepid Traveller (aka Ken Babbs) is standing next to her.

Double-breasted suit for women, by Yves Saint Laurent, 1971.

David Bowie, glam-rocker, 1972.

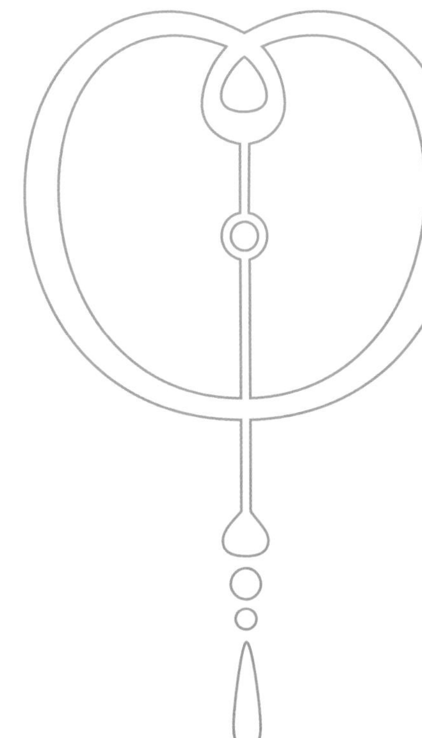

Vivienne Westwood (right) and two girls wearing her designs, 1977.

John Galliano for Christian Dior, Spring 2006 Couture.

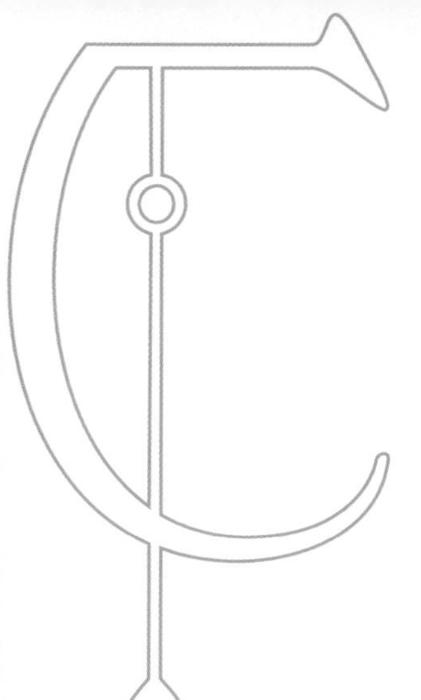

Models display creations by Indian designer Rohit Bal at India Couture Week, Mumbai, September 2008.

Eva Longoria attends the Art Costume Institute Gala Superheroes: Fashion and Fantasy at the Metropolitan Museum in New York City, May 05, 2008.

Mark Cheung's high fashion design at the China Fashion Week in Beijing, November 2008.

Marie Antoinette, Queen of France (1755-1793), as a young woman.

modern architecture died." The entire United States could see on television as the 33 towers of the Pruitt Igoe housing project in St. Louis were dynamited (Figure 10.5). The housing project of more than 2,000 apartments had proved to be a disaster of modernist urban planning and came to be a turning point for antimodernist sentiment in design. The beginning of the 1970s was in this same (if slightly less explosive) way a turning point for many of the progressive dreams of the first half of the twentieth century.

{ LOOKING FORWARD LOOKING BACK }

Art, Business and Modernism in Fashion

The crisis of modernism in the arts developed in large part from the mismatch of the priorities of corporate capitalism and the arts.* When the success of creativity is judged by the profits it generates, the creative artist is simply a creator of commodities and the nature of the artwork has little significance beyond that of any crafted object.

It was part of Charles Worth's brilliance (and conceit) to adopt the stance of "artist," thereby increasing the mystery of his "genius," placing his authority outside the reach of his clientele, and rationalizing his significantly higher price tag. Fashion design, however, was right from the start a creature of industrial capitalist society and is now, for the most part, a subsidiary of multinational corporations. Like the gallery-arts industry, the global corporations have a limited interest in the creative nature of their commodities beyond how it affects their bottom line. However, before being critical, one must question by whose standard "success" is measured: If I run a business, I want it to make a profit. If I am an artist, I want to create significant, challenging, and engaging work. The two do not always (and frequently cannot) meet.

Recognizing that high-fashion design was a business *and* a craft clearly contributed to the modernist ideal working so well in Chanel's designing of women's wear. Her work before World War II certainly rivals that of the most brilliant architects of the day in terms of its stripped down functionality, elegant construction, and rejection of old-world ideals. Also, couture is focused on individuals. It cannot go to where mass-architecture went

* Suzi Gablik, *Has Modernism Failed?* (New York: Thames & Hudson, 2004), 148.

wrong, while ready-to-wear can and therefore often echoes the bland, depressing featurelessness of much modern architecture.

The architecture connection presents a perfect metaphor: Chanel is an elegant skyscraper or modernist villa, while ready-to-wear often becomes Pruitt Igoe. The next time a modernist building complex is dynamited, perhaps it could be packed with polo shirts and khakis?

Saint Laurent: Tradition Flickers

The hundred years of high fashion were ending, and Yves Saint Laurent was right on the cusp of tradition and innovation. The remarkably astute designer was right in tune, as he had been since the late '50s, and his designs turned away from the modernist vision right along with the tide.

Saint Laurent's Chanel-inspired collection in 1964 heralded the breakdown of modernism. Knowing what we now know, to see that he was referencing Chanel also signals the coming inward-looking spiral that high-fashion design went into. Saint Laurent's collection in 1965 featured the famous "Mondrian" dresses, and in 1966, he exhibited pop art dresses inspired by Warhol's work. That same year he opened his "Rive Gauche" boutique, selling ready-to-wear. The next Spring/Summer he moved into African, to be followed by "gypsy" themes. In '71 he seems to have begun to look back, when he tried out a '40s theme, but that was not well received, to say the least, and he subsequently went back to the "ethnicities" of the late '60s.

Saint Laurent brought this kind of postmodern eclecticism to the front of fashion design and reached the apogee of his development in 1976 with a collection that caused great excitement. In hindsight, one can see the beginning of the end in the Spring/Summer and Fall/Winter collections from 1976, where the theme was, amazingly enough, Ballets Russes, the ballet company that had created such a stir in Poiret's day with its orientalist costumes. The look backward had gone beyond simply referencing a period. By referencing costume designs that had radicalized fashion before he was born, and by referencing so specific an event in the history of design, Saint Laurent closed a circle, confirming that the past had authority over the future, and just as he had opened the door to influence from the street, he now opened the door to the past.

Two revealing comments show where things were headed. First, from *Vogue* in September 1976: "What Yves St Laurent has done, with his latest collection, is to remind us that fashion, in its radical form of haute couture, *is* costume. . . . It's not nostalgia for the past, but for the eternal present which lies on the other side of the past." The idea that high fashion is costume is not news; this was evident to anyone who wished to see it from the Second Empire on. However, what this comment also suggests is that there is an image that transcends time: "The eternal present" is an idealized image of society that is not tied to a particular time but is about a type of time, of a specific flavor of existence, a *feel.* If this is so, it can be a truth only for a very limited group in each instance and can be neither universal nor eternal. In Saint Laurent's case (and presumably the *Vogue* writer's), it is the "Search for Lost Time," as described in Saint Laurent's favorite reading, Marcel Proust's *Á la Recherche du Temps Perdu* (*Remembrance of Things Past*).[6] Proust's novel describes an emotional, philosophical memory of a time that may or may not have existed in reality, but that has achieved an idealistic reality in memory and can be called up through experience of the now, just as easily as any "real" memory.

Second, Saint Laurent had been remarkably in tune with the spirit of the times since the beginning of his career, and in the early '80s, he became more conservative, once again anticipating and reflecting the attitudes around him. In an interview late in 1983, he said that he was growing tired of the constant movement of fashion and was searching for some stability. He added that it was this search that had led him "to bring back the ideas and points of fashion that were out of fashion."[7]

We can see Saint Laurent going down the same road as Worth and Poiret, in that the latter half of his career became a search for a connection to not only his own past but to an idealized past of Western European culture as imagined in Paris in the decades leading up to World War I (Figure 10.6). Indeed, the very next year Saint Laurent seems to have been acutely aware of this himself, when he said of that season's Chinese-inspired designs:

> It was a deeply egocentric show! I returned to an age of elegance and wealth. In many ways I returned to my own past. I put into the collection all my favorite painters and operas. It was theatre! It was also what is still hidden inside me. I grew up in a generation and a world of elegance. Tradition still flickered! And yet at the same time, I wanted to transform it. One is caught between the past holding you, and

FIGURE 10.6. Parisian designer Yves Saint Laurent poses with his models after showing his Spring collection in Paris in 1964.

the future pushing you. It's why I'm split in two. And I always will be. Because I knew one world and felt the other."[8]

The "world of elegance" that Worth, Poiret, Dior, and Saint Laurent exhibited such longing for, and along with Chanel and Schiaparelli believed they constantly created, seems to be integral to the design vision of high fashion. The world these designers grew up in relied so heavily on the social patterns that required the elegance of haute couture that a world without it seems to have been unimaginable to them. Even Poiret and Saint Laurent, who willingly and actively broke the rules and did their best to redefine the world, stayed within the strictures of *couture* traditions in their approach and choices of materials.

This longing for lost times does indeed seem to be more than a simple nostalgia. It seems to include in it a deeper element of longing and be applied to a larger world than that which mere personal nostalgia for *temps perdu* would embrace. Perhaps this is a necessary element in the makeup of a major designer. Perhaps this need to see a world created that brings back or embodies an imaginary golden age is the force that lies behind the creative drive. The absence of such longing in today's culture of irony and detachment might therefore account for the seeming lack of large movements. With neither a past to mythologize nor a future to drive toward, the commercial needs of the business wind up being the only operative force, and the art of fashion design becomes only another marketing tool.

When Yves Saint Laurent retired formally in 2002, a friend of his said, "It is the end of an era. There will never be anything like it again. There are very talented designers around, but Yves also dressed a world—a really good world, where people cared about chic, great refinement and the art of living. That world is gone. And it's gone even more since Sept. 11. Who today wants to talk about Mme Rothschild's ball at the Hotel Lambert?"[9] Pierre Berge, Saint Laurent's partner and the driving force behind the brand, put it in equally strong but more personal terms: "We have entered the era of marketing, at the expense of creativity." Alluding to Saint Laurent's status at the top of the fashion world, he added, "It's not very fun to play a tennis match when you are all alone."[10]

Saint Laurent, who died in 2008, had become an institution at the time of his retirement (both literally and figuratively) and his last 25 years are the story of the final transformation of high-fashion design. It was in 1983 that Yves Saint Laurent became the first living designer to have an exhibition of his work at the Costume Institute of the Metropolitan Museum of Art in New York. He had celebrated 20 years of the House of Saint Laurent the year before, and the past had now enveloped him as it had his predecessors. He had gone from being a vital designer to a museum piece.

Fashion as Museum Display

The act of placing a living designer's work in a large-scale museum retrospective is a dramatic statement by the cultural class involved. This is perhaps especially strong when the designer in question is the primary designer of clothing for the high society that is now exhibiting the clothing. If dressing the empress was the ultimate accolade for a *couturier* in a nineteenth century France, a retrospective at the Metropolitan might be seen to be the full sanctification by (at least) New York high society.

The dramatic shift implied by the YSL exhibition in 1983 is quite remarkable. What does it mean for a segment of society to be dressed in clothing that has been decreed "museum-worthy" by the agents of consecration? The cultural significance of an institution such as the Metropolitan Museum gives enormous weight to the work chosen for display (possibly even more so some 25 years ago). In the case of high-fashion design, the enshrinement of the designs completes the separation from the world of daily experience. The enshrinement of a living designer also creates a powerful position for designs to come, and the label itself now has a status equal to the aura of a grand master artist. An original Saint Laurent could now rank as an original Matisse painting, for example.

The consecration of Saint Laurent in this way can be seen to be at least equally significant as the choice of Charles Worth to dress the court of Eugénie and Louis Napoleon. The sociologist Pierre Bordieu points out that the act of consecration in the artistic sphere can be seen as part of the maneuvering for power in society.[11] The consecrating of the designer, not only to the position of couturier as in Eugénie's day but to the exalted position of artist in the grand temple of culture, gives him status; however, the main function is to convey power to the class that does the consecrating. The exhibition at the museum takes

FIGURE 10.7. Art, design, cultural artifact? Couture as a museum piece: evening gown, Spring–Summer 2002, from Yves Saint Laurent Rive Gauche by Tom Ford, brown silk chiffon.

the place of the action of designing for the royal balls or summer retreats (Figure 10.7). By wielding such power over society, the consecrator (museum curator, fashion editor) and the class of cognoscenti that surround the action have now achieved an increased level of "symbolic capital" or status with which to maintain their place in the social hierarchy. Again, just like the power that Pauline Metternich and the Empress Eugénie—or even Marie Antoinette—could wield over court society in Paris through their control over sanctioned fashion, by being able to sanctify a couturier or style, so would increased social power flow from the ability to create a "modern classic" in a museum. The authority that then rests on the acquired symbolic capital can assert itself through further sanctifications, and so on. This also, as Bordieu points out, "condemns those agents whose province is most limited to a state of perpetual emergency." Those whose social power relies on being able to recognize the "next big thing" in art or fashion are now condemned to continually do that or lose their power: "haunted by the fear of compromising their prestige as discoverers by overlooking some discovery, and thus obliged to enter into mutual attestations of charisma, making them spokespersons and theoreticians, and sometimes even publicists and impresarios, for artists and their art." It is therefore only logical that high-fashion design would eventually end up as a museum piece.

However, this now more often results in as the elevation of a young designer to the status of being the next this or that iconic designer, well before the designer has even been able to do much beyond create a degree show or début at a fashion week. This is reminiscent of the so-called "Saatchi Effect" in the art world, where the art collector Maurice Saatchi had, by virtue of his buying power and art collection, become the ultimate creator of "the next new artist" in Britain after creating a whole generation of what are now called Young British Artists, or YBAs, in the late 1980s and '90s (the artist Damien Hirst being perhaps the most famous of these). Saatchi, whose fortune was built on his advertising agency, understands well the power of the image, and the strong, often controversial art produced by the YBAs has generated much publicity, which in turn has driven up the prices for the art.

It is still very viable for the art world to work this kind of cultural positioning, but the YSL exhibition at the Metropolitan seems not to be easily repeated. Recent exhibitions of Dior and Poiret have revived interest in these designers, but no living designer has been similarly enshrined in a solo show at the Met. Designs have been shown in group shows, but no one has yet reached the sanctified level of Saint Laurent. A similar exhibition for Giorgio Armani at the Guggenheim in New York was heavily criticized for the perceived conflict of interest between the subject of the exhibition and the funding that Armani was providing for the museum. The perception of commercial interests buying their way into the temples of art put a damper on further such shows.

However, this is all part and parcel of the maneuvering for cultural capital on one hand and market share on the other and can only be expected to continue and grow stronger, with increased influence from all sides. We can even expect the educational establishment of the design schools to become involved soon in terms of deciding who should be included in the pantheon of "classics." To go back to Bourdieu:

> Academies (and the salons in the nineteenth century) or the corps of museum curators, both claiming a monopoly over the consecration of contemporary producers, are obliged to combine tradition and tempered innovation. And the educational system, claiming a monopoly over the consecration of works of the past and over the production and consecration (through diplomas) of cultural consumers, only posthumously accords that infallible mark of consecration, the elevation of works into "classics" by their inclusion in curricula.

That high-fashion design enters into this position at the end of the hundred years of fashion is hardly surprising. The finality that seemed to hover over the discipline after Saint Laurent's departure abated somewhat, but even so, after 2002, the general feeling is that an era is definitely over. Therefore, the discipline is more museum-worthy now than ever, the more it is under threat, and hence we have the full collusion of museums and industry in this development.

A social structure that relies in part on symbols provided by high fashion is still with us.

But it is not the same as the social structure of Eugénie's court, nor is it that same as the structure of Saint Laurent's, Dior's, Chanel's, or Poiret's youth. The reactions it has to change are the same though, and when faced with radical change, it falls back on the ritual with which has maintained its structure so far. In its defense, it begins to create new systems in place of the old and strengthens those that it can. If it cannot stop the forces of change, it at least can create, as in Paris of the 1860s, a temporary enclave of revised or invented tradition, and through the introduction of new methods or stricter guidelines, draw new lines of orthodoxy. These new orthodoxies will either open up and lead to new systems or die out with their practitioners.

In Chapter 11, we will explore what the current situation of high fashion looks like from the ground level and, with all the hindsight we can muster, try to trace the path that led to the present in order to project the next few steps.

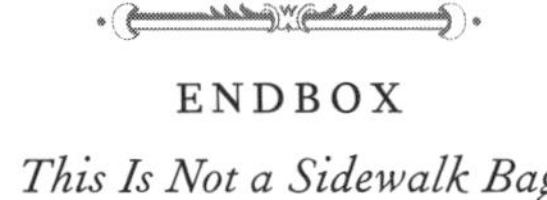

ENDBOX

This Is Not a Sidewalk Bag

A . . . question came up in the minds of some who, making their way past the police guard outside the [Brooklyn] museum, found themselves in a forecourt where a group of ratty stalls, the type one sees all over Chinatown, had been set up. Inside such places—with their graffiti-covered riot gates, dubious signage and with touts outside hissing in Shanghai-accented English—out-of-towners have thronged for years, to participate in the racy but highly illegal game of scoring cheap counterfeit luxury goods.

. . . Here, in a bit of surreal museum theater, the stalls were mocked up again. Standing outside them were men who resembled the African immigrant vendors who haul around telltale bundles of alluring, cheapish and almost-right copies of stuff from Gucci and Louis Vuitton. This time, however, these characters were playacting. The goods laid out on trays and tarps were real Vuitton accessories. They cost, as they do in the stores, a bomb.

"There is nothing good" about the gray market in counterfeit goods, said Edward Skyler, the deputy mayor for operations, addressing a small crowd of early arrivals who had almost certainly never bartered for an $80 copy of a $1,400 bag off a blanket on the sidewalk. "There are billions of dollars in lost sales tax and revenue lost," Mr. Skyler said as people nodded blankly and then raced inside the museum to get warm.

And there the partygoer was met by a fresh set of dilemmas, of the more manageable aesthetic sort. It seems almost passé to bring up the controversy that erupted when the Museum of Contemporary Art in Los Angeles, where the Murakami show originated, set up a shop inside the museum selling Vuitton goods. A headline on this newspaper's review of the current exhibition framed the overarching issue well: "Art With Baggage in Tow."

The baggage in question, made since 2002 in a collaboration between Mr. Murakami and Louis Vuitton, has generated sales estimated to be in the hundreds of millions, by far the most successful such venture in the label's history. "Vuitton has a long tradition of these collaborations, of relationships with artists, going back to the Impressionists," Yves Carcelle, the chairman of Louis Vuitton, said on Thursday night.

Still, nothing the company ever did hit the jackpot like Mr. Murakami's cherry-ornamented and "Multico" bags, which came about, as Mr. Carcelle explained, after 9/11, when the Vuitton designer, Marc Jacobs, suggested to his corporate bosses that it was no good to mourn forever: fashion had a responsibility, ahem, to help people past their grief. "Marc said," Mr. Carcelle recalled, "'If I work with Takashi, and we do something colorful, I think it will help make New York strong again.'"

Source: Guy Trebay. "This is Not a Sidewalk Bag." The *New York Times*. April 6, 2008, p. ST1.

Discussion Points

1. Is high-fashion apparel design an art? Does it belong in museums?
2. What is the connection between Dada and fashionable clothing in museums?
3. How can a handbag help strengthen a city?

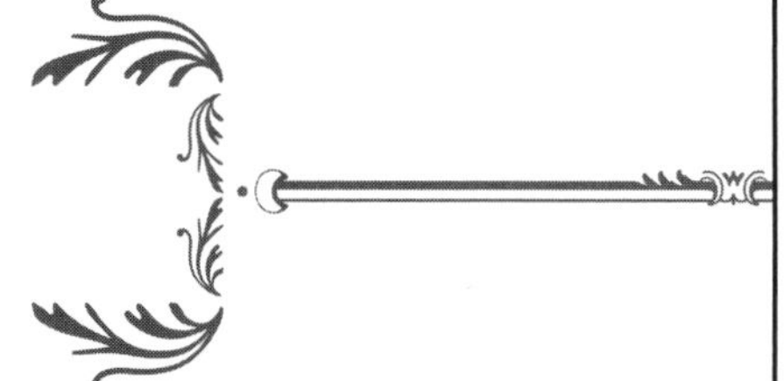

CHAPTER 11

The "End of History" That Wasn't

The fashion system of today functions inside a myth of its own creation, where twice a year, a cycle of pageants is held in the form of the various "fashion weeks" of Paris, London, New York, and Milan. Other cities, such as Moscow and Rio de Janeiro, have begun to hold their own weeks, but the "big four" still manage to hold center stage through their economic and media clout. Through these pageants, the various labels are exhibited, in varying degrees of connectivity to the world outside. The relationship of one designer's work to another's is no more than of any artist's to another's, as the notion of the designer-artist has gone to its furthest extreme, and the trends and proliferation of designers resemble the world of fine art much more than they do Poiret's world of fashion or that of Worth before him.

In this chapter we will look at the *mechanics* of this situation. The chapter will suggest that the answer to "How did we get here?" is not only in the fashions themselves demanding changes or simply by virtue of the designers' visions. The place we find ourselves in is a construct resulting from the changing of our perception of time and space, through our use of and familiarity with electronic media.

This is not to be taken as a call for any kind of rejection of technology or a wish for a "simpler time." No such time exists or can exist. The world is what it is, and for those who decry the use of technology, it suffices to point them to a world without communications and ask whether they would choose to live without the capabilities of our day. Any longing or nostalgia about an old system is misplaced. We are simply in a situation that is inevitable, natural, and a logical consequence of the technology we use. Just as nineteenth-century trains and telegraph drove changes in the social and political situation of Europe and the United States, so do our gadget-driven, media-saturated days influence how we now navigate and interact with the world.

Following on from our look at the idea of the postmodern condition as set forward by Jean-François Lyotard (see Chapter 6), we will see views of another French thinker of the late twentieth century. Jean Baudrillard will help us understand the state of affairs as a situation in which there is no actual history or reality behind anything that's done and allow us to understand that we have arrived (for better or worse) at a place where there is no central truth from within which we can securely operate. This closes the little French circle as it brings us back to Lyotard's notions, which involve the lack of overall narratives in our "postmodern" world.

We will then see how the ideas of Marshall McLuhan, a Canadian scholar who considered the effect modern electronic media had and would have on our culture. His thoughts from the 1960s and '70s speak remarkably clearly to our age of the Internet, cell phones, and iPods, in which we have extended our sensory mechanisms way beyond our bodies to circle the globe in a network of 24-hour wakefulness, streaming information everywhere at once.

The End of History?

The title of this chapter evokes a book from 1992, *The End of History and the Last Man,* by the historian Francis Fukuyama. The book came out after the dissolution of the Soviet Union and was rather misunderstood as a neoconservative tract claiming that democracy was the natural course of human events. Fukuyama later explained that what he posited to be universal is " . . . the desire to live in a modern—that is, technologically advanced and prosperous—society." This, then, he said, drives demand for political participation with "liberal democracy arriving in that process, something that becomes a universal aspiration only in the course of historical time." Fukuyama continues to say that he "presented a kind of Marxist argument for the existence of a long-term process of social evolution, but one that terminates in liberal democracy rather than communism . . . "[1]

But what else could follow such a process? The other half of Fukuyama's title "The Last Man" refers to Nietzsche's writings in *Thus Spoke Zarathustra*, where he presents the end result of systems based on equality and liberty (Figure 11.1):

FIGURE 11.1. An unlikely fashion influence: the German philosopher Friedrich Nietzsche. In his view, the so-called "civilizing" achievements of the Western world had made us into a passive, apathetic, and servile people, living only for day-to-day comfort.

> I tell you: one must still have chaos in one, to give birth to a dancing star. I tell you: ye have still chaos in you. Alas! There cometh the time when man will no longer give birth to any star. . . . Lo! I show you THE LAST MAN.[2]

In Nietzsche's view, European civilization had turned man into an apathetic creature of small desires and timid appetites with no passion or drive for anything but the mundane. Whatever this Last Man would be given, he would receive meekly and without complaint, happy to be left alone.

They have their little pleasures for the day, and their little pleasures for the night, but they have a regard for health. And like Herbert Hoover's ad-saturated Americans:

> "We have discovered happiness," say the last men, and blink.[3]

Like Marx, Nietzsche describes the development of mankind into a monstrous machine, and it is the serving of this machine of modern industrial man that has become the only meaning in life.[4] The desire for comfort and well-being can lead to a denial of reality, and it is in the strange relationship Western culture has with reality that we find our next set of clues. We must consider whether our passive reception of media information and our relationship with the market have brought us to a point where we no longer question the progression of history and our place in it. Worse still, we may have become passive observers of our own experience.

We can start with a brief examination of the writings of Jean Baudrillard, with a view to their significance for the analysis of fashion design.

Simulacra and Simulation

An understanding of the state of high-fashion design at the beginning of the twenty-first century can be much improved by examining the world in the light of the writings of the French sociologist Jean Baudrillard. Two of the essays in his book *Simulacra and Simulation* point to a way of explaining how current high fashion, having reached the "End of History," can maintain its illusory existence without collapsing under the weight of its contradictions.

When Charles Worth set out to design for the court of the Empress Eugénie, he based his creations on the styles of the day, and when he needed a new idea, he went to the paintings in the Louvre for inspiration from historical styles. His son and grandson after him continued to look backward. Jean Worth, as we have seen, was extremely willing to give up on modernity altogether and return to a time he perceived as harmonious and peaceful. Poiret maintained his link with the past, using the Empire line as a base for many of his designs. He broke with the established culture when he referenced a theatrical and imaginary "Orient," but toward the end of his career, he seems to have had nowhere to go and increasingly looked backward. It was Chanel who provided the break with history, but she quickly settled into a history of her own that has since become one of the touchstones of fashion (Figure 11.2).

Baudrillard suggests that there has not so much been an end *of* history as an end of the *perception* of history. Media, and specifically in his discussion, film have delivered and redelivered history to us to such a degree and in such a fragmented and out-of-order fashion, that we have lost any sense of historical progression. History has become "History," a collection of images and references that can be aligned any which way to build whatever construct we chose. To this he adds the notion that our image-driven culture has reduced all cultural experience to images of culture, rather than any direct experience, and in fact, he maintains there is no direct experience to be had. All our culture is a perfect copy, a simulacrum, of a reality that is no longer available.

FIGURE 11.2. Coco Chanel wearing her "sportswear" in 1929. ("For watching sports, not playing them!" she said.)

We can apply Baudrillard's four stages of the image[5] to a definition of the problem of the state of high-fashion design. High-fashion design has long gone past what Baudrillard defines as the first stage of image: *reflecting profound reality*. This it may have done for only a brief while, before its modern implementation—that is, in bourgeois Pairs and London in the decades prior to the House of Worth, when the newly formed fashion houses created apparel according to clients' needs. Haute couture's beginnings in the hands of Eugénie and Worth found it quickly at the stage of *masking and denaturing a profound reality*, which was its largest function in the Second Empire. Once the Second Empire fell, it would then seem to continue through Baudrillard's phases, *by masking an absence of a profound reality*, while it pretended for almost a hundred years that there was a reality underneath its carefully crafted and elaborate mask.[6] Then, once the absence of reality could no longer be denied and the word "death" began its annual appearance in the reviews, the mask and myth became the reality. The frame pulled us like Alice through the looking glass into the image that has no relation to any reality whatsoever: high fashion *is its own pure simulacrum*. Baudrillard's phases imply that there is nowhere to go from here.

We can take, for example, the designer Ralph Lauren, in whose case we have a set of images that derive their impulses from an imaginary version of a patrician society that never really existed. That is to say, except in some idealized afterglow of the 1920s, such as in the 1974 film *The Great Gatsby*, for which Lauren designed the men's wear. This idealized vision of East Coast upper class was also brought to the 2008 Olympics, when Polo Ralph Lauren became the official outfitters for the U.S. team. The athletes' clothing was a look back at an imaginary 1930s of white shorts and knit-vests. "[The US Olympic Committee's] vision was to do something elegant, refined and appropriate—very 'Chariots of Fire.' We saw the Olympics as a chance to put America out as statesmen, the athletes as representatives of our country and our way of being," said David Lauren, son of the designer and the head of marketing. "We wanted to reference the glory days of the Olympics and then bring it to a very modern silhouette.... It's a combination of looking back and looking to the future."[7]

Ralph Lauren himself said of his designs in 2001: "Whether that world exists or not, I don't know. I saw things as they should have been, not as they were."[8]

{ LOOKING FORWARD LOOKING BACK }

Ralph Lauren Revives—or Re-creates—the Past

"Can't repeat the past? [Gatsby] cried incredulously. "Why of course you can!"

He looked around him wildly, as if the past were lurking here in the shadow of his house, just out of reach of his hand. "I'm going to fix everything just the way it was before," he said, nodding determinedly. "She'll see."*

Ralph Lauren's iconography of the mythical 1920s as they "should have been" is one of many examples of designers revisiting the *temps perdu*, the bygone times of their own or their society's past. The choice of Polo Ralph Lauren Co. to dress the U.S. Olympic team in 2008 invites interpretation: what to make of costuming the athletes—who use cutting-edge technology in textiles and equipment while competing—in outfits referencing the years between the twentieth century's World Wars?

Ralph Lauren contributed much to the mythological self-image of the United States in the late twentieth century and again presented his vision of what America should have been. Like Fitzgerald's Jay Gatsby, he wishes to regain the dream of America as it was before the Crash of '29. But there is another layer of meaning: Entering the grounds in Beijing, the crisp Cape Cod whites and newsboy caps represent the high-tech athletes as belonging to a tradition of gentlemanly athletics on university playing fields. Most will recognize the reference to a supposedly more innocent time, having seen some version on

* F. Scott Fitzgerald, *The Great Gatsby* (New York: Simon and Schuster, 1995), 116–117.

TV, and will not question its veracity. It actually doesn't matter: The image is all. Just as our personal memories contain "golden moments" that may not have been just so, so does our society's collective memory. Designer fashions are a repository for our myths, to be revisited and re-presented until they seem real and the past that should have been is finally gained.

The Fictional Buzz Rickson's

The writer William Gibson, who coined the term *cyberspace*, wrote in his novel *Pattern Recognition* about a fashionable trend spotter, who, on entering a department store, observes a rack of Tommy Hilfiger clothes:

> My God, don't they know? This stuff is simulacra of simulacra of simulacra. A diluted tincture of Ralph Lauren, who had himself diluted the early days of Brooks Brothers, who had themselves stepped on the product of Jermyn Street and Savile Row, flavoring their ready-to-wear with liberal lashings of polo knit and regimental stripes. But Tommy surely is the null point, the black hole. There must be some event horizon, beyond which it is impossible to be more derivative, more removed from the source, more devoid of soul. Or so she hopes . . .[9]

Gibson's *Pattern Recognition* prompted the creation of a garment that, although a very special case, in some ways illustrates the strange direction fashion design is heading in. In the book, his lead character, the trend spotter named Cayce Pollard, has a deep aversion to logos and branding. She wears a black military jacket made in Japan. It is an exact replica, a simulacrum, of a 1950s jacket known as the MA-1 (Figure 11.3). The MA-1 is an iconic garment and has been popular in a number of subcultures since its initial military issue in the '50s. In Japan, there is a company, Buzz Rickson's, that makes precise replicas of MA-1's to the degree of obsessive accuracy that it spent a million dollars, when the company started up, on machinery to reproduce 1950s USAF-spec Crown zippers.

> The jackets are expensive, but, as Gibson wrote later, you would have to understand the degree of sheer lunatic obsession that goes into these things. You are very un-

FIGURE 11.3. Trends can create their own reality and frame of reference: Buzz Rickson's MA-1 in black. A simulacrum of an anti-fashion military jacket described in William Gibson's novel *Pattern Recognition*. The jacket as described by Gibson never existed. Now it is copied and knocked off high and low.

> likely to ever wear another piece of clothing this well-made. I know I never have. (They are actually better than the 1950s USAF originals, which were only finished to military contract standards.) Nobody outside of Japan is very interested in paying for that, they told me, smiling. They have found their niche-market, bigtime.[10]

Gibson knew of them, but what he did not consider was that the MA-1 had actually never been made in black for the military and hence not by the obsessive crew at Buzz Rickson's. He, of course, was writing fiction and could make it any color he liked.[11]

When the novel came out, Gibson "received a very puzzled letter from the folks at Buzz Rickson's, who had been getting requests for black MA-1's. Once [he] had explained what was happening, they amazed and delighted [him] by asking [his] permission to make a repro of 'Cayce's' jacket, to market as their Pattern Recognition model." He said that would be fine, if they would make one to fit him, and now he wears an authentic reproduction of a jacket, which never existed until he wrote about it. In this one jacket we see the layers of fiction and invention that underlie the myths of "authentic" fashions.

Gibson concludes the story on his blog:

> Recently we have been discussing an entire Pattern Recognition line, which would consist of all of their classic reproductions, but in black. People have been requesting other jackets that the USAF never issued, like a black version of the coyote-snorkel N3-B USAF

> parka. Ninety per-cent of their product sells within fifty miles of their Tokyo workrooms, they tell me, and they really aren't very interested in foreign sales. They are just, well, nuts. Divinely and magnificently nuts.[12]

This twist of creation, from fiction to reality, seems slightly odd (if not magnificently nuts) when seen in the context of a single military jacket in a novel becoming an icon in its own right. It seems less so when viewed in terms of costumes for Olympic athletes, and even less so—if at all strange—when considered through a high-fashion lens. The design shapes reality from the wish for a world that might have been.

TALES FROM THE HYPER-REAL

Getting back to high fashion, the year 2007 saw a remarkable series of illustrations of the hyper-reality of high fashion. The first moment was right at the beginning of the year at Giorgio Armani's Paris couture show. Armani Privé broadcast a show on the Internet—an event that was perhaps doubly surprising in the fact that designers did not do this on a regular basis, despite Yves Saint Laurent having shown his Spring/Summer show online already back in 1996.

"Now through the democracy of the Internet, we can provide a front-row seat for everyone," read Armani's statement,[13] deftly skipping past the question of why this generous act of democratic largesse was necessarily a good idea. Given that the entire market for haute couture numbers only in the hundreds, and the main clients were most likely all represented at the show anyway, the benefit to Armani is clear only when one remembers that the couture show is a PR exercise, an attempt to frame the event in a context of inviting everyone to be in the front row with the fashion royalty. The fantasy of sitting in the front row might, of course, be slightly dampened by the fact that the garments on view are completely unaffordable to the majority of viewers. However, the show's purpose, just like the purpose of couture for years, was not to sell the clothes but to be a media event to publicize the accessories, cosmetics, and perfumes associated with the label. (See Figure 11.4.) Now that cell phones had become an accessory, it was inevitable that a designer cell phone—in this case Armani's—would hit the market, and then of course, the associated couture-event would have to be broadcast over the cellular network (Figure 11.5). Early 2008 then

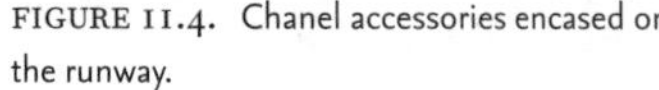

FIGURE 11.4. Chanel accessories encased on the runway.

FIGURE 11.5. A fashion show on a handheld screen must deliver something other than the intimacy of texture and detail that is such a large part of the couture fashion experience.

saw the immediate—and inevitable—arrival of designer cell phones from Dior, Prada, Dolce & Gabbana, and more. The irony of displaying couture, which prides itself on detail, fit, and fine fabrics, on a low-resolution 2-inch cell phone screen, seems to have been lost on everyone. Even Anna Wintour, the editor-in-chief of U.S. *Vogue*, pitched in: "I think it's wonderful, it helps [fashion] maintain a glamorous image and I'm all for it."[14] How this move contributes to the glamour was not explained.

The removal of exclusivity, however, is enormously significant. By broadcasting the show, in real time, into the most accessible arena in history, the idea of haute couture as media event is laid on the table. Given that other labels' respective phones are coming out at the time of this writing, it is fairly certain that they will broadcast their shows. Then, it is also fairly certain that the shows themselves will begin to be staged with this broadcasting in mind, and the performance aspect will eventually override the apparel considerations completely. That Armani's subsequent show was meant to be rock star inspired, with bright colors and glitter, shows a definite tendency in this direction. Armani's press release (again with a complete lack of irony) explained that the collection was inspired by David Bowie's Ziggy Stardust era of 30 years before and called it "the beginning of a new age."[15]

The performance aspect has, of course, been part of the game ever since Poiret took his models on a tour of Europe, the difference being only the technology involved. But before we explore the effect of media and technology more closely, let us look at more of the hyper-real events of 2007.

Mouret

Roland Mouret, a young designer who, in 2005, resigned from the fashion house that bore his name, returned to the runway as RM because his former business partner and financial backer owned (and still owns) his full name. He showed where the marketing of high fashion may be headed. He published his 21-piece collection online for orders the very next day, four months before it would actually hit the stores. A reviewer noted that "we will have a chance to see it, for real, when [Spice Girl] Victoria Beckham does her first American TV interview with Jay Leno next week."

Apparently Mouret's new backer, Simon Fuller, was also the impresario behind the music group the Spice Girls, which included one of the "it-girls" of 2007, Ms. Beckham. She had already seen the collection and supposedly bought nearly every piece.[16]

Just as the Armani collections have for years been mainly about dressing a few actresses for the Oscar ceremony, Roland Mouret's collection was seemingly designed for one woman to wear. Each designer has his empress.

Valentino

Our next designer in hyper-reality, Valentino, certainly had his share of elegant ladies: Jacqueline Kennedy Onassis, Elizabeth Taylor, Audrey Hepburn, Gwyneth Paltrow, Jennifer Lopez, Scarlett Johanssen, and Keira Knightley, to name a few, and the significance of this list of seven women containing six actresses should not be lost after what we have seen in the preceding chapters.

In 2007, Valentino celebrated his 45th anniversary as a designer with an event so ironic that Baudrillard could not have invented a better illustration of his notion of cultural simulacra (Figure 11.6). In January 2008, Valentino presented his last show in Paris and was subsequently presented the medal of the City of Paris in recognition of his services to

FIGURE 11.6. Valentino at his retirement party, standing in front of a display of mannequins bearing his designs.

fashion in the city. The previous summer, however, he was in Rome for the anniversary celebration. With a lack of irony that outstrips Armani's PR team, the celebration—a dinner for 500—took place in a fiberglass replica of the Temple of Venus, created by a set designer inside the ruins of Rome's Coliseum: A simulacra, inside the real thing, masking the actual ruins! Even the designs of the master, displayed around the area on mannequins, underscored the loops and layers of referencing involved:

> During the cocktail party for the opening, a guest, pointing to a silver dress edged in feathers, asked Valentino if it wasn't a famous number once worn by Jennifer Lopez.
>
> "No, that was Jackie Kennedy's dress," he said with a shrug. "We made Jennifer a copy."[17]

When Valentino had sold his name and company to financiers some years before, he and his partner kept creative control, but after his retirement, the design responsibilities were distributed among several designers. However, only two seasons in the new head of design was fired only hours after presenting her spring 2009 show in Paris. Her designs were "not appreciated" by Valentino as they were too abrupt a departure from the "master's" style. With the decrease overall in luxury markets in the fall of 2008, any changes in an established brand were not considered wise. The new head of design learned of her firing from the press and was replaced by the "two accessories"—designers who had worked alongside Valentino for many years.

Valentino was among the last of a type. Few, if any, designers will be celebrating decades at an eponymous label in the future. As more and more labels are bought by investors, whose primary goal is expansion of a brand and a diversification into multiple markets on many continents, the place of the "star-designer" at the head of the label has become redundant. The myth will survive for a while, but the corporations that own the couture houses are putting less and less emphasis on the designer as part of the appeal of their brand. The designer is more and more seen to be subservient to the brand's identity rather than the creator of a vision. The myth of the founding designer—or the myth of the brand itself—suffices, and the current designer stays in the background. This arrangement also serves to keep the designer from outgrowing corporate control.

GALLIANO AT DIOR

A few nights before Valentino's celebration in Rome, the house of Dior celebrated its 60th anniversary with a grand show at Versailles. It was also John Galliano's 10th anniversary as the label's lead designer. The show was in itself a complete step outside any current reality, and suited Galliano's grand theatrical style, as well as the celebratory nature of the evening. Guests were told to dress "elegantly," and the expectation was that a tribute would be paid to the "New Look." However, Galliano did not go into full retreat into Dior's myth but celebrated Dior by referencing his art collection, with the silhouette and detailing of each creation reflecting the style of a Picasso, Monet, Degas, Rembrandt, or other art from the late designer's collection.[18] Odd as this might seem at first, the statement that couture is the designer's canvas is highly appropriate for Galliano's larger-than-life and highly imaginative creations. His catwalk styles are often so divorced from the reality of clothing as it is worn today that he may just as well be approached as a painter, sculptor, or conceptual artist (Figure 11.7). After all, his creativity is geared toward creating a buzz and an image, and not to send mundane suits down the

FIGURE 11.7. Galliano's designs have always tended toward the fanciful and wild, creating a "feel" for the label.

runway. He proved this with some flair a few years before, when apparently the management at Dior asked him to create something more wearable. He responded with a collection that included fairly low-key pantsuits in a beige color scheme. His audience and the critics were appalled, and Dior's sales figures dropped. As soon as Galliano went back to the mad costume spectacles that his fans expected, sales went back up. To be a Dior customer is not about wearing the wild creations of its designer, but about being associated with his artistic creativity.

But one might ask: Where does all this leave high-fashion design as a discipline? If the ultimate goal of a high-fashion designer is to create fireworks to draw an increasingly distracted audience to its merchandise, then Galliano is pointing the way. High-fashion design will continue to place itself on a hyper-real plane, and the designs will go further into the realm of costume designed for multimedia consumption. Where Galliano went, others are following. With couture becoming more and more openly a part of the PR side of the apparel and accessories business, the extreme language of spectacle will no doubt prevail.

GLOBALIZATION: YOU ARE HERE (AND HERE, HERE, AND HERE)

Despite worldwide consumption of globally marketed media and goods, there is still enough diversity among people in different parts of the world that the expansion of a market requires adaptations to local styles and consumption habits. One advantage to removing the high-end design from the context of the brands' other, less extravagant wares is that it is then only the logo that binds them together. It then doesn't matter what differences need to be brought into the merchandise for each region or market segment. The design is authenticated by the logo, and as long as the logo is sanctioned by whatever local authority of fashion holds sway, the brand is safe. Local trends and changes in local needs can then be addressed without disturbing the entire market.

The contradiction this leads to becomes obvious: In an increasingly connected and globalized market, the tendency is toward fragmentation, not unity. We will explore the implications of this re-tribalization in Chapter 12. There is also the problem that Paul Poiret warned his American audiences of almost a century ago: "Take care! You are being deceived. You imagine you are being provided with the fashions of Paris; but you do not see them! You send to Paris emissaries commissioned to inform you, but they do not tell you what they see."[19]

Only now the tables are turned. There is no need for emissaries, even though we still read fashion writers in newspapers and blogs. We can see the shows for ourselves online and even on our cell phones if and when we so choose. Now we can see the show as it happens, but what are we seeing, and does it bear any relation to any other experience we may have? How does what we see on the cell phone screen or in the media window of our laptops relate to what is happening in the designer's studio or on the streets? Am I actually watching it live, or is it edited and scripted? Does it matter one way or another, when I can click on links to show me shows from the last ten years anytime I want? The critics and press releases may help us interpret what we see, but given the nature of the PR machines of the large corporations, there is perhaps less to be had there than one would hope. The experience is of yet another show, a "media moment" of which there are millions to choose from and that disappear into the digital cloud the moment we are linked elsewhere.

McLuhan's Global Village Revisited in the Age of IT

Writing in 1968, Marshall McLuhan pointed out that the late twentieth century technological revolution is greater than that of the wheel in its power to reshape human outlook and human organization. The wheel and other classical tools are extensions of the human body, but computers and electronic communications are an extension of the human self.[20]

This insight, published years before the advent of anything resembling the Internet and wireless connected world we live in today, is remarkably prescient. We are able to move ourselves, the core of our perceptions and experiences, to events and people practically anywhere on Earth, and are no longer limited to our geographical space or time zone. The technology we have adopted has not only changed our methods but has changed us as physical beings on a fundamental level. The fact that we can communicate and experience events over distances, regardless of real time, changes how we operate in society and relate to the world and each other. The technology we use also directly affects our experience of the world.

The Arc of an Icelandic Grandmother

My grandmother, a seamstress in Iceland, who was born in 1907 and lived to be almost 90 years old, can serve as an example of the kind of change wrought by technology. When she was starting out in the '30s, making dresses for middle-class ladies in Reykjavik, information about the latest styles in Europe would arrive via magazines and pattern books from the mainland. They would come by ship and would be anywhere from weeks to months out-of-date. Fashions did not change so rapidly, so this was not considered any kind of problem, and there was no alternative anyway. To see the actual style icons, she would have to wait for the Hollywood films to arrive in one of the two movie houses. These could be up to a couple of years old when they arrived, but their arrival would be greeted with the same enthusiasm as if they were fresh off the block. The outside world was seen as a distant place that an occasional glimpse could be caught of, and from these occasional glimpses a world view was formed at a slow and steady pace (Figure 11.8).

She went on to live through the arrival of air travel and air freight, which brought the world closer and delivered the magazines within days, not weeks. She saw television, which could show her events in foreign countries, first within a day or two and then live as they were happening. (I watched the first live broadcast on Icelandic television in her living room as Neil Armstrong took the first human step on the moon.) In the final years of her life, she enjoyed magazines that brought her fresh images at the same time as the rest of Europe, live television broadcasts of, say, Academy Awards shows, and knew of the Internet, although she was rather mystified by it.

To her, the world had changed, not just the technology. She had changed in her regard toward the world as well. She belonged to a world that was much larger, faster, and open to

FIGURE 11.8. The author's grandmother (second from right, standing) and her sisters ca. 1935: nineteenth- and twentieth-century styles in comfortable proximity.

inquiry than the world of her youth. Waiting for information was, of course, still part of her interaction with the world. Now we are wired and connected to a degree that has moved us even further than the shift my grandmother experienced. Information flows around us faster and thicker than we can process or even accommodate.

The Past Has Been Abolished (for Now)

Another insight of McLuhan's is that the information revolution we are in abolishes the human past by making it entirely present.[21] This echoes Baudrillard's notion of nonexistent history. By allowing us access to all recorded events, archived writings, and bits of information, the wired world obliterates the linear motion of time. We can experience history in any order and at any pace we choose. And it is all available all the time. Not only is there no waiting, there is no order to the line. Galliano's latest show can be had along with his last 20 at the click of a mouse. Instead of a progression of experience that relies on time, consideration, and memory, we can view his work as a collage divorced from the reality of the world, or as Baudrillard might put it, there is no world within which to place it. It has its own temporal reality without connection to anything.

To continue with McLuhan for a moment, it is worth noting his comment that "when a new technology strikes a society, the most natural reaction is to clutch at the immediately preceding period for familiar and comforting images."[22] It is tempting to see the tendency that we have observed in the preceding chapters for fashion to continually look back in this light. On might wonder, then, what could be the next step, once the tensions of the globalized media and connectivity have settled. What we are seeing may well be a period of adjustment, as style and design adjusts to the capabilities of "anywhere and anytime." If every direction is in order, then no direction may well be the answer for a while. Societies are coherent structures, and what grows in a society comes from a society and stays in a society. We cannot separate ourselves from our experiences, and new technology is always absorbed along with the changes it has brought to the human experience.

ENDBOX

Milan Style Undimmed by Recession

It's unlikely that Miuccia Prada, Giorgio Armani, or any of the other designers showing in Milan over the past week have been pondering the effects of dizzying utility bills, surging inflation or the American sub-prime mortgage crisis. In fact, while the collections last week may have been restrained in mood, they were certainly no less luxurious than usual.

Consider Fendi, which came up with everything a billionaire ski bunny could wish for next winter, from highheeled, fur-trimmed moon boots to a mink-lined pushchair. Or Italian knitwear firm Loro Piana, who showed ultralight "baby" cashmere overcoats combed from the bellies of baby goats (mere cashmere is no longer de luxe enough). On the catwalks things were just as precious. The exquisite hand-made Swiss lace that made up most of Miuccia Prada's clothes costs more than £400 per metre.

As the commercial heart of the fashion industry, Milan should be a pretty accurate barometer of how luxury brands are squaring up to an economic downturn, yet most designers are adamant that their customers are in an elite that won't be affected by a recession.

"For a luxury brand, like Versace, the recession wouldn't have that much impact because our client doesn't feel the effects," Donatella Versace said after her show on Thursday evening—a stance shared by most designers last week. Versace can afford to be optimistic; this week the company posted strong sales for last year with revenue up by 7.7 per cent to €310.6m (£234m).

However, that does not mean that luxury labels are not taking note of changing economic conditions. "We do feel a demand for more unique and exceptional pieces, so of course it becomes more challenging for a designer," she added.

. . . Versace is not the only brand feeling confident. Both Prada and Salvatore Ferragamo plan to take their companies public this year, despite jittery markets. This week the industry paper WWD reported that, on average, fashion companies listed in Milan have lost a third of their value in the past three months.

So why are luxury brands feeling so perky? It's largely down to the rapid growth in newly emerging markets such as China, the Middle East and Russia, which will offset any dip in sales to America or the UK.

But while some designers are chasing new markets, others are trying to refine their message for customers closer to home. Luxury houses may not be feeling a downturn in consumer spending just yet, but they are noting a shift in mood. However, they are not responding with more affordable fashion. Far from it.

Source: Clare Coulson. *The Observer*. February 24, 2008.

Discussion Points

1. Why do high-fashion designers not need to respond to economic downturn?
2. What would need to happen for the fashion world as we know it to change dramatically?
3. When has this happened in history?

CHAPTER 12

The End of the Century That Wasn't

In this chapter we will briefly summarize points to consider from our histories in earlier chapters as we begin looking toward the future state of affairs, anticipating the prospects for high-fashion design. As part of this discussion, we will look at how the millennial ideas of the twentieth century did not come to fruition—that is, how fashion design was meant to be but wasn't. We will then begin examining the rise of the new capitalist economies in Russia, China, and India and their implications for the future of the fashion business in general and fashion design in particular.

Not Your Mother's Apocalypse

Twentieth-century visions of the year 2000 were generally—even until the last decades of the century—wildly off the mark. Reality managed both to overshoot some expectations, as in communications and microtechnology, and to underwhelm completely, as in transportation, energy technologies, and fashion.

Possible Futures

The tendency up through the 1970s was to view the future as some logical projection of the present, so images of the future can generally be dated quite quickly by reference to their styling. This can be seen in the first decade of the 1900s, when the future looked Edwardian, and all the way into the 1970s, when the future looked distinctly created in an American design studio—replete with hairdressers galore.

As the modernist vision failed, the future grew progressively darker and an odd thing happened to the future vision in the 1970s,. It grew dark, but it also turned away, seeking its design cues in the past. It can be seen that this is common to all arts and design, but the clearest illustration is in film, when the dark dystopian design of *Alien* and *Blade Runner*

FIGURE 12.1. A still from the film *Blade Runner*: In the late '70s the image of the future in popular art and design began to darken considerably. The dystopian vision has continued.

(Figure 12.1) changed the way the future would be seen in film, with their contemporary, gritty feel. Future visions began to assume the dystopian look that became the norm for the 40 years that followed, at least.

After modernist fashion design came to an end in the 1970s, the direction taken in punk fashions provided the cue for the concluding statement of twentieth-century fashion design. Punk style, as we have seen, could not be appropriated by high-fashion design as the mod and hippie fashions had been. As it was the inevitable end result of the progression of youth fashion, there was nowhere else to go, leaving high-fashion design with no street reference to work from. High fashion did what it had done before the '60s: It turned to the past.

At the end of the twentieth century, high fashion, for the most part, did not recognizably belong to any particular continuum of development in art or design, with references to iconic designers and "homages" to style icons replacing the creation of new styles. The trend became more to revive and revisit, than to invent or rethink.

Y(awn)2K

The future, as we knew it, did not arrive at the turn of the century. The primary fashion for what passes for high society in the media glare is mostly a reconstructed image of a mythical mid-twentieth century: an unstructured amalgam of Hollywood glamour of the 1930s to '50s. Meanwhile, those who actually buy high fashion kept to a fairly low profile of proven styles that have no connection or reference to anything but themselves.

The sleek, antiseptic styles projected in sci-fi films of the 1960s and '70s never arrived. Nor did their attendant metallic and monochrome vistas, such as the black-and-white future Poiret envisioned. The modernist vision in clothing was even less well in touch with reality than that of architecture. Human civilization, in an uncommon disconnect, seems to be unable—or at least unwilling—to quickly adapt its appearance to the design of the technology of the times. Modernists fashions, for both men and women, essentially stripped down and streamlined Edwardian fashions. After that, not much has changed, apart from an increased casualness and use of denim. Wearing a Chanel suit, the sportswear of the polo fields, or even the crisp suits of the Dada artists (Figure 12.2), an avant-garde couple of the early twentieth century could walk into a swanky café anywhere in the Western Hemisphere today without attracting undue notice (except perhaps for their sense of style!).

FIGURE 12.2. The highly modern Dada artist Emmy Hennings in 1916.

As the 1990s drew to a close, a swell of millennial unease hit the Western World. It was an inverted media-amplified version of the turn-of-the-century euphoria that had, one hundred years before, led to all sorts of imaginings of what the twentieth century would be. Those visions tended to the optimistic, technological, and highly confident in the continuity of the Western vision of culture and society.

The millennial visions of the late twentieth century were not so optimistic, or to phrase it in a typically late-twentieth-century fashion, naïve. The underlying fear of technology that had become a signature element of late-twentieth-century popular culture came to the front, in fears of a millennium "Y2K" virus that would wipe out the newly established Internet by taking down all the world's computers at once. The end of the Cold War left history's path wide open again, ready to be redirected by whatever was going to happen next. The uncertainty over what this was going to be added to the generally anxious undercurrent. Heading into the twenty-first century, Western culture seemed simultaneously apprehensive and relieved. On one hand, this problematic, violent century was over. But, on the other hand, what was to take its place was not clear at all. The societal underpinnings for a "century of Worth" or a "King of Fashion" are simply gone from Western society, at least for now. In the rising economies of the world, the images and systems of late-twentieth-century fashion are presented by global corporations, film, and media.

However, while turning away, fashion seems to have taken this millennial dystopia to heart. Designers seem to have been searching for a way out of the increasingly tighter circles of reference with the kind of overemphasis that has characterized periods when fashion has come to an impasse. High fashion elements have been referenced in ever-tightening circles for so long now that the vernacular of fashion design contains all the elements of twentieth century high fashion. Meanwhile, as the market for high fashion decreased, the corporations who own the labels have pressed hard to move the brands to ready-to-wear and the gap between high fashion and street fashion has been decreasing from both sides. A remarkable example is when the avant-garde designer Rei Kawakubo of Comme des Garçons appeared in a 2008 "guest collection" for the chain store H&M. This joining of high-concept creativity and high-street retail takes the relationship of high fashion and street fashion into new territory. If high fashion brands are dissolving as independent entities, perhaps designers such as Kawakubo will increasingly practice their arts in the mass-retail sector.

Rei Kawakubo stated in the press release for the collections launch, which coincided with H&M's first store in Tokyo, that she is interested in the balance between creation and business. Here again is laid down the question with which high fashion design has grappled from Poiret onward: How to balance the demands of the market with the ideals of creativity? Neither all about business as Chanel would have it, or all about the impulsive creation of Poiret, perhaps the meeting of high street and high concept will bring a new approach. If it finds the balance.

{ LOOKING FORWARD LOOKING BACK }

Futures Uncertain and Unrealized

A safe (albeit disconcerting) bet about the long-term future of a society is this: Any current situation was never on any list of predicted futures. Given the number of variables involved, this is not surprising. Given that our future vision is more often than not a projection of our wishes, desires, and fears, it is certain that predictions will be at best approximate.

Past difficulties in visualizing the magical year 2000 abound. Fin de siècle images show people in flying machines wearing impeccable fin de siècle fashions; the mid-twentieth-century envisioned everyone as healthy and fashion-conscious, and then there's my favorite: a textile science textbook from 1972 predicting that cotton would be phased out as men's shirt material by 2000—at which point the men's suit would also have disappeared. A current problem seems to be in guessing which way Chinese fashion will trend, and yet the future of high-fashion design is directly linked to that trend.

The big picture is easier, as human behavior does follow patterns, but even this, as any political pollster can attest, is tricky. Specific predictions about any society's behavior are now best-guess situations, choosing between likely scenarios. Therefore, to predict twenty-first-century fashion long term is near impossible. The rate of change in the fashion system, media saturation amplifying trends before they take, and the market manipulation that is often at odds with the situation on the ground, coupled with the multitude of scenarios, makes choosing anything by any logic, before the parameters change, a nearly random move.

The current lack of long-term vision acknowledges this near-impossibility. Meanwhile, the presentation of styles in seasonal shows—a system long ago irrelevant in terms of any reality bar its own—seems almost a random effort, in which each label attempts a wild throw of garments and accessories at a moving market, hoping something will stick.

Pop Goes Fashion: 15 Minutes of Fame, or the Disappearing Designer

When it became clear in the 1970s that the couturier was disappearing breed, because of lack of business and a change in societal norms, the business of high fashion responded with ready-to-wear and licensing, and then branding took over. The star designer was ingrained in the system, and the couture section of the business was needed to attract attention to the brand, but as the eponymous houses became corporations or were bought up by multinationals. The story of the designers themselves becoming a cog in their own machine became a familiar theme. The core concerns of the designer didn't change despite the altered landscape, and just as with Poiret in his day, the designers' reluctance to play by the rules of the marketplace would bring them into conflict with the corporate order.

John Galliano at Dior, for example, has twice deliberately brought out collections of completely uncharacteristic blandness in response to corporate requests to design more "wearable" collections. (See Figure 12.3.) Neither collection sold well, and even sales of accessories and perfumes were down in the following months. Said Galliano, "I did that show with complete conviction. I gave them what they wanted. The results were I had to refit every single jacket." His following collection was back on form, and record orders were placed.

Galliano may well be one of the last few designers to carry such weight. As the brand becomes more diversified and distributed, the cost of the haute couture operation becomes

FIGURE 12.3. Galliano's "bland" collection (left) was created in response to corporate requests for more "marketable" designs; a design from Gallliano's "Madame Butterfly" collection (right).

harder for the corporations to accept. To have a designer on board who, with old-world methods, creates whatever he or she likes and presents it however he or she wants is too costly and unpredictable for most boards of directors. Young designers are recruited but do not receive the same kind of rollout given to Galliano, Alexander McQueen, or Stella McCartney when they were brought to Givenchy, Dior, and Chloe, respectively. Now the corporations play the cards much closer to the chest and sell the logo, not the designer, saving costs and exerting control over their product at the same time.

IT ISN'T ABOUT CLOTHING

The near total lack of connection of high-fashion design of clothing to the daily life of the Western world is perhaps not surprising, given the history involved. The discipline came into being as an answer to a specific need and set of circumstances in a resurrected aristocratic society whose last vestigial structures have turned into simulacra of themselves. Instead, design now functions mainly on the middle level of production. High-fashion design creates iconic images to stimulate consumption of the derivatives, whether they be clothing, accessories, perfume, or luxury goods of any stripe. For example, Versace accessories accounted for 4 percent of sales in 2005, compared with around 40 percent in 2007. An interesting direction is that Donatella Versace herself developed a lucrative business customizing the interiors of helicopters, yachts, and sports cars for the super rich (Figure 12.4).[1] With such ventures proving lucrative, there was no reason to expect other brands not to follow. The demand for luxury goods was steadily rising in the early years of the twenty-first century as the global markets cranked up global wealth. In early 2007, Chanel, Lacroix, and Dior also reported strong double-digit growth in sales, as did markets for fine jewelry, art, and private yachts, showing that demand for Versace's opulence was not an isolated trend.[2] The global economic crisis of 2008 only slowed down the growth of luxury market, but did not cause it to halt—luxury yacht sales were up, the highest end of luxury accessories was up. However, every other aspect was down, which may result in a re-establishing of a wide gap between the work of high-end design and the street, especially if ventures such as Kawakubo and H&M's collaboration prove unsuccessful. Business inter-

FIGURE 12.4. An August Westland helicopter with a customized interior by Versace, on display at the 29th International Furniture Expo in Milan, Italy, April 2007. "I believe that today lifestyle is important. It is no longer expressed with handbags or shoes. You express this with your travels, with your car, or helicopter. You express it in 360 degrees," said Versace CEO Giancalo Di Risio.

est will follow the money and if it is only coming from the super-rich, then high-design will be for the super rich while the current business models hold.

Apparel design, as we've seen, now concerns itself mainly with mass production of ready-to-wear. When the economic center of the world moved across the Atlantic to the United States, the business model involving department stores demanded different methods, and even the system of selling couture models for reproduction could not answer the demand. Soon labels devoted to the mass manufacture of all levels of design took over, assuming the mantle of couture, but in fact trading on the status value of the label and logo.

As the chain store and branding became the dominant model, the requirement for students of fashion to have detailed knowledge of couture traditions has likewise become increasingly redundant. For example, the traditional dressmaking skills are, at many schools, now a quaint addition to the education of designers, who are primarily being trained for mass production (akin to calligraphy courses offered to graphic designers). Many students, in fact, find themselves slightly confused regarding the purpose of such training. They find that their internships or entry-level jobs require them mainly to sit at computer screens, creating spec sheets, and altering the previous year's patterns for production halfway around the world. They enter a world where "design" is about keeping a distant production line fed with new versions of previous lines, where "the market" gets what it supposedly demands. Knowing what that market demands then becomes the designer's function, changing the focus of the designer's work from that of the creator of a vision to that of a trend forecaster—or follower. Not having a societal ground to connect with, trend-development-as-designing can become the kind of overstressed seeking that typifies high fashion in the early twenty-first century.

A New Electronic Tribe

Forecasting trends in the current market requires knowledge that designers of previous generations did not need. To begin with, the clients of high fashion came to them. From Worth onward, the designer's *atelier* was the center of gravity. At most they would venture across the ocean to New York or take the occasional trip to the capitals of Europe, but these trips would be in order to sell, with observations as an added result. The desire to imprint the designers' styles was often larger than the need to assess the market. They could assume, with some confidence, that the market would come to them.

The New York-Paris axis of fashion power, which developed right at the beginning of Poiret's career, strengthened and continues to this day. Its centrality is, however, greatly lessened as the fashion market globalizes. One might say that as the centers of gravity multiply, each one has a diminished capacity to influence the whole, but this is in need of some discussion. It is in fact wrong to say that there are multiple centers of gravity in today's fashion world. It is too simplistic to say that Paris was usurped by New York and Milan, and then all were diluted by the influence of London and Tokyo. Initially true in each case, what has taken place is not a diminishing of the business, but a diversion of the audience's attention and design's focus. With all the big names competing for a share of each market, the audience in each location is getting an adaptation of each designer's vision, and each local market has its focal point. However, each audience can also observe, instantaneously, the trends and movements in the other markets, rendering the separation rather moot (Figure 12.5). In other words, if I would like to dress in the Italian style, I can be just as up-to-date as the Milanese, even though I am thousands of miles away, and neither look nor

FIGURE 12.5. International style.

speak Italian. Is the "Italian Style," designed by an Englishman for a French conglomerate and made who-knows-where, Italian, or merely "from Italy" or perhaps just "shown in Italy"? Questioning whether it is an authentic "Italian" look or one that is designed by evoking some 1960s film version of Roman youth generally doesn't occur, except, perhaps, as an afterthought. (It is beside the point, as our sense of what is "Italian," "French," or "American" style is derived from various pre-packaged images.)

FIGURE 12.6. Stage artists dance as Bollywood star and former Miss World Priyanka Chopra shoots a scene for the Indian movie Plan in Bombay.

The centers of gravity therefore do not pull audiences away from each other as much as they each exert a new influence over the whole, weakening each others' influence. They are not the same, and yet they are not different, and for the brands to address both sides of the equation, they must have their finger on the pulse of each market and the total market at the same time. The corporate solution is therefore to not follow local markets. As with any other product, if the desire can be created, the market will take what it is given, and a new identity will be created. This task is made considerably easier with the global connectivity and dissemination of media that now has the same images streaming worldwide. Paris, Milan, New York, Hollywood, or Bollywood (Figure 12.6), all can be referenced from anywhere at any time. Two nearly opposing results stem from this situation. One is the increasing homogenization of fashion, high or otherwise. The other is the intensifying of existing differences. The former results from the globalization of commerce, the latter from the globalization of communication.

In order to maintain a global market with the most efficiency and, therefore, profit, an industrial product such as mass-produced clothing needs to be created and marketed uniformly and consistently. What results, in brand-name fashion, is production that is not unlike Charles Worth's, but on a much larger scale: A specific set of basic models is adapted slightly for different markets' needs and produced in sufficient quantities for that market. Different physiques and local customs and needs are thereby addressed. Depending on the sophistication of the inventory control, this strategy can be taken to a regional level. The determining factor is the marketing, especially in the creation and maintenance of the brand's image. Whereas the distribution of the actual manufactured items can be fairly tightly controlled, the distribution of the image cannot be. A global brand needs a global image. Local variances can be created through the placement of print and television ads, but the variances can never be so large as to make a significant difference. For this reason, image campaigns tend toward the nonspecific iconography that we have become accustomed to. Someone becomes the "face" of the label, or there is an overall "feel" to the "look" of the campaign. The role of the designer, if there is one, becomes one of "stylist," but more often than not, the designer is only one of many voices in the creation of the brand's image. In this way, the "look" and the "feel" become the product, allowing the corporation to market anything it wants under that banner (including helicopters!).

The globalization of commerce and communication therefore decreases our choices, but it also has the effect of enhancing any differences that are available. On one hand, the global connectivity allows a trend or an image to spread anywhere there is access to media, increasing the homogenization. On the other hand, the spread of media, online or otherwise, allows a segmentation of culture, as each of us can pick and choose our influences wherever we find them. This has the effect that any subculture or local trend has the possibility of "breaking out" and becoming a larger trend. So all historical periods, foreign cultures, virtual realities, innumerable films, and any fashions past and present offer themselves as possible influences.

How Does Our Past Become Future?

The question that is staring us in the face is, Now what? The 40-year death-watch for high-fashion design must end soon. But in human culture one thing transforms into another, rather than ending. A system shuts down, only to reveal another in its place. We have seen the hundred years' fashion come to a close, but the system of high fashion for high society live on as simulacra. Now what, indeed?

Trying to see the shape of the future has clearly not been an easy task, so to try may be futile. It is also entirely possible that the global corporate system can keep things going for quite a while, and despite the global economic crisis that erupted in late 2008, the Versace-

FIGURE 12.7. The arc of the hundred years' fashion.

flying set will certainly keep luxury in business, but there are several scenarios that could play out. The past can inform the future, not by the "look" of fashion, but by the method of approach. All of our iconic designers became so by being placed against a set of historical circumstances and using their talents, insights, and quirks of their personalities to create something that has endured. Their example may show where a break can occur in the current situation (Figure 12.7).

Beginning with Worth, we might examine what it was that caused the change in the system in his day. Framed large, his ascendancy resulted from the converging of technology and politics in a society that required a solution based on the talents he could provide. The world he entered in Paris was in a state of transition. Manufacturing was going to a larger scale than ever before, requiring more management of operations but also allowing for larger scale in sourcing of materials. High society was reforming in a previous image and was threatened from within and without. The need for ostentatious fashion was thus both societal and economic. Couture could keep the wheels of production turning and give the upper classes fashions with which to identify themselves and display their status to others.

The Aristocracies of the Twenty-first Century

Clearly, high fashion has continually served this purpose, and it is not to be expected that it will stop even with the remaining couture operations closing down, one by one. On the political front, the beginning of the twenty-first century contains nothing close to the turmoil that European society was experiencing in the mid-nineteenth century (up until the middle of the twentieth century, for that matter). All signs currently point to a shift in global economics, but one might view the moving of the center of world commerce as a broadening of the capitalist system, not a restructuring. Donatella Versace's example shows that there may very likely be an increase in the demand for deluxe fashion and that this demand may go into territory that begins to resemble the early days of capitalism, with the gap between the wealthy and everyone else being exhibited in spectacular displays of consumption. This will happen in the areas where the growth of wealth is at its most rapid and where the politics of new wealth, with its attendant class differentiation, are backed up with enough authority to keep worries of social unrest away. Recently this was borne out in Russia, China, and Dubai. Soon after the year 2000, when the Versace label courted clientele in Russia and China, the fashion world reacted with some hilarity and disdain. Now this looks to have been the right move at the time.[3] There is nothing new here, however. There may be a boost in business, but nothing essential will change, except perhaps the transformation of the large labels into full-blown luxury "lifestyle" providers: Ralph Lauren to the nth degree. What will change, if this trend moves ahead, is that the corporations will follow the money, and the New York-Paris axis will look increasingly irrelevant as the axis moves east. If China's economy takes off in the way many predict, then all bets are off, and there could be the big change calling for a new system.

Twentieth-century Designers as Change Agents

A quick look at each of our designers following Worth is in order. We should then consider the scenarios that may follow these designers in the twenty-first century.

Poiret, the Artist

Poiret broke out of the Worth mold by restructuring the clothes and bringing in the artistic influences around him. He showed how the twentieth century might have looked had World War I not happened. With his Oriental motifs, bright colors, and playfully anarchic approach, he was right on the artistic trend against the dark, structured urban culture of nineteenth-century Europe. But after World War I, he like many others thought life could go back to way it was, and he was identified with the old world rather than the new. Poiret's big failing was not to understand (or not want to understand) what America was about. He felt that the old-world system could survive unchanged in the new world. This failing seems to presage a lot of what has gone on since. Not being able to see that the world is changing around you and not adapting to the change is a fatal evolutionary mistake, one that the business of fashion design may have been guilty of for years. But what is the necessary change?

Chanel, the Modernist Businesswoman

Coco Chanel brought in the much-needed change at the beginning of the twentieth century. Even before World War I, her modern simplicity provided a new direction. There was no pretense to ownership of a time gone by in her work. In that sense she was perhaps the only real modernist of the designers featured in this book. Her outlook was very practical, and businesslike, and yet it was by following her initial instinct of what a woman really needed that allowed her to create a feminine image for the twentieth century.

The question of whether the twenty-first century should offer women something new does not seem to be asked very loudly. The need for a break from the past that seems to be underlying much of today's fashion chaos is not addressed directly—or even at all. One might say there is no demand from the clientele for such change, but it could then be pointed out that neither was there any "demand" for Coco Chanel initially. The need becomes obvious when the solution to the problems it poses presents itself. Fashion generally works on the principle of discovery, and discovery implies a moment of recognition of an existent truth. What will we recognize as the new mode of dress when it arrives?

Schiaparelli, the Artist

Schiaparelli's model may not shed much light on this question. Like Poiret, she adopted the artistic stance and, in doing so, firmly established the high-fashion-designer-as-artist image. Just like Poiret, her artistic vision was too narrow in the end, and her vision and her business could not be sustained once the world moved forward from the place where that statement had resonance. However, it may well be that our time is ripe for a healthy dose of strangeness, and the Eastern nations that are taking up Western capitalist commerce with gusto may eventually react as a whole in a nationalist, traditionalist way and turn back to their own "lost time" for reference. The Western world may at that point find itself on the receiving end of some very unfamiliar fashions indeed.

Dior, the Reactionary Revolutionary

After World War II, the surreal intensity of "Schiap" was not what the women of Europe and America wanted to see. It fell to Christian Dior to take fashion back to safer, less aggressive places of femininity and glamour. His amplification of the reactionary fashions that had begun to surface in the 1930s was exactly what seemed to be needed. This kind of reactionary revolution is perhaps less likely in the twenty-first century, as the reactionary is commonplace, and the emergence of a singular authority in the manner of Worth or Dior seems unlikely, at least in the West, for now.

Saint Laurent, the Last Haute Couture Dictator

The genius of Yves Saint Laurent was to react to the real growth market, one that didn't want to be identified with Dior's bourgeois femininity. But against what would a disaffected generation rebel, and how? Saint Laurent redirected the styles away from the preciousness of Dior, but with that high fashion lost control and the center dissolved. Perhaps what punk styles attempted is the only way out. What may be required is a complete recontextualization of designer fashion. Before we look at the previously stated questions in some detail, let's look at the catalyst to all of the scenarios that may play out in the decades to come.

New Empires on the Horizon

FIGURE 12.8. A model shows off the latest from Chinese designer Guo Pei during the China Fashion Week in Beijing, China, in November 2007.

It seems the gravitational center of the world's economy is moving away from the Western Hemisphere, or at least diffusing over the globe. Russia, India, and China are all now key players in what happens next. The incredibly rapid development of capitalist mechanisms, replete with massive, conspicuous consumption has turned all three into places of great potential for the manufacturers of luxury goods. This point was brought vividly home at London Fashion Week in the beginning of 2008, when counted among media in attendance were both *Vogue Russia* and *Vogue China*. These two titles would have been considered science fiction a generation earlier; now they were only 2 of 80 publications from Russia and East Asia at the shows. The interest from these markets was happily seen to compensate for the slowdown in buyer attendance from America, where the weakened dollar was reducing interest in European imports.[4]

One system goes; another takes its place. To assume that the fashion system born at the Court of Empress Eugénie would continue without change seems absurd, and yet this is the premise on which the myth was resurrected after World War II. The European class system is gone, the economic model is gone, and the societal structure that allows the investing of authority in a few voices is also gone—but only from the Western Hemisphere. Out of Russia, China, and India, new versions of bourgeois society are emerging, basing their systems and fashions on the mythical media-model of Western society.

One of the difficulties of the discussion of this moment in the short history of high fashion is that much of the writing assumes a very Western, Eurocentric stance. The economic and political situation in the Western Hemisphere led to and supported the development of art and design, and much of what has happened in the past century and a half has been very focused on the experience of the ruling elites of this culture. Now it is clear that economic and political developments require a widening of the focus of this examination.

If high-fashion design has indeed come to an impasse in the Western Hemisphere, as the twentieth-century model of society transforms, then perhaps the arc of development will be seen elsewhere (Figure 12.8).

Currently China is in the position that the United States, France, and Britain were in at the beginning of this story. Massive industrialization is taking place, with an attendant transition from agrarian to urban culture. An affluent class is rising quickly, and wages in the manufacturing sector are rising, slowly but steadily. The technological sector has developed in the past two decades, and decades-old film and fashion industries are beginning to make themselves felt worldwide. Meanwhile, Russia, more so than the other countries of the former Soviet Union, is developing its own version of robber barons, in a remarkable reversal of roles. Russia's transition is, on the surface at least, rockier than China's, as China's move to industrial capitalism is managed by a centralized government, attempting to balance centralized authority with free-market operations. Russia, meanwhile, suffers from mismanagement and tensions between factions of an oligarchic elite, who are battling for control of the country's immense resources. India seems to be steadily on an upward path, nothing is certain. In the late 1980s, writers of thoughts such as these would have bet everything on the rise of Japan. For a while, Japanese fashion was the "next big thing." With the older generations of Japanese affecting a very conservative high-fashion stance, the youth were appropriating elements from everywhere to create intensely new and exciting fashions. The two together were producing a sense of style that was seen to be the model for future developments worldwide. Japanese designers such as Rei Kawakubo and Isse Miyake became the ones to watch, while Chanel, YSL, and Paul Smith, to name a few, made huge profits in Japan. Science-fiction and cyberpunk film and literature feature a Japanese-influenced culture to an almost clichéd degree. But Japan's economic boom did not last; the bubble burst, and Japan has not recovered. Following the money, attention has moved elsewhere.

Predicting the future is not something I would gladly propose to do, given that the past has been so spectacularly unsuccessful at it, but imagining scenarios based on previous events may allow us to approach the future with more confidence, and with Chapter 13, we will look at projected scenarios based on the arcs of our designers and the emerging global situation. Perhaps we can see what new fashion paradigm may grow from the new capitalism of the twenty-first century.

ENDBOX

Two Madmen in Paris, Maybe Just a Little Bit Lost

Many fashion houses find it profitable to offer parallel realities: clothes made for the runway and the red carpet, and a second, modified group called the commercial line. Some houses like Prada and Comme des Garçons make a point of selling what they put on the runway, partly in the belief that customers are too well informed, thanks to digital technology, to accept a toned-down alternative.

Though fashion journalists admit the importance of commercial lines, and even understand their increasing role in a global marketplace, they have a see-no-evil policy about them and feel a childlike sense of disappointment when such clothes pop up on a top designer's runway. There is still the belief that a little stage madness can transcend everything.

For this reason alone, the collections of John Galliano and Alexander McQueen were noteworthy. They are true madmen of genius, and individually they have changed our notions about clothes. Mr. Galliano has also done a great deal for LVMH Moët Hennessy Louis Vuitton and its sister company, Dior, creating exciting fashion that made front-page news.

But now these designers seem in limbo, and it's having a decidedly dampening effect on the Paris spring collections. "I feel it's the end of something," an American editor said, a bit dramatically, after the Galliano show. Other guests were not willing to believe their eyes: two-tone strapless party dresses with awkwardly draped bodices and ribbon-embroidered beige suits with a stiffened net flower exploding from a shoulder. They would defy anyone familiar with Mr. Galliano's style to guess they were his.

Maybe the explanation for this sedate mainstream turn is self-evident: Mr. Galliano has to try something different because his clothes aren't generating the numbers the company wants. A designer doesn't throw out a successful formula.

Source: Cathy Horyn. The *New York Times*. October 9, 2006.

DISCUSSION POINTS

1. Can history end?
2. Can fashion end?
3. Can you define what "end" means in both of these cases?

CHAPTER 13

We Are Caught

Trend Spotting in the Early Twenty-first Century

In this chapter we consider the different paths the world of high fashion may take, given the history we've seen and current conditions. We consider possible futures that may arise from the current state of affairs. After a discussion of the state of high fashion and trends in the first decade of the century, we look at the elements that define trend movements in our time and speculate about the possible effect of technology in the years to come. Finally, we consider a few scenarios of where all this may lead.

Signifiers: The First Decade and the Next

Examining the development of fashion over the last quarter century reveals that the primary characteristics of high-fashion design in the late twentieth and early twenty-first

FIGURE 13.1. Mid-to-late twentieth century influences in the first decade of the twenty-first century dress.

centuries were its enormous diversity (Figure 13.1) and its reliance on previous periods for inspiration. With no linear progression to attach to, trends head in every direction they can, and the knowledge of trend development also allows marketers and designers to attempt to manipulate fashions in order to be seen as authorities and trendsetters, rather than followers. There is a constant search for the "next big thing," and a coveted mantle of authority is placed on those who can correctly indentify this elusive beast, even if only briefly. The search for the future of fashion generally results in any number of equally probable statements being uttered each season, most of which are then amended or ignored in the next round, and no one seems to ever be any closer to any clarity at all.

As the fashion cycle dissolved into this cycle of self-reference and quick turnaround, "trend" became the buzzword around the definition of each season's designs. Given that no one knows where anything is going, this is really not surprising as a "trend" is a direction of things, and therefore easier to spot and easier to shrug off if it changes. When high-fashion catwalk looks show up in the malls two weeks after their appearance in Paris, London, or Milan, and new looks show up every couple of months without any necessarily visible through-line, a direction is all one can ask for. A definitive style is impossible to spot. To be in the know is to know which of these mini-fashions is accepted in the right circles and which is not. In a strange way, this in itself contributes to the exclusivity of high fashion. The level of expertise required to keep track of the trends from one season to the next requires a stylist or full-time devotion to the fashion press. As one critic wrote of the Paris shows in October 2007:

> So the mood in Paris last week was uncertain and a little bewildered. . . . [W]hile there is no one mood, no single direction to be gleaned from Paris this season, this does not mean that all outfits are to be deemed equal. Far from it. There will still be a fashion in-crowd—it's just that this season, you can't hope to join the club simply

> by buying the key piece, the puffball skirt or mustard-coloured jumper. The look of the moment is as exclusive as ever: it's just going to be harder than ever to pin down.[1]

Where Are the Trends?

Largely, the lack of any major trends, apart from that of general dissolution, may be ascribed to the following.

First of all, very few of the trends touted point to the future; most are a return to some past, either real or mythologized. The trick of trend spotting—and creating—then requires picking the most viable past. This can go on for only so long because a return to the past is inevitably a dead end. Once the fascination with a particular period diminishes, the next move must be in a direction far enough away from it, or else the move isn't considered a significant artistic statement, and the design is criticized as unoriginal, weak, or worse. This leads to a complete lack of linear progression, without which there is no trend to be seen.

Secondly, it is one thing to identify a trend and follow it. To develop it is another type of endeavor altogether and requires a stable base on which to work. In design, this may mean working through several iterations of a product in order to establish the movement of the trend and then bring it into a new state that moves the trend forward. Today's market does not have the patience for this process, primarily because it is expensive. Large corporations such as those that own Chanel, Dior, and YSL look at quarterly balance sheets and have little patience for subdivisions that lose money over several quarters. The demand for the apparel division to turn a profit becomes too intense for any kind of careful development of a vision. With the intense competition in the high-fashion sphere, the need to make a big splash overrides any thoughts of an artistic development that would continue until such a time that the designer has established a following. Slow and steady is not a method that modern marketing has tended to operate within. If a collection does not sell, the requirement will be to do something different, more often than not the opposite, to see whether this is how the market can be captured.

Also, the demand for originality of vision in the education and critique of high-fashion designers has led to designers staking out a claim to a certain territory as soon as they can. They establish themselves (or are established, through being brought in to design for an established label) as a certain type, identified through references to the past. Their collections are then quickly categorized as a specific statement geared toward a specific image. Having established a strong identity, either individually or by having one delivered, the young designers then must either stay within the parameters of that identity or make a dramatic break. This then requires a re-identification, which means that the "image" being sold now must be reframed for marketing. This can be extremely difficult and costly in the case of established brands. Only at the moment when a strong enough designer comes in to an established house can such an image overhaul take place, such as when Tom Ford took over at Gucci. But do that too often and the established house loses its aura.

As a result of these factors, the authority of designers is greatly diminished, still further decreasing the likelihood that a strong trend will develop from their work. With less authority, the voices must be louder or the congregation smaller. Either way, any large-scale trend is made increasingly difficult. We also saw, in the discussion of the ritualistic aspects of designer fashion, the diminishing of authority leads to diminished relevance and the increased ability of challengers to step up to authority positions. The multiple voices of equal authority will then prohibit any pronounced direction to develop, with each voice pulling the attention of the audience away from any common understanding. This has a multiplying effect, in that the less authoritative designers are, the less clear their role is and the less daunting the prospect of becoming one seems. Thus, the number of voices increases still until none is clearly heard.

What Is Designing, and Who Is a Designer?

The authority of the high-fashion designer is undercut further by the confusion in the public mind about what exactly constitutes "designing." Partly this is due to the confusion created by licensing, which began early, and partly by what later became known as branding. So effectively executed by Ralph Lauren and Tommy Hilfiger, the idea of placing the designer's name on objects entirely unrelated to clothing had already begun during Poiret's day. The name of the designer became a "brand" that could be applied to anything at all. The brand was the designers name reified—that is, turned into an object.

The late 1970s, which seem to be a watershed period for high fashion in so many ways, brought a new twist to the branding game when the idea of celebrity branding took hold.

It became clear to marketers that no longer did the name on the label need to be that of an established designer. Given the level of celebrity adulation in increasing media, a celebrity would carry the same authority. Placed on denim jeans, Gloria Vanderbilt's name created "designer jeans" by associating a stylish name with a product that had no relationship at all to the world of high fashion. Vanderbilt, along with the Jordache brand, popularized the term *designer jeans* (Figure 13.2). They were fitted and cut differently from the standard jeans, which hadn't changed much since the nineteenth century, but to equate them with a sense of couture was absurd. In fashion, however, logic is rarely an issue. The lack of fashion authority by the 1970s allowed the art of design to become "styling."

FIGURE 13.2. Designer jeans: Gloria Vanderbilt's 2008 campaign harks right back to the label's beginning.

The next development was inevitably that couture would continue to lose its cachet as its qualities got confused in public perception with the label itself. If "designer" meant "label"—as in the name on the back pocket of the jeans—then to "design" was not about the creation of anything, but merely about placing your mark on something. This was where America really shone, and by the time the century ended, it was a commonplace for pop stars and actresses to try their hand at "designing" by choosing looks put together by a stylist and branding them. The media treatment of these "designs" allows the public perception of this action to be the same as the work of, say, John Galliano (who could be said to be doing the opposite at Dior by placing his designs under the brand). What this misperception creates is again the weakened authority of the designer through sheer overload of "designer." The labels and brands are fluid in their identity, and to the marketers, this is in many cases a good thing. The harder the labels are to pin down, the easier they are to adapt to the market. More anonymity on the design side doesn't matter, because the brand is all. Worrying about the 500-odd customers of couture won't bring in enough sales to sustain the large corporations of fashion, so if the sizzle of high fashion can be sold without having to have an actual high-fashion designer behind it, so much the better.

The Message from the Red Carpet

In the twenty-first century, we are all joined by global brands and logos. These are the identities that bind people all over the globe to a single culture of commerce. Those who would say that this is not enough to bind people together would have to consider that even when high-fashion design was coming into its own in the nineteenth century, it was already an artificial construct. Charles Worth is romanticized, as are those who came after him, but we have already seen that the wearing of Worth's designs was as much about the wearing of Worth the designer, once he was established as a "brand." The difference today is that the message is much more overt, being completely visible and acknowledged. Worth would never have considered placing his label visibly on a garment, but then he didn't need to. His position was clear enough and secure while the sanctity bestowed on him by the Empress Eugénie was maintained. It was known "who was wearing whom," and the message of the fashions was clear. Worth gowns were a medium that radiated a message of the existence of a secure and affluent high society to itself.

So, what message —if any—does high fashion deliver 150 years later? "Status" is the obvious answer, but that unleashes other questions. Status implies a hierarchy, and to use clothing to signal status means that the wearer of the garment is identifying with a level of society through the garment. The garment therefore must have an element that is available only to persons of that level, even though the signals need be recognizable by other levels in order to place the person correctly. The recent return of Gilded-Age-levels of ostentatious display (such as Versace's helicopters) makes this level an easy one to place, but for most of the market, the signals have been unclear for a while and getting murkier. The difficulty with placing high fashion in modern society is that this function has become distributed to any number of other commodities, and that the ownership of sanctified labels has not been very exclusive of late. The availability of products bearing various logos sees to that, not to mention the fact that ready-to-wear styles are generally derivatives of high fashion, if not simulated high fashion, and that the significance of the difference is often lost, even on the consumers themselves. The status value of high fashion may therefore be perceived only by a fairly small group of people who identify with each other through designer clothing and accessories. The high fashion seen on celebrities has its own status value, of course, but as a red-carpet moment is essentially another performance; the status is temporary. A film star's status doesn't rely on such signaling anyway, and the red-carpet faux pas can be equally counterproductive.

High fashion's status message is of course more subtle than the straightforward wearing of the garments as in the time of Worth. The message is contextual, especially after the 1960s and 1970s, when the political message of fashion design reached its inverted climax. High fashion has been disengaged from politics since then to the extent that making political statements through high-fashion clothing is seemingly impossible, as only through its negation can fashionable clothing make a statement.

What Purpose Does High-Fashion Design Serve?

High-fashion design cannot, at the beginning of the twenty-first century, be said to contribute to nationalistic or political purposes, given that its products are distributed all over the world and are consumed on all sides of whatever political divides exist. One could say that the desires it creates serve to increase demands for luxury goods and thereby keep the wheels of capital turning by encouraging commerce. This could be said to be a political purpose, but that is problematic, as it doesn't differentiate it from any other manufactured product and therefore goes into a realm of larger-scale economic politicizing that isn't really helpful to a discussion of this sort. If serving the purpose of commerce is political, then so be it, but that waters the statement down to an almost meaningless degree, given that consumerism is the driving force for nearly all nation's economies.

Given the amount of attention that is paid to high fashion, its purpose in society actually seems rather limited. Let us look at its phases throughout the "hundred years of fashion" and see whether this is indeed so.

Holding the discipline today up to Worth, we find that, yes, there is an element of societal control through exclusivity, but there are no "Worths" today, nor are there empresses. There are designers and muses, but high-fashion design does not serve the political purpose of a regime except to further oil the wheels of commerce. Indeed, after Worth, that direct connection was no more (with, as we have seen, one brief, notable exception in Jackie Kennedy). Today's designer cannot be said to resemble Poiret either. His willful breaking of molds is not to be seen, although the implications of hedonism are in many cases there. However, Poiret's revitalizing links to art, and his orientalisms, were aimed toward creating a mode of being in society that high fashion finds difficult to achieve today. We live in a time of cynical and ironic dispositions. Anyone bringing such statements to the table today would need to couch them in ironic or self-deprecating terms. Poiret's achievement in freeing women of the technical constraints of dress was unique. Parallels in this regard for today are hard to conceive of.

Chanel is probably the closest parallel to today's designers at work. Her businesslike attitude, and her modernizing of Edwardian fashions brought in the sensibilities with which designers have worked since. However, her revolutionizing simplicity has again no parallel in the business of fashion design at the beginning of the twenty-first century, and the same can be said about Schiaparelli's art connections. So it is only when we get to Dior that we recognize some similarities. Today's situation may perhaps be understood somewhat by placing it alongside his circumstances: The discipline requires the creative individual, but the creative individual is too small to deal with the global proportions of the business. Furthermore, an individual designer working from his creative impulses is inevitably feeding off his or her own environment, being inspired by concerns and movements in his or her immediate community. Unless the experiences are all the more universal, it is highly unlikely that the spirit the designer taps into is shared by clients worldwide.

In the disconnect of the years immediately following World War II, Dior's fashions took hold by appealing to a sense of a lost past regained. Just as Worth had appealed to a past age and Poiret had rejected Chanel after World War I, the designs looked back to a myth of a time of more security. Dior's silhouettes recalled the corsets and crinolines of Worth, and his extravagant use of fabrics denied the austerity of the postwar years. The fragmentation of Western culture at the end of the twentieth century, with its lack of historical continuity and decentralization of culture, certainly provided impetus for a return to familiar pasts. Revisiting each past decade individually and en masse, designers of the turn of the century have certainly made a large effort to identify what was good about the past, even when the past they are holding up is a nostalgic fabrication.

It is interesting to note that Dior's myth has now lasted five times longer than the decade his reign as "King of Fashion" spanned. He, as the archetypical fashion designer of the twentieth century was, as we saw, the last of the nineteenth-century designers (Figure 13.3). Perhaps we need to see a divide appear, such as the one between Dior and Saint Laurent, or better still: between Jean Worth and Poiret. Perhaps there is a designer on the hori-

FIGURE 13.3. Christian Dior, "the King of Fashion," with his models at a fashion show.

zon who can synthesize early-twenty-first-century global street fashion and deluxe apparel in a way that provides a new vision of how we dress. Before we consider scenarios to suggest what might be needed for such a transition to take place under today's circumstances, let us consider what the early twenty-first century is historically, so far.

{ LOOKING FORWARD LOOKING BACK }
The Fifth Shift

The history of the hundred years' fashion contains four societal shifts: its own beginning, two major break-points after 30- to 40-year intervals, and the shift of its own ending. Clues as to where we are headed may be found here, as each shift involves new economics and a change in clientele and market demands.

First was the relatively slow shift from monarchical agrarian society to industrialized city dwelling, which allowed first for an amplification of courtly society and then of manufacturing to answer increased demand for luxury goods. This shift brought Charles Worth.

Then, during Worth's time, French society shifted from monarchical to democracy driven by industrial wealth. This amplified trends and led to an international style that molded Poiret. Mixed with modernism and American wealth, the international industrial society produced Chanel and Schiaparelli and finally, in reaction to too much modernism, Christian Dior.

Aprés Dior marked the third shift, as the last vestiges of aristocratic society became irrelevant, and youth culture became the driving force in an international system. The American era had begun, and Paris produced Yves Saint Laurent to acknowledge the generational change.

And then, in the late 1970s, came the end of the "hundred years." This fourth shift has international fashion becoming transnational, then global and corporate, leading to fragmentation.

And here we are, seemingly at the end of the American era. America is becoming the old world. We must ask: What does the old world of the first decade of the twenty-first century represent that the new world will react to? Who will come along, look at the current system and styles, and, like the Shah to Emperor Napoleon, say, "You must change all that!" Taking the reactions of Poiret to Jean Worth, Chanel and Schiaparelli to Poiret, and Saint Laurent to Dior, one might wonder what we have in our day to produce the same departure.

Technology Ascendant

The early years of the twenty-first century have been a time of transition and shift. The economic centers of the world are moving east. The political map of the world is being redrawn to a north-south axis, and religious fundamentalism is on the rise, along with nationalism. None of these movements were widely anticipated a generation ago, and the strength of their trends is debated, although only as a matter of degree. All of these conditions point to an increased tension and polarization until a new mode is settled on.

One transition that was foreseen was the increase in technological capability, although even that was underestimated. Technological and scientific discovery has accelerated exponentially, that is, the acceleration is speeding up as it goes. The futurist Ray Kurzweil, for example, has suggested that this acceleration will continue until it reaches what he terms "the singularity." This he defines as the moment when artificial intelligence develops to such a degree that computers surpass human brains in cognitive power, with the effect that humans no longer fully understand the operations of their own technology. He predicts that this will take place before 2050.[2]

There is good reason to believe that given no unforeseen global catastrophe technology will accelerate at such a rapid pace that the equivalent of the developments of the past 100 years will take place in the next 20. In other words, the changes the twentieth century saw, from development of the first automobiles to exploration on Mars, will be equaled many times over for the next generation.

Changes in communications, transportation, medical science, manufacturing, and more may render the experiential scene of 20 years hence as different as that of the year 2000 compared to the year 1900. Constant, instant connectivity and information flow will continue the transition into McLuhan's Global Village. Technological change means societal change. No historical period undergoing such development can remain constant in its identity. There will be change; that much is certain. But where will it be coming from?

Historical Parallels: Are We There Yet?

Perhaps other moments in history may parallel these times and may shed light on where fashion design is going. There are historical periods when a culture has developed a very elaborate and organized fashion system that has then turned in on itself until the only way out was a radical transformation of norms.

FIGURE 13.4. As the Roman Empire fell apart, its courtly fashions ossified into a heavily ritualized form.

As the Roman Empire grew, so did its fashion. Each new territory conquered, each tribe encountered added a—sometimes momentary—change to the high fashions of Rome (Figure 13.4). Changes in hairstyles, for example, became rapid enough for marble busts to have interchangeable sections for the hair, during the final years. The Romans, as their Empire declined, took up more and more of the "barbarian" fashions until the East Roman Empire ossified into an Eastern hierarchical court. Societal structure was embalmed in rigid dress codes. Meanwhile, the western part of the Empire was gradually overrun by the tribes from the north, and the cumbersome fashions of Rome were supplanted by more practical tunics and layers. In other words, a simplification of clothing followed the dissolution of society.

In the late Middle Ages fashions lost all sense of proportion as an extremely wealthy class of feudal lords competed in fifteenth-century conspicuous consumption, displaying how much fabric, dye, and embroidery they could afford to let go to waste. Hems dragged on the ground off horseback, shoes grew so long as to impede motion, and headdresses ballooned into caricature. When the first hints of urban modernity began to appear, this could no longer go on. The demands of larger societal units with more frequent interaction required a simplification of styles, and the styles transformed into much more practical forms in an extremely brief period of time.

Marie Antoinette's fashion games began this story, but in the absence of strong central authority, no such games are played for power today. The French revolutionaries, who put an end to Marie Antoinette's life and reign, reacted to the overloaded fashions of the French court by "modernizing" their fashions. They stripped their garb of any decoration and suggestion of aristocracy such as lace or embroidery, with the most extreme elements doing away with all color as well. Male fashion was transformed into dandyism, where cut and fit became the touchstones. Elegant structure overtook decoration, in other words. There were moments of political symbolism in revolutionary fashion, when women would wear red ribbons around their neck to symbolize where the guillotine would cut their head off, and the sansculotte, who in the manner of many a revolutionary since, adopted workingman's clothing.

Each of these examples contains elements that may leave a thought or two about where fashion in the Western world may head in the first decades of the twenty-first century. The overarching thought is a simple one: In a world of change, fashion always (eventually) reacts. A society that has lost its bearings may wander around for a while, going in circles, but once it finds how to move outside the circle, dramatic changes happen.

Scenarios

A fairly safe bet from where we are standing is that high fashion will continue to follow the money, and this is probably the key to its revitalization. The Western world is in transition (some would say crisis) and needs to be shown the way out. The money has been followed to three main locations: Russia, India, and China. The overall effect until the end of 2008 had been an upward trend in profits of luxury brands in an otherwise difficult world economy. Bottega Veneta, a brand owned by Gucci, showed, for example, a 32 percent sales increase in early 2008, opening stores in Vilnius, the Ukraine, Shanghai, Beijing, Moscow, Dubai, and Mumbai.[3] However, the world-wide economic crisis that developed in the fall of 2008 led to forecasts of a downturn in the European and American luxury market.

Initially it was believed that this would be offset my continuing growth in the emerging markets in Russia, Asia, and Brazil. But the crisis spread through the globally-connected financial systems and soon these regions were experiencing a slowdown of their own. China's economic uprising, thought to be more powerful than most, came to a grinding halt in late 2008 when orders for goods for Western markets became greatly reduced. Not having an internal market that could buffer the loss of business, factories began closing causing massive unemployment.

The Russian Scene

China, India, and Russia are dramatically different in terms of history and culture, and Russia stands out specifically in that it had modernized to a further degree, earlier in the twentieth century. However, years of Communism left its systems and infrastructure in a bit of a mess, and with the privatization of its industries, wealth was gathered into the hands of a small, elite class of people. With 1 in 12 of the world's billionaires in Russia, this relatively small section of the Russian population has made a large impact on the luxury industry as the reaction to all the wealth was to go west and buy everything they could to create as ostentatious a lifestyle as possible. All Western fashions and luxury goods became must-haves for the new Russian upper class, and recent art auctions have seen record prices set by Russian bidders. The Russian upper class has essentially joined the Western fashion system and gave it a much needed injection of wealth. The effect of a parallel resurgence of Russian nationalism could bring a demand of specific "Russian" styles.

The Chinese Scene

China and India have been moving rapidly to modernize their cultures, and now, through increased technology and education, they are reforming as an urban culture in the same way Europe did in Worth's day. The question is this: Will they go through the same social patterns? Once the incredibly swift urbanization is over, will they begin to experience the same growing pains as, say, nineteenth-century Paris? The factory closures of late 2008 and the resulting spike in unemployment led to protests and sit-ins and Chinese authorities feared riots. The dark side of the industrialized free-market system was sparking a disillusionment in 2008 that was no less than that of a century before, although no rise in anarchist sentiment could be seen by the end of that year. Will China have a restless working class, joined in their restlessness by a disillusioned middle class against the overly wealthy and ostentatious upper class? More to the point of our discussion, will this restlessness produce a wealth of artistic statements and radical design? Some sort of street answer to the designer helicopters, perhaps?

FIGURE 13.5. Chinese teenagers in fashionable clothing.

Furthermore, will Chinese youth need a rebellion of their own against the staid old culture, in the same way the '50s led to the '60s in the United States (Figure 13.5)? If China begins to form an active artistic counterculture, all bets are off. The commodification of culture has already begun in China, with artisans becoming artists in a gallery system. This may simply not go anywhere. Any burgeoning counterculture may simply be bought and packaged in the new commercial society. However, if the Chinese artists go the same way as the French in the nineteenth century, they are now right on the verge of an explosive period. But either way, a professional artist class, comfortable with commodity culture, will lead to a professional designer class, based on local modes and systems. This is not to say that these don't already exist, but what is there seems more to be a version of what has been imported from the West. In order for China to fully become a force, it will need to develop its own from-the-grassroots-up system, and odds are that it will.

With the increase in production of goods for personal use, a status system of conspicuous consumption follows in a commodity culture. Once the current generation of old-guard communists leaves the scene, interesting things may begin to happen, when China will develop a class system of fashion and design, based on Chinese tradition. Currently, however, the Chinese are adopting commercial culture and Western styles as fast as possible. There seems to be such a rush to modernity that the styles and methods are being appropriated without any attempt to blend them with local traditions. There is very likely a tipping point when Chinese fashion culture will reach a point of no return, and Chinese designers will design the styles that are being sold and worn without regard for local identity or tradition. This point is very likely within two generations of urbanization, when the "old life" begins to be forgotten. If designing fashions takes serious hold in China before then, it is highly likely that we will see a shift in fashions worldwide. Chinese designers will begin to design Chinese ideas for Chinese manufacturers to be sold to a Chinese economy instead of a pastiche of what is being manufactured for Western consumption.

The Indian Scene

India, like China, has an enormous past to work from. Unlike China, India already has a blossoming fashion and design scene. It just hasn't made it to the West, with Indian markets choosing instead to appropriate Western fashions in the same manner as the Chinese. Indian influences in film, music, and style have been creeping into Western culture, and one would expect an increase in flow back and forth. However, the tilt is toward the West, and if India is to become a fashion influence on the world, something more than the incidental input will be needed.

What needs to happen is the reaching of a tipping point, where the cultural influence begins to flow the other way. India has already attempted this on several occasions, with a middle-class interest in cultural preservation preceding the time of separation from British rule after World War II. The nationalist sentiments became most visible in literature but extended to visual arts and cinema as well. However, high-fashion design in India, when it references tradition, has a flavor all its own and has not been able to mix with Western styles to any significant degree. It would seem that the economic shift toward India would need to be far greater than it is today for the wealthy customers to influence the direction of the Western brands. There would also need to be an upsurge in nationalistic identity, which would be reflected in choices of traditional influences in high fashion. With India's upper class generally accepting international styles as their fashion, and nationalist sentiments gearing toward the ethnic and religious rather than a pan-Indian, and therefore kept under control by the ruling parties, this may seem an unlikely development in the near future.

Questions about Possible Scenarios

One thing to remember is that all three of these cultures, the Chinese, Russian, and Indian, have extremely long historical memories. A decade here or there is not so much in a long history, and the emphasis on "the new thing" is less prevalent than in the rootless culture of the United States. Some questions to ask are the following:

- Will their main market be import or export while starting up? If their designs are for a domestic market, their tradition will shine stronger than if they cater to perceived "foreign" tastes. With a strong internal market, they may begin exporting the domestic styles. Otherwise, they will cater to the tastes of wherever they are selling to.
- Where is the money? If the money is in the hands of Western corporations, it is likely that Western markets will call the shots, no matter what. Whatever sells will be the direction things will take. The same holds if the money begins to be controlled primarily by non-Western corporations, and then a cultural tipping point may well follow, as long as local demand has not become accustomed to Western-influenced styles.
- Where is the sociological need? Do any of these three societies have any needs that resemble the situations we have examined in the West? Just as one might have inquired at the beginning of Worth's career: Who *needs* their fashion? What is the class system? Who are the icons? Who can anoint the accepted designers?

Jokers

When trying to predict how the cards will fall, it is always good to know that there are jokers in the deck. One must keep in mind that there are whole swaths of the world where high fashion just doesn't matter *all that much*, under current conditions. With increased technology, these areas could well become modernized, and then who knows what will happen? History happens. Britain was a small island in the Atlantic that became an Empire

FIGURE 13.6. The broken column at Place Vendôme. The column, with its statue of Napoleon I, was toppled by the Communards after the end of the Second Empire. The Place Vendôme was the center of Paris's fashion district.

that, through advanced technology, ruled over the entire globe in less than a century. Then that Empire fell apart even faster than it had come together. The Second Empire in France, which, at the height of its grandeur, allowed the Empress Eugénie to become the fashion icon of the Western world, collapsed within a decade of its high point. (See Figure 13.6.) It is amazing how history can quickly and cruelly twist itself around and equally amazing how hard it seems for a dominant culture to remember that. At the height of its reign, the high-fashion system that originated in Paris seemed invincible, and yet it has gone into its slow decline simply by the world changing around it.

Signs of Green

A point I have made several times before (and it's worth repeating) is that few predictions about the twenty-first century have actually come true (yet). There are always unintended events and consequences, and nothing is as linear as anyone imagines. But how to expect the unexpected? This is the key to trend spotting as the twenty-first century enters its second decade: to not only watch the styles as they arrive but to read the signs of politics and society. By keeping watch on the movements of markets and noting changes in the politics of class and wealth, one might see the structures that will define the movements of fashion. This may not eliminate surprises, but it will at least show from which direction the unknown will arrive.

For example, the discussion of sustainability in design burst onto the scene in the first years of the new century after decades of association with counterculture politics. Was a point finally reached where the environmentalists of the 1960s had enough clout to make an impact? Was there a new generation that felt it was time to make their mark? Had a tipping point been reached when just enough people finally actually cared? Attitudes are slowly changing, and the politics of "green" are going mainstream. This could change everything. If "green" becomes fashionable among the trendsetters or if the mainstream population simply begins buying into sustainability, then the markets will adapt and follow the money. With the luxury brands following the money to the wasteful lifestyles of the super-rich, this has not seemed likely. The historical record is not on the side of the environmentalists, and conspicuous consumption will probably continue to win out over responsibility. There is a scenario, however, that may play out between the "old world" of the West and the new money of the East that relies on the inner politics of upper-class social distinction. Perhaps some historical irony will be seen and "green" will become an expensive status symbol for the "old money" of the West, while the new money of the rising economies takes on the proscribed role of upper-class ostentation. With high fashion and deluxe goods being strong elements of the language of class distinction, perhaps this is how the old money will distinguish itself from the new. All it would take is for environmentalism to lose its last remaining overtones of eccentricity and hippie-ness is for wealthy customers to begin demanding it of high-fashion design firms, or for the high-end design firms to make it the cachet of their brand. Incongruous as it may seem, it would take only one high-powered client or one profitable firm to start the trend. As soon as someone began to profit, the rest would follow. To expect high fashion to become the opposite of the wastefulness of consumer society may be too much irony to expect even from this history, but this would definitely be one of the signs to watch for.

With the bottom fallen out of the housing and stock market in 2008, investors still needed to put their money somewhere. These were indications that the next "hot" market for venture capital would be "clean tech" or "green tech" investments. If "green" becomes the next financial hot spot, then this would very quickly translate into trends in accessories and apparel. "Green fashion" could easily become a status symbol if "green tech" becomes the next high-profit area. It would presumably begin on the U.S. West Coast and quickly make its way around the fashionable world from there.

ENDBOX

Designer Bows Out in Style—of the '80s

Fashion designers aren't known for having a sense of humour about themselves and Valentino, who held his final show in Paris yesterday having announced that he will retire after 45 years in the business, is probably one of the least self-mocking around. This is a man who will tolerate only certain women, such as Gwyneth Paltrow, wearing jeans in his presence—and only if they have just had their hair professionally blow-dried.

So it was either a show of heretofore untapped irony or simply a lack of self-awareness that made the designer close his final show with the song Kiss by Prince, with Valentino taking his bow as the singer belted out: "You don't have to be rich to rule my world"—an odd final cry from Valentino, considering that is precisely what one needs to be in his universe. This show emphasised that.

It would be easy to dismiss Valentino as the in-house dressmaker for the princesses of European countries one didn't even know had royal families. That is part of the story, but few designers can cut as elegantly as he, or make a red-carpet dress that is guaranteed not to land an actress in the feared column of "Oscar fashion disaster".

Because of these strengths, a recent poll in a US magazine showed that Valentino is the third most recognized luxury brand in the increasingly important Far East market, beaten only by Rolex and Lacoste.

But for his final show, Valentino made the bizarre decision that instead of emphasising these modern strengths he would remind people of his '80s matchy-matchy heyday. Cue endless cocktail dresses with matching coats, heels and handbags. Dresses were given a Dynasty twist with puffball trims and giant rosettes, which might have looked great on Ivana Trump in 1987, but seem less appealing now.

Every '80s cliché was on show: cocktail dresses with giant polkadots, boxy jackets and frilled long dresses that made the models look like lumbering mermaids.

If ever there was an argument for why a designer needs to retire, this was it. In a recent interview in Time magazine Valentino claimed that he would like his successor to be Tom Ford, Nicolas Ghesquière or Alexander McQueen, all bizarre choices, being far too modern. Fortunately, others felt the same way and Alessandra Facchinetti, who was briefly at Gucci and less of a wild card, has been named as his successor.

Source: Hadley Freeman. *Guardian*. October 4, 2007.

Discussion Points

1. Why was it necessary that the successor to Valentino not be "too modern"?
2. Why is it important to not be an "Oscar fashion disaster"?
3. What is the relationship between the Oscars and high-fashion apparel?

CHAPTER 14

Thresholds

Our story does not have an end, nor should it. High-fashion design has been in a liminal state, hovering between the past and future, for decades, but this is not an ending; it is a transition. We have seen the discipline carried by six of its most iconic and mythical designers from its origins at the court of Louis Napoleon and the Empress Eugénie. For each of Worth, Poiret, Chanel, Schiaparelli, Dior, and Saint Laurent, a number of others could have been discussed in detail, but in the grand scheme, these six drove our story through its stages. Other designers, fascinating and affirming as their inclusion would have been, can be seen as being integral to their stage of the discipline's evolution if these six are considered archetypes of the high-fashion designer of each period, as much creating their world and being formed by it.

Where Have We Been?

Starting in Paris during the tumultuous realignment of society that was the nineteenth-century in France, we saw high-fashion design become a profession serving the needs of an entrenched upper class in need of legitimacy and a solid projection of identity. The discipline was founded there on a principle of conservatism and reactionary politics. The Age of Worth, having set the standard for couture and created the image of the *couturier,* was then abruptly interrupted when the society it helped create crumbled and was swept away.

Worth: The Original Couturier

FIGURE 14.1. Charles Worth projecting an artistic image in his Rembrandt cap.

Charles Worth created the original type. Myth-maker extraordinaire, he, more than anyone else, is responsible for the image of the fashion designer as a temperamental bourgeois artiste. How calculated a move this was is hard to tell, as documentary evidence is not available and Worth was notoriously careful about revealing anything about himself. The Wagnerian and Rembrandt-like stance and attire in his portraits certainly tell their story (Figure 14.1). The stories of his attitude in the fitting room mainly come from his detractors, but he did cultivate a dictatorial air and, with his refusal to discuss his process, created the myth of the "magical" designer, conjuring up works in flights of inspiration.

Poiret: The Artiste

Paul Poiret stepped in with his wild vision of color and oriental mystique, shaking up the dusty backward look that the house of Worth had become. Poiret couldn't sustain his business or his vision and returned from World War I dislocated from the modernist vision that was changing everything. War or no, his disorientation was compounded by the arrival of American business practices and American consumers. Poiret could not understand why anyone would not want to be elegantly dressed by couturiers, misunderstanding the nature of American consumer culture, or at least refusing to acknowledge it. Poiret followed Worth's lead in the artiste department, while Chanel didn't care who saw her working intensely on her craft. Poiret reveled in being an "authority," but bristled at the American magazines and newspapers when they portrayed him as an oracle and had no tolerance for American sensibilities (or the lack thereof).

Chanel: The Haute Couture Revolutionary

Coco Chanel had no such problem. She embraced the emerging global culture, and if any high-fashion designer of the twentieth century can be called a true modernist, her career up to World War II would be the model. She outdid or at least equaled in her approach to women's wear anything that the architects and designers of industry were doing in the masculine enclaves, creating a style of clothing that has informed almost an entire century of women's elegance. Chanel and Schiaparelli both had little patience with the myth of couture, although "Schiap" reveled in the artistic. Chanel's contribution to the image was in the *hauteur* that seems to have been an integral part of her nature. Whether her disdain for everyone but Chanel may have been playacting in the French artistic mode is really neither here nor there. Her seriousness as a truly revolutionary designer is what counts, and her legacy may perhaps be the last one as far as the twentieth century is concerned. The complete transformation of not only silhouettes and structure but also of *approach* to women's fashion inside and out was as radical as any of the major changes in fashion of the preceding centuries.

Schiaparelli: The Experimenting Artist

Elsa Schiaparelli was no less influential to the design approach of the late twentieth century, but from a different perspective entirely (Figure 14.2). Her association with the avant-garde of art allowed her to bring an edge into women's fashion that Chanel shunned and Poiret had avoided. However, she, like Poiret, came out of World War II with her

FIGURE 14.2. Schiaparelli wearing a white dress with a white coq feather boa, 1932.

heart in the culture of prewar Europe and could not connect to the desires of postwar Europe, much less those of America.

Schiaparelli broke in a different direction from Chanel, and her contribution, while also strong, was more philosophical. She opened doors that would not be closed again. Without Schiap, fashion would have been a much duller place, and her more sculptural pieces opened up possibilities in designers' as well as in the public's minds that would later allow for more experimentation.

DIOR: INTERPRETER OF THE PAST

Dior's understanding of the desire to return to the past was already active in him in the prewar years, when he aligned himself with a group who turned away from the reigning artistic direction of Picasso and the Cubists. Despite the deceptively named "New Look," Dior's high fashion openly turned toward an imaginary past of Dior's childhood. Not that this kind of reactionary design hadn't been evident in the House of Worth's later years, but now the contrast with what was actually happening on the street and in society was such that two distinct worlds had formed. Maison Worth had a "living" aristocracy to dress that was expected to wear the uniform of conservative dress, but Dior was dressing his wasp-waisted women in yards of layered and structured fabric at the same time as "Beat" fashions were appearing on the streets. Fashion had become pure spectacle.

Dior continued the counter-trend that had begun to take shape before the World War II. In reclassifying women as little fancy things swathed in fabric, he enraged Chanel enough to bring her out of retirement, but he hit all the right notes, especially where it counted, in America's middle class. Through the power of media saturation and advertising, this new consumer powerhouse wanted a taste of European elegance, not modernist simplicity. So Chanel and Dior split the market until the market disappeared into fragments.

Saint Laurent: The Anti-Dior

Yves Saint Laurent swung the pendulum as Poiret had done, became the anti-Dior, and brought the happening world into high fashion. From there, there was nowhere else to go but into nonfunctional space. High fashion could not tolerate democratization, nor was there a basis for a reestablishment of the ritualistic approach, when the street-fashion invasion was also a part of a general questioning and dissolution of societal norms. Saint Laurent followed, almost regretfully it seems, the transition of Western society into an inverted pyramid of social influence. No longer would fashion be the exclusive domain of the upper class, and Saint Laurent created, followed, and contributed to the opening up of all subsequent possibilities. (See Figure 14.3.)

State of Play

We have seen the game played out, from the Second Empire through the fin de siècle revolutions of politics, class, and arts, followed by two world wars, and finally to social revolution, allowing the questioning of everything. High fashion answered all challenges until the

FIGURE 14.3. Yves Saint Laurent attends the opening of the Yves Saint Laurent Foundation on March 5, 2004, in Paris.

basis for its existence as strong class structure was finally obscured through the overload of commodities in our consumer culture. Now, with capitalist society having created a system of multinational market-states rather than political empires, we find, at a time that was meant to be the "end of history," that the road could be leading almost anywhere from here.

We are not able to disengage what is happening today from that larger historical procession. The economic transition that our fashion culture developed from may in fact be seen to be only now coming into its fulfillment, having begun to gather steam at the time Charles Worth was crossing the Channel to Paris. When the sanctification of Charles Worth became the solution to the fashion problems of Eugénie's court, the story had in fact been written all the way up to the eventual enshrinement of Saint Laurent at the Metropolitan Museum. As designs go into museums, so does the culture that created them. It is worth noting that among Warhol's iconographic portraits, such as those of Jackie and Marilyn, there is also a portrait of Saint Laurent.

We are supposedly all equally celebrated in this new age. Hierarchies of class, education, or (oddly enough) income do not stop anyone from indulging in some version of high fashion as long as the capability to buy and sell is there. The inequality that caused tensions on the streets of Paris during the Second Empire has been outsourced, and the laborer who creates the fashionable item has, in many cases, no idea what this thing looks like in its day-to-day environment or where it is going. The alienation is so complete that the fashionable accessory might be literally anything for all the impact it has politically. The astonishing contradiction of our post-industrial fashion society is that while the hippies won the fashion battles, the capitalists won the war.

Modernism

So, the hippies won the battles and yet we are all modernists now, supposedly choosing form according to function, and disregarding ritual and decoration. While women may be the true modernists still, the odd notion of an almost nonexistent men's fashion remains on the sidelines. This odd identity crisis is perhaps best exhibited by a fact such as this: It is, with one exception, not until the final chapter of this book that the men get a mention. Given that the emphasis is on the journey of high fashion and our main characters are the top couturiers of history, this is not fair, of course. Men's wear never was a "fashion" in the way women's fashion evolved after 1850. Men's wear *was* couture by default, but the aura created by Worth et al in Paris was never elaborated in the tailoring shops of London.

Modernists we may be, but are we *post*-modernists? High fashion has largely resisted modernity, and what postmodern games have been played, they are mainly that: games. Post-modernity is perhaps as nonexistent in fashion design as it is in industrial design. At best, one could perhaps talk about fashion design as being in a late-modern stage, but as high fashion seems to have generally dug in its heels at any thought of the modern age, this discussion may have to await further developments and a clarity that comes with historical distance. However, the constant resistance of high fashion to modernity begs the question of whether the discipline has ever really moved out of the methods and philosophy of its inception during France's Second Empire. (See Figure 14.4.)

Perhaps that is overstating the problem. Perhaps fashion has not achieved any kind of "post" anything, because it has never arrived at a point of establishing itself for long enough to create a presence against which the next wave can be firmly "post." Of course, punk tried and came very close. But punk fashion could not be translated into high fashion, and that was its strength and its *raison d'être*. McLaren's punk derivatives and Vivienne Westwood's resulting fashions notwithstanding, the fusion never happened. However, punk opened the door to the angry response that had been brewing under the failure of the '60s to deliver on its promises. Those promises included a doing away with egalitarian

FIGURE 14.4. French President Nicolas Sarkozy and Carla Bruni-Sarkozy attend a banquet at the Guildhall with the Lord Mayor of the City of London (center) and the Duke of Gloucester (third from the right) in March 2008 in London. Mrs. Sarkozy wears a new Dior creation. Other fashion influences range from the Middle Ages onward.

dress codes and "oppressive" fashion systems. As a precedent, punk has been extremely effective. Without punk fashion there would probably have been no such fun as Galliano has had at Dior or none of the games played by Alexander McQueen and Paul Smith (all three Englishmen, of course). So while punk did not revitalize the failed promise of "Won't get fooled again!" from the '60s, one could at least paraphrase Orwell: "If there is hope, it lies in the punks." The kind of free-for-all aggression that is exemplified by early punk may after all find its way into the canon, in the way Duchamp's "R. Mutt" *pissoir* is now a classic and yet retains its absurd power to amuse and bewilder.

Globalism

One cannot say that there is currently a "global fashion," only a global *market* for fashion. The rapid acceptance of French-derived styles during the early twentieth century goes hand in hand with the explosive distribution of modernist architecture and industrial styles. The search for identity that followed industrialization and urbanization in Western

Europe and America created a semi-homogenized market-state within which global commerce could operate without running into cultural contradictions. The rapid adoption of modernist fashions and architecture point to a need for cultural identity, and the shortest route was through identification with media images. In this way, the global market self-perpetuates itself by simultaneously stripping culture of its local identity and creating a need, which it then fulfills by the very same mechanism with which it has obliterated local identities.

However, local identities also put their mark on the international. Just as local customs are integrated into the local menus of global fast-food chains, so do local fashions eventually insert their needs into globalized franchises and even couture. Color schemes, fabric choices, sizes, and context all vary once fashion goes "in country."

WHAT SIGNS HAVE WE SEEN?

There have not been any signs of late that the shape and direction of things is changing from what we have seen since the late '60s. When Balenciaga quit, he was rumored to have said there was no one left to dress, and as we saw, this was echoed by Pierre Bergé when Saint Laurent retired: there was no one left to play with.

However, there is definitely still a market out there. The ostentation of the newly rich citizens of Arabia, Russia, and India is soon to be magnified, and it is only a matter of time before the shift to capitalism in China produces a consumer society of unprecedented magnitude. So, even while the reluctance to display wealth that the '60s produced in liberal capitalist countries faded in the early twenty-first century, the resulting upswing in conspicuous consumption may pale by the explosion of spending that begins to take place in the former Communist China. Economic shifts and political developments may slow Chinese development or even change its focus, but the center of gravity is shifting from the Atlantic and heading east. The business will shift with it.

When the Germans wished to move the fashion industry from Paris to Vienna during World War II, the most compelling argument the French could make against the move was the need for local talent. It would be impossible to relocate all the skilled workers from Paris. Now, of course, this is not a problem. The skilled work is not done in the West anymore, and there is no reason to move the corporate headquarters either, given that the companies are all multinationals. Any node on the global network can become the main point, which means that the locus of design can easily move to wherever the action is. And the action is where the money is.

If the trend continues for high-end ready-to-wear to replace couture as the flagship operation of a fashion house, then the logical progression, if the markets expand and diversify, is for couture to disappear altogether and for ready-to-wear to become layered into strata based on target markets. Couture may continue as a relic and survive—as it visibly has begun to do—on red carpets and at government events. The House of Worth survived very comfortably on this kind of reliquary business for a generation by essentially becoming a costume maker for court pageantry in Europe. This scenario is, of course, heavily reliant on the economics being viable, and that requires an infusion of wealth into the community that walks on red carpets. Likely as this is, we must remember that it is all highly speculative, and predictions are a dime a dozen where the fashion industry is concerned.

FIGURE 14.5. Paul and Denise Poiret at "The Thousand and Second Night" party, June 24, 1911.

However, we must not forget Poiret: It's about having fun (Figure 14.5). It may well also be the saving grace of high fashion to remember that. Given that the main reason for high fashion's continued existence is an aging and increasingly alienated clientele of fewer than 1,000 people, the fun will have to come from a new generation of clients that has more reason to wear such items than just a yearly debutante ball or museum openings. However, the slowdown in the luxury markets, and the crisis of credit in 2008, made such developments unlikely—at least for a while. High fashion designers can only burst out if the economics of luxury are active.

New Participants in the Spectacle

The society of the spectacle will continue until it hits a wall, and that unlikely wall, despite the economic downturn of 2008, is the reformation of the capitalist system. Therefore, it is most likely that we will continue on as we have for the past decade or so, fully participating in the spectacle, but all the while wondering where it is taking us. The only way to combat the spectacle, as the Situationists attempted, is to take it on from the inside or out-weird it. This might seem like overkill if one questions the need to fight the spectacle at all. It may have seemed inevitable in the 1960s that capitalist society would be fought, and the attempt to take that fight to the streets of Paris created a myth of fashionable resistance that lives on. However, the riots of the late '60s were just as much a generation claiming its ownership of culture and demanding an acknowledgment of its voice and identity as it was a fight *against* anything. The student protests were displays of social significance as powerful as any the world had ever seen. Fueled by media and global communications, the youth of the late '60s banded together and said, "This is who we are." But they were as much a part of the spectacle even as they were railing against it. However serious the situation on the streets of Paris may have been, the experience of revolt was, for most of the world, through media images. (Note how the more dangerously armed riots in America were not equally romanticized.) In creating the "image" of street protest, they removed from the barricades their image of terror. The rioters acted their part and the police theirs. There was nowhere else to go but back home, once the riots were over. After 1968, revolution in the West was the new chic and a marketable style.

New Technologies

The new media technologies that arrived at the end of the twentieth century could both heighten a style by speeding its dissemination and, at the same time, limit the depth of its effect by distancing it from its original source. This double effect is then compounded by the fact that a spectator to the events where a style is introduced is alienated from the source, while simultaneously, the source of change does not get the benefit of feedback from the participation of the removed spectator. A true mass movement becomes harder and harder to sustain as more and more sources of information pour more and more different images into the mix and the spectators to the spectacle become more and more distant.

Subcultures of fashion that manage to evade the media long enough to establish a strong enough core in one place will avoid being watered down too soon. In this way, the big fashion movements of the past 30 years have emerged from the localized street cultures of urban rock music rather than originating in design studios.

A New Question

The hundred years' fashion that was haute couture was a distinct historical event with a clear arc of its own. The question in the air for 40 years is this: Is it over? Is haute couture dead? To this we can add: If so, will it come back? The question is brought out every couple of years but has still not found a definite answer. However, the fact that the question has been asked for more than 40 years without a clear answer must be indicative of a problem with the question itself. There is the distinct possibility that there is no answer found simply because it is not the right question. What is the problem with asking, "Is high fashion dead?" and what does it tell us that the question cannot generate an answer that is satisfactory? Three possibilities present themselves: The question may be too obvious; it may be meaningless; or it may simply be misdirected.

The Old Question May Be Too Obvious

The first possibility is that it cannot be answered because the answer is too clear and it doesn't make sense to ask the question in the first place. It is akin to asking oneself, "Am I dead?" Any answer must be either rhetorical or delve into the linguistics or philosophical issues implied (What do you mean by "dead"? What is this "I" that lives and dies?). The situation can be separated into three distinct (and equally obvious) possibilities: It's dead, not dead, or in indeterminate state. Simply put, one of these must be the true state of affairs, as there are no other possibilities.

It is true that the world of design of Dior and Chanel was already over by the early '60s, but the designers continued to produce and if the business of high fashion is dead, it certainly is a lively corpse indeed. The labels are making money hand over fist. Ready-to-wear and accessories are selling at record levels, with waiting lists of months and years for the most coveted items. It is only the couture divisions that are not making money. But this may be a temporary state.

A number of crafts that came into being as profitable commercial enterprises in the nineteenth century are no more. Technology did away with quite a few. Others simply were supplanted by different modes of living. High-fashion design was no more or less alive in the Second Empire than carriage making. It was practiced over a period of time, and now it is simply not practiced as much. What practice there is, is enough to satisfy the existing market. That market is getting smaller, but at the same time a larger market is developing for the derived goods. Carriage makers found other things to do; so do couture houses. Perhaps the discipline is actually still transforming into whatever it needs to become, but only not fast enough. We of the late twentieth century just aren't comfortable with a transformation that takes a couple of generations, and the rapid rate of change in today's world also means that anything that cannot change quickly winds up behind the wave. The mechanics of high-fashion design may need a longer cycle of renewal than the market will allow.

The Old Question May Be Meaningless

The state of the discipline cannot then be fully determined beyond that it is in transition from one state to another. The question of whether it is dead or not has therefore no real meaning, because the answer will be a meaningless "yes and no" or "maybe" and thereby contain no information. Maybe the question should be reformulated, as there is a clear possibility that it is simply flawed linguistically. Perhaps the word "dead" does not have a relation to the reality that is being investigated. Try asking "Is high fashion frozen?" or "Is high fashion empty?" Perhaps it is *dry*? "Dead" may be simply be a misleading word choice that comes from a tradition in the arts to pronounce the previous generation's art "dead" whenever a renewal needs to take place. Critics and younger practitioners race to be the first to deliver the news. Painting was declared dead several times during the course of the twentieth century; poetry was "dead" for a while; and so were sculpture, rock 'n' roll, classical music, opera, musicals, television, film, and the novel. In other words, high-fashion design is no more or less dead than any other artistic discipline of the twentieth century. What is meant is that the current state of affairs within the discipline cannot stand. When the death notice is given, whatever was going on has lost its energy, and the next thing must happen. Then it usually does happen.

The Old Question May Be Misdirected

The question may also need to be directed to a different place. Something definitely departed in the early '60s, but it wasn't the discipline that died. What has been "dying" is a lifestyle and a society. The world of pre-World War Europe on which the whole system was modeled and based had in fact been losing ground from the end of the Second Empire onward. What was difficult to do was to recognize that the couture business model itself was unable to function in the commercial world of mass production and mass media. Poiret refused to believe it; Schiaparelli gave up; Chanel didn't care; and both Dior and Saint Laurent, heavily financed, rolled with it. But in the absence of aristocracy, there were only a precious few clients or events after 1870 to sustain the type of operation Charles Worth had created. In the mid-1960s, when the question of the "death" began seriously to be raised, the clientele had begun losing numbers. The last pre-boomer generation—a generation that had a connection to the old world—had reached adulthood by the time YSL upended the cart with his "Rive Gauche" collections, and the world of fashion was simply not the same after that.

The question of a discipline "dying" is itself part of the "search for the lost time" (Proust's *récherche du temps perdu*) problem—a circular reference of sorts: If we question the vitality or validity of a creative discipline in the current moment, we imply thereby that it once existed in a better state at a previous time. Following that logic, the way to keep it alive would then have to be to resurrect the discipline as it was before, not to keep it moving forward in its lifeless state. The seeking of the perpetuation and perfection of its vital years therefore deepens the problem and establishes the notion that the craft is "dead" at the present time. But the question should really not be "Is it dead?" but "Does it seem lifeless; if so, why, and what is keeping it this way, and what do we do to revive it?"

New Histories

It must also be noted that high fashion as conceived during the Second Empire was already behind the wave of history. Yes, it was an innovation, but that innovation was one of production and marketing. In social and political terms, it was a defensive action, both reactive and reactionary. By virtue of its impact on the large-scale industries of the time, it managed to survive the elimination of the society it served as the market took over its reason for existence. What remains of its structures still exists because of what remains of the political and industrial structures of the nineteenth-century world it lived in. The fact that the industrialist elite that followed the Victorians and the Second Empire modeled its high society on what it had learned at the courts of Europe meant that the system could be continued as a framework. But again, without a clear authoritative structure, the cohesive message of rank and status became diluted and confused when too many voices shouted directions.

FIGURE 14.6. Bee Shaffer (left) in Nina Ricci and her mother and editor of Vogue, Anna Wintour, in Chanel, at the Metropolitan Museum of Art Costume Institute Gala *Superheroes: Fashion and Fantasy* in New York City, 2008.

This new upper class, created as it was by capital and not birth, needed something to bind it together as a social group, just as the elite of Paris under Louis Napoleon, but it did not have the core of royal tradition (real or imaginary), only the possessions of its members and each other. Given that the upper class of today is made up of people who are where they are also by virtue of money, not royal birth or ancestry, the identification with post-Empire Paris is fully valid. The Second Empire had a court around which the newly minted upper class could gather, but the twentieth century did not produce a viable alternative social model for the upper class that could apply to urban capitalist society. The mold in which its social life had been created disappeared, and therefore, it had to make its own royalty system to act as its social core. It could buy all the trappings and fashions, but its continuation could not be sustained because aristocracy traditionally relied on hereditary land-based power. A new aristocracy needed to be developed, and it was based on wealth and media exposure. (See Figure 14.6.)

High fashion was a gift to the emerging American marketplace in the 1920s. It had a high turnover rate, low labor costs, and a seemingly nonstop supply of producers. This system will continue, of course, as long as it is economically viable, and so it is as long as there is cheap labor to be had. "Cheap" is, however, relative. So, as labor costs rise in Asia, the manufacturing will move elsewhere until all continents of the world have experienced this initial side effect of the transition to a modern economy. Presuming that visions of robots running on cheap energy will still be only science fiction, a new system will have evolved. What that will be will seem logical in hindsight, but currently there is no operable projection available, and I should not attempt one. (I won't bet on the robots.) However, it seems that any new system is going to come from the need for radical re-thinking of how things are currently done and considered.

New Understandings

Long-term projections are notoriously tricky and historically, more often than not, wrong, if not just ridiculous. The "grand doubters" of the nineteenth century, Marx, Nietzsche, Freud, and Darwin, seem like unlikely trendsetters in a discussion of high fashion, but it is to these four that we may look, not for their theories but for their willingness to question the state of society and put them forward. Regardless of the "accuracy" of their writings in light of subsequent developments, we must credit them for their willingness to challenge the reigning intellectual and societal standards of their time in order to point out larger forces moving humanity. It is this kind of radical questioning and redirection that our culture again seems in need of.

One attempt at shaking our culture out of its shell is taking place in (where else?) San Francisco. There the Long Now Foundation is working on a number of projects that are geared toward propelling people out of their "faster/cheaper" mind-set by focusing on long-term projects and concepts. One such project, for example, involves a clock that is to be installed in a mountain in eastern Nevada (Figure 14.7). The clock is a result of the following rumination by the computer scientist Daniel Hillis:

> When I was a child, people used to talk about what would happen by the year 2000. For the next 30 years they kept talking about what would happen by the year 2000, and now no one mentions a future date at all. The future has been shrinking by one year per year for my entire life. I think it is time for us to start a long-term project that gets people thinking past the mental barrier of an ever-shortening future. I would like to propose a large (think Stonehenge) mechanical clock, powered by seasonal temperature changes. It ticks once a year, bongs once a century, and the cuckoo comes out every millennium.[1]

FIGURE 14.7. Must we rethink our time cycles? The clock of the Long Now, designed to measure time in millennia.

In a world of increasingly shorter trend cycles, this is remarkably refreshing, if not liberating, and may well be one of the models that will supplant the system that we currently see breaking down around us. It is difficult to imagine our culture thinking in millennial timescales, but there have been cultures before ours that have done so, and they lasted longer than ours seems to want to. We must not fall into what has been called the "Tyranny of the Present" where the current state of things becomes the model for all future projections.

{ LOOKING FORWARD LOOKING BACK }

Tyrannies of Past, Present, and Future Are There to Be Fought

We are at the end of a cultural era, at the beginning of something new. The future must be approached it with an open mind. This can be done by freeing ourselves not only from the tyranny of the past but also from the tyrannies of the present and future.

Escaping the tyranny of the past means letting go of the system that began with Charles Worth. Could there be a reasoning for design that is a part of the reality of *now* and not of a mythical elite on an artificial timetable? The seasons of fashion are artificial constructs based on courtly life's social calendars that create an artificial rush and a constant pressure for "new." The constant schedule from show to show is debilitating to young designers today who have no time to grow into their art and burn out in five to six years.

Then there is the deadening myth of the "New Look." The desire to be (or own) the next anointed designer is harmful, as it instills in young designers an impossible hope. With so many authorities, self-proclaimed and otherwise, and fashion icons created by stylists, who has enough authority to anoint the next anything?

It is the tyranny of the present that causes designers to lose their direction. Born from anxiety, arrogance, or even complacency, the assumption that the future will be a continuation of the present causes the designer to freeze when faced with change. Looking over the past history, the lesson is clear: The world *changes*. To imagine that what is now cannot change leads to paralysis when change inevitably overtakes us.

But into *what* does the world change? By this question we become enthralled by the tyranny of the future: the *expected* future. The idea that a culture must fulfill a specific agenda is dangerous in any context. It leads to a lack of flexibility and illogical ideologies. The dangerous idea in the corporate fashion world has continually been that everything will continue to get bigger and better; the entire world will become a marketplace for accessories; everything can be a labeled accessory. This frenzy of pseudo-design, when incessant branding overtakes all conceptual logic and integrity, devalues the designer's creativity. Business or art, design must be consistent. But consistently running after every market to fill it with logo-encrusted stuff has no merit beyond the balance sheet. If high-fashion design's purpose continues to be only to fill the marketplace with stuff, it is in danger of being culturally irrelevant and eventually it will become another quaint relic of a lost time. Considering its reputation for extravagance and wastefulness, this may be a good thing in a time where there is both economic contraction and an increasingly louder call for sustainable practices. Now would be the time to turn things around. What is needed is a return to a purpose. Perhaps not repeating past designs, but rather repeating past *motivations* is what we need. Can design go back to being a force in society? I believe it can and should. Worth, Poiret, Chanel, Schiap, Dior, and Saint Laurent all had the drive and the bravery that was needed to use their craft, their art, and their vision to deliberately engage with the character of their society. They knew that what they did mattered and acted on it with passion.

People don't change; only technology changes. The hundred years of fashion will not return, but there are equivalents of our six designers out there somewhere, trapped in the tyrannies of time and the market. Tyranny is overcome only with passion, and yes, clothes *do* make the man. Get up. Change the world, one garment at a time.

New Philosophies

The new philosophies of the twentieth century certainly point to a shift from a mechanistic model of constant forward motion. The dissolution of centers of authority and meaning that have been described as postmodern are themselves a product of modernity and may well be the next phase of human society. The excitement generated by modernity had its demons that led to the next idea, which is that perhaps we don't hold all the keys. Perhaps, in all the technological and scientific progress, we have lost connection with something essential to our being that can be recovered only by stopping and refocusing. There may be more to this thing called existence than the frantic scramble to obtain things and information.

What Do We Need?

Given that we may have exhausted the possibilities of the nineteenth-century system, and admit the futility of a strong prediction, let us look at factors that may affect the next step taken.

It is entirely possible that the grain of truth that can be found in the fashion revolt of the late '60s and '70s was a search for a more symbolic content of everyday dress. That both the hippies and the punks implied a heavy tribal element in their styles (Figure 14.8) may well be read as a clue as to what the next wave will bring ashore. However, the wait for that next wave is proving to be long. The music scene has not produced anything of fashion interest since punk, and the elements of grunge or hip-hop that were appropriated into ready-to-wear designer fashions did not make it into high fashion. Both styles were marketed wholesale into ready-to-wear and stayed there. As both styles were themselves appropriations of previous styles, their outward force to create high-fashion styles in the mode of Saint Laurent's treatment of Beats and hippies was limited.

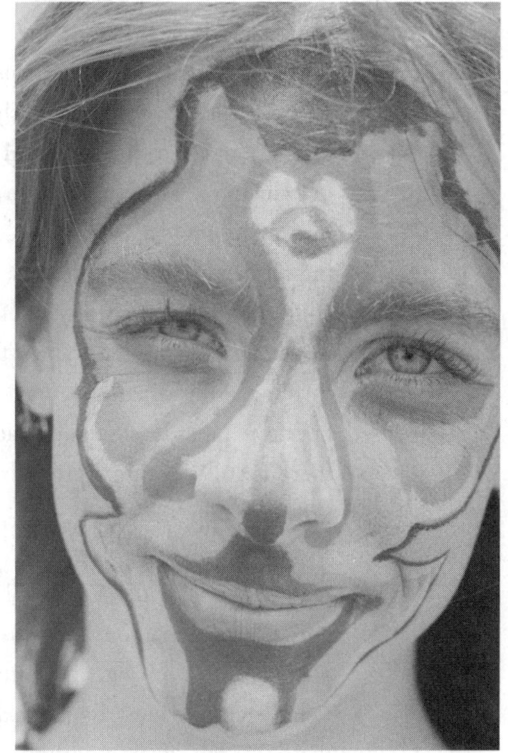

FIGURE 14.8. A tribal look for our time: a Grateful Dead fan in face paint.

After the idealism of the '60s turned to the malaise of the '70s, irony and cynical detachment became signature elements of the cultural scene in the United States. The postmodern program, which questions all centrality, feeds directly into the resulting disassociation. With no overall narrative to guide us, there are only two options: Accept the absence of overall narratives (Lyotard's metanarratives) or invent new frameworks in which to place our larger cultural identity.

However, at the same time that the overall picture fragments, there has also seemingly developed a need for consistency, which is—not surprisingly—sought in the lost times of recent history. Much of the dilemma of current design, apparel, industrial, or otherwise, stems from a lack of continuity, which both reflects and amplifies the inconsistencies of existence in the early-twenty-first-century life of Western culture.

With modern life molded by sentiment that was largely invented in previous centuries for cultures living under different political and technological systems, we find that our notions of being in the world and relating to our fellow beings are informed by models that are no longer fully valid, if not completely out-of-date. Our media-fueled notions of family, friendships, and love are formulated from centuries-old models. Our culture's relationship to nature is distinctly of the Enlightenment, even when informed by non-European philosophies. Our politics are still run on nationalist mottoes that came into being while the royal courts of Europe were in decline. To top it off, it is on this toppled royalty that our fashion system is based. One might well imagine that a twenty-first-century attitude adjustment is due.

This adjustment will perhaps not come quietly. Let us consider what blew up in Paris in the 1870s when the last such "adjustment" was made, and consider where the fault lines are in the capitalist world today. The politics of our day are themselves in a state of transition. The liminal state that capitalist culture finds itself in after it lost its defining enemy involves a violent conflict with a culture that is itself seeking an identity in the modern world. From this conflict, with its overtones of religious zealotry, could come a redefinition of both cultures. A change in the self-image of both could result in a reevaluation of the values that drive their politics. If our consumer society goes through a reevaluation of consumer culture on par with that of the 1960s, there are bound to be at least equally radical results. Even though the results prove short-lived, there is still a residual effect from each revolt, and each successive layer adds to progressive change.

Changes in technology have been the driving force in modern culture, and there is no reason to assume that there will be any slowing down of this in the decades to come. Robotics, nanotechnology, and the explosive developments of communications technology will continue to change the nature of manufacturing, commerce, and, indeed, daily living. Once again, we must avoid the danger of future vision, especially with such predictions as these that fall squarely into the "And there shall be many Wonders and Ye shall be much amazed" department of prophesy. However, if robotics become overwhelmingly cheaper than human workers or nanotechnology becomes viable, the resulting changes in economic models and social structure will make the nineteenth century's industrial revolution look like a warm-up exercise.

Is There a Green Element?

The looming question these days is the environmental one. If our trust in technology and science proves not to be valid in the face of the ecological disaster that is now predicted, then our use of resources and our manufacturing will have to cease. The model of human society and economy that has been built stage by stage for the past 600 years or so will have to be scrapped, with resources rationed (and probably fought over). The current market-state model will not function without constant expansion, and so it will go. With it will go every model we have of commerce and consumption that hadn't been thought of in the late fourteenth century. This is, of course, a very large "if," but one worth stating in order to drive home the point that no human system is constant or even stable.

So, more to the point of our discussion, *if* there is a sudden demand on markets and manufacturing based on ethics of consumption and conservation, then a new model will need to appear for apparel design. It might even first appear as a new model of social distinction based on environmental ethics. This does seem to be the only politics that could conceivably arouse as much passion as religion or royalty. If it does appear, it splits the world into layers, depending on environmental sensitivity and dedication to long term thinking. (Could recycling ever be the new black?)

There is no model to fall back on in this case. There is no precedent for the environmental threat that is increasingly dominating the discussion. There will therefore be a new historical outcome, for better or for worse. Threats of doom and destruction are nothing new, of course, but never before has the option for humanity been to modify daily nonreligious behavior in response to visible threats to the environment.

Where Would Ritual Return?

Here may be where the ritual returns to fashion, and this may be the next phase. If high fashion in the age of Worth arrived on the scene as a visible signal of societal cohesiveness, no matter how "true" it was, it certainly found a way to serve that purpose. That society failed for numerous other reasons, and despite what we might hope, fashion is not a strong enough glue against such forces as those with which the high society of the Second Empire had to contend, once it was under attack. However, it is possible that we need Eugénie's solution again, only applied to a different problem. With high fashion going the way of other nineteenth-century societal finesse, a space is opening for the strengths of the designers to go to other purposes. The power of design in society is not open to question. How it is put to use is.

One could question whether modern society is capable of concerted change, and that is what we shall see in the coming decades. To willingly jettison centuries of habits in order to take up a long view and a different relationship with the world at large may just be too tall an order. Perhaps we are too bound up with fashion as a part of the politicized class system of symbolic power to rethink its design strategies toward a different world. But with the signs becoming increasingly clear that something needs to change, perhaps it is inevitable. Perhaps the decision will not be in our hands at all.

FIGURE 14.9. Iggy Pop: What next?

What Are We to Look for?

So, what signs should one look for that the world of high-fashion design is going to return to a place of influence? One clear sign would be to see fashion arbiters, such as editors and celebrities, team up with creators and designers to advocate radical change and then actually do it. This would be the most powerful move and would reestablish high fashion as a force in society.

Conversely, we may be on the lookout for a new realignment of insider/outsider culture. If the equivalent—not a revival—of Beat, hippie, or punk shows up for more than a year or two, and this is coupled with true advocacy of change, then things may be on the move. Notice how increasingly violent the reactions have become over the last century. The

Beats look positively genteel in their khakis and suits compared to the hippies, who look relatively harmless compared to the punk styles. If the next wave can make Iggy Pop and his cohorts look tame, we are in for some fun (Figure 14.9).

Fashion does not end. History does not end. Technology changes, conversations shift, and futures are multiplying as we speak. What we may be seeing in the end of high fashion is a signal that the world of the nineteenth century is finally departing. If this is the case, what of the other nineteenth-century models by which we live?

. . AND WE ARE CAUGHT

There is a virtue in returning to beginnings when the way ahead is unclear. High-fashion design cannot return to court life, but it can return to its beginning principles. Leaving aside those of direct commerce, which are still valid and will continue to be so, let us consider what these may have been and see whether there is any problem there that requires a solution.

The first place to look would be to the inherent craft involved. With the manufacturing practices of today, designers are increasingly separated from the craft of textiles and apparel construction. Rethinking the approach to these is part of the environmentalist agenda, along with the life-cycle analysis of product development, and may bring a new life to the discipline if reducing the environmental impact becomes a major design constraint. But design is only one element in the life cycle; the change must come in the entire commercial cycle and in the behavior of the consumer as well. Again, we come to the philosophical notion of our relationship with the world.

The French philosopher, Maurice Merleau-Ponty wrote at the middle of the twentieth century:

> When people demand a "solution," they imply that the world and human co-existence are comparable to a geometry problem in which there is an unknown but not an indeterminate factor and where what one is looking for is related to the data and their possible relationships in terms of a rule. But the question we face today is precisely that of knowing whether humanity is simply a *problem* of that sort.[2]

If the questions of human behavior could be solved geometrically, then such ponderings as have been exhibited here would all lead to a single, clear solution. The vagaries of human society and the impulsiveness of its inhabitants are so clear to us that we need not think about this except with some amusement, although there is a darker side to such thinking. That society could be ordered theoretically with logical, geometric precision was the extreme of the modernist dream, and the politics that resulted were at times terrifying. Society-by-decree has not gone out of fashion, although fashion design's part in such politics was over even as it began. Politics and fashion can mix, but clothing involves desire, and desire cannot be regulated or even predicted, except in either an extremely limited or an extremely broad manner. The in-between is where the unexpected happens.

But we are fortunate in that what we need is not a "solution." Needing a solution implies that there is a "problem," and there really isn't a "problem" in design. The problem is in the relationship of design to society and the marketing forces' relationship to both. The art of apparel design must continue to evolve with the society it operates in. The problem itself is simply that of finding out how to move out from under the legacy of the hundred years' fashion. What is needed is a way forward that allows designers to express their creativity in a way that does not rely on myths created in worlds now gone.

WHAT IS THE WAY FORWARD?

These days, there is no "future." Instead it is now common in business and politics to speak of "sets of futures."[3] Business and politics have in this way come to the language of twentieth-century physics, where probabilities rule, and all events are probable, but some are more likely than others. Trends could follow this path or that, leading to some conclusion or other, but the point of interest is where the trend begins to change direction or "bend." It is at this point that the trend is no longer the trend it was, but is "trending" somewhere else.

The problem with predicting the future is that trends are often assumed to continue based solely on the present situation when, in fact, the present situation is not by any means permanent or even stable. This involves a kind of wishful thinking on the forecasters' part. It is, however, not intentional. Our future-vision is developed by our past, to which our present is continually adding new layers. We are caught in the shifting earth that continually buries and yet at the same time builds and affirms the past ground that we ourselves have covered.

Karl Marx's *The Eighteenth Brumaire of Louis Bonaparte*, which we last saw in Chapter 1, comes again to mind: "Man makes his own history, but he does not make it out of the whole cloth; he does not make it out of conditions chosen by himself, but out of such as he finds close at hand. The tradition of all past generations weighs like an alp upon the brain of the living."[4]

Marx was addressing the historical moment at which our story began, the creation of the Second Empire. The resonance to our present situation is remarkably clear. We find that our present does not allow us clarity on the future, and therefore we continually look to the past for guidance, inspiration, and even identity.

Like Marx envisaged social revolution of the nineteenth century, the social revolution of the twenty-first century "cannot draw its poetry from the past, it can draw that only from the future. It cannot start upon its work before it has stricken off all superstition concerning the past."[5]

If high-fashion design served its purpose in the late nineteenth century, and the historical necessity that drove its emergence onto the scene is no more, it will simply continue its slow disappearance. It will fade until all that remains is the nostalgia for the mythical vanished era of elegance so sorely missed by Poiret, Dior, and Saint Laurent. Looking at the field today, one might think we are reaching that point.

"Former revolutions required historic reminiscences in order to intoxicate themselves with their own issues," Marx continues. Our time does not have "issues" that are driven by such romantic energy. The only place "Golden Ages" are seriously treated as models are in fashion and pop culture, and even there we have come to a place of ironic detachment. The way for the discipline of design to continue to flourish as a creative discipline rather than a cog in the marketing machine of a culture of consumption is for the discipline to rebel against the weight of the past generations.

Maurice Merleau-Ponty also wrote in 1960 that philosophy "will never regain the conviction of holding the keys to nature or history in its concepts."[6] The dissolution of the concrete world view of the preceding centuries would also play out over the coming decades in art and design. There is no reason to believe that the certainty of its inception will ever return to the world of high fashion. But this is a good thing. Such certainty in a creative discipline is deadening and leads to stagnation.

Creativity in any field must be based on uncertainty that leads to questioning and a search for new descriptions of the world. Our world is demanding a new description. If there is to be a revolution in design in the twenty-first century, it will come with the turning away from the world of the nineteenth. Whatever high-fashion design is to become will rely on finally putting the ghosts of Marie Antoinette, Eugénie, and Charles Worth to rest.

ENDBOX

Why British Designers Are Looking to the East

With a week to go until London Fashion Week begins, the cream of Britain's new designers are holed up in the East End, living on Boasters and Diet Coke and crashing out under sewing machines for three hours' sleep a night.

. . . Until the end of last year it looked as though the coming round of London shows would be the most exciting and unmissable in a decade. But with the sudden chill wind blowing through fashion retailing, the massed talent of Hackney, Dalston, Shoreditch and King's Cross might well feel that, this time, they're designing for their lives.

Hilary Riva, chief executive of the British Fashion Council, has been monitoring the likely attendees at fashion week for a month. "We have a load of publications coming in from China, Russia and other emerging markets," she says. "And buyers from Europe and the Middle East. But on the Monday the stock market dropped, we were taking calls from American buyers cancelling their trips. It's that issue of London just being too expensive."

. . . The good news, from the risk-limitation point of view, is that they are not wholly dependent on the fluctuating American economy. The "emerging markets" have, in the past two years, zoomed ahead in both wealth and fashion. Russians, Chinese, Koreans, Greeks and shops from the Middle East are turning up to place orders—and they're not looking for anything wishy-washy.

"Russians are quite experimental," says Aliona Doletskaya, editor in chief of Russian Vogue. "There's a lot of optimism around, a crowd who are young and happy, who do not have 75 years of Soviet rule on their back. When they earn money, they spend. There's something very special and quirky about the English they like, that you can't find with a Chanel or Louis Vuitton."

As a representative of the market potential of the new China, Sarah Rutson, fashion director of Lane Crawford (which has branches in Hong Kong and Beijing), is flying in to visit designers in their showrooms with a large budget at her disposal. "I feel very strongly that the creativity from London needs to be supported. The talent pool is incredible and over the years I've seen many designers develop unique looks women find approachable. Our clients are incredibly knowledgeable and nuanced in what they want to buy."

Meanwhile, even at home the rich, it is to be remembered, are always with us. Joan Burstein, the octogenarian owner of Browns of South Molton Street, who has serenely weathered every economic downturn since the three-day week, certainly isn't panicking about the prospects for London Fashion Week or for her sales.

"Truthfully, many of our customers are in a bracket where it's not going to affect them," she says. "I don't think people are going to spend money flippantly on clothes, but they're not buying conservative either. The London designers we buy have something different and fashion-forward. I'm making sure my team covers everything. But the main one for me is Central Saint Martin's. It's so important to see what the young people are doing. It's the future."

Source: Sarah Mower. *The Observer*. February 3, 2008.

Discussion Points

1. How can the emerging Eastern markets change the "hundred years' fashion" as we have known it?
2. Could it possibly be the other way around? Can the Western fashion system imprint itself on emerging markets in the East? How?
3. Can young designers be influential in today's market?

A TIMELINE

This timeline is a collection of dates mentioned in the text, along with other culturally significant events. Some entries may seem more logical than others. Some appear simply for curiosity's sake. Each event listed here is a building block of some large, sprawling structure that is really unclear and cannot be seen at all except as a sum of its parts.

A timeline can just be an entertaining collection of facts for trivia games or for whiling away the time on the Internet. However, a timeline can also create insights into the flow of ideas and influences, and by putting events into historical context, can give us a sense of the continuity of thought in the world. Meander around and let the combination of things begin to create patterns of events and technological developments.

Be careful not to read too much into the list (for example, Disneyland opening and Ginsberg publishing *Howl* both occurred in 1955). The fact that two events share a year does not necessarily mean anything, but taken over the course of many years, large-scale patterns emerge. One sees the shape of the *Zeitgeist* over the decades, forming the world we live in and the future we are approaching.

1825

Charles Frederick Worth is born in England (d. 1895).

1844

Friedrich Nietzsche is born in Prussia (d. 1900).

1845

Charles Worth leaves London to seek his fortune in Paris.

1848

Revolution in Paris: France's Second Republic established. Louis-Napoleon Bonaparte becomes President of France.

1851

Great Exhibition—decorative extravagance of Victorian design—takes place at the Crystal Palace.

Bally begins mass production of footwear in Switzerland.

Isaac Singer is granted a patent for his sewing machine. Although not the only one working on the development of sewing machines, he builds the first commercially successful version. He is promptly sued for patent infringement by Elias Howe, with whom he then enters into business.

December: France's Second Empire established. Louis-Napoleon Bonaparte becomes Napoleon III, Emperor of France.

Charles Frederick Worth marries Marie Vernet.

1852

Emma Snodgrass is arrested in Boston for wearing pants.

1853

First electric telegraph in use, Merchant's Exchange to Pt. Lobos.

1855

Napoleon III and Eugénie are invited for a full state visit to the court of Queen Victoria in England. Napoleon is legitimized; Eugénie is established as a fashion icon.

1856

William Perkin discovers the first synthetic dyestuff, manuvine, which produced violet tones that could not be obtained from natural dyes. This leads to a mania for all things violet, and begins a rush toward the development of other synthetic dyes.

A cage-like frame of metal strips, the crinoline, is patented, leading to enormous skirts becoming fashionable for the following ten years.

Charles Worth and Otto Bobergh set up the shop Worth et Bobergh in the Rue de la Paix.

1857

James Gibbs patents the first chain-stitch, single-thread sewing machine. Ready-made clothing now becomes commonly available. The spread of sewing machines in middle- and lower-class households later leads to increased demand for patterns and new fabrics. This also speeds up the fashion cycle, as the high fashions are now quickly copied, requiring society women to put more effort into staying ahead of the shopgirls.

1859

Ground broken for Suez Canal in Egypt, which eventually joins the Mediterranean and the Red Sea. It opens for shipping ten years later, allowing transport between Europe and Asia without circumnavigating Africa. It has an immediate effect on world trade, increasing European penetration and colonization of Africa.

Charles Darwin publishes *On the Origin of Species*.

Jules Leotard performs first flying trapeze circus act (Paris). He also designed the garment that bears his name.

1860

Arts and Crafts movement: John Ruskin, William Morris, and Gustav Stickley consider machine production degrading to both workers and consumers. To fight the deadening hand of industry on design, they advocate and put into practice an aesthetic based on traditional methods of craftsmanship.

Marie Worth brings sketches to Pauline Metternich in Paris. Soon Charles Worth is the court designer for the empress.

1861

First transcontinental telegram sent. The telegraph not only ends the Pony Express but allows large amounts of information to move faster than humans, ending the connection between information and the human capacity for travel.

1863

Chenille manufacturing machine is patented by William Canter, New York City.

Patent granted for a process of making color photographs.

1865

Édouard Manet's painting *Olympia* is hung in the Salon of Paris. A departure from the idealism of the preceding century, its realism and rough technique shock and outrage the public and the critics. Guards have to be stationed next to it to protect it until it is moved to a spot high above a doorway, out of reach. Some consider *Olympia* to be the first modern painting.

1866

Atlantic cable ties Europe and United States for instant communication.

The color "Bismarck Brown" is all the rage in Paris.

1867

The Paris Exposition sees heads of state strolling about and eating at restaurants. Japanese art is exhibited at the Paris Exposition. Painters such as Van Gogh and Gauguin are heavily influenced by what they see.

Assassination is attempted on the Czar of Russia in Paris.

Emperor Maximillian of Mexico executed by rebels. Empress Carlotta goes insane in Paris.

1868

Worth founds the Chambre Syndicale, which will later become the Federation Française de la Couture.

1869

Empress Eugénie formally opens the Suez Canal.

Bloody riots occur in Paris.

1870

Napoleon III surrenders his army to the Prussians at Sedan

The Second Empire ends with the collapse of government in Paris following the end of the Franco-Prussian War.

The Empress Eugénie narrowly escapes a rampaging mob in the Tuilleries in Paris. She flees to England.

1871

Communards rule Paris for three months. Charles Worth waits out the rebellion by the seaside.

Hints on Household Taste is published in the United States. Published three years earlier in England, it preaches "simplicity, humility, and economy" in design to replace the extravagance of the popular revival styles of the time. The American edition states, "We take our architectural forms from England, our fashions from Paris, the patterns of our manufactures from all parts of the world, and make nothing really original but trotting wagons and wooden clocks."

1872

Metropolitan Museum of Art opens in New York.

1873

Emperor Franz Jozef opens fifth World's Fair in Vienna.

1874

In France, the Impressionist painters have their first show.

1875

Charles Garnier's new Opera opens in Paris.

Georges Bizet's opera *Carmen* premieres in Paris.

1876

The telephone is introduced and quickly becomes an indispensable part of daily life and business.

1877

First news is dispatched by telephone, between Boston and Salem, Massachusetts.

1878

Full-page newspaper ads appear.

1879

Paul Poiret is born (d. 1944).

1880

Advertising copywriter becomes an occupation.

The anarchist writer Kropotkin bewails the pursuit of fashion in "Appeal to the Young."

1881

The first photographic roll film is produced.

1883

Thomas Edison invents the lightbulb, which eventually changes the concept of the workday, alters architecture, and becomes a significant aid to communication.

The first significant Impressionist exhibition in the United States is held in Boston, featuring works by Manet, Monet, Pissarro, Renoir, and Sisley.

The magazine *Ladies Home Journal* is founded, offering readers to look into the homes of high society and observe the difference between good and bad taste in home furnishings.

Karl Marx dies (b. 1818).

1884

The Stebbing Automatic Camera, the first production model to use roll film, is introduced.

1885

Redfern, an English tailor, with shops in London and Paris, introduces the women's tailored suit.

The Home Insurance Building, in Chicago, is completed. It is the first building to incorporate the principles of the modern skyscraper, with a steel skeleton above the sixth floor, and curtain walls. The building was designed by William Le Baron Jenney, in whose offices Louis Sullivan completed his apprenticeship. Sullivan would later formulate the maxim of "form following function."

Friedrich Nietzsche publishes *Also Sprach Zarathustra* (*Thus Spake Zarathustra*).

1886

The H. Taylor house in Newport, Rhode Island, inaugurates the colonial revival building style in homes. It becomes the most popular home style in the United States and remains so for 70 years.

1887

Thomas Edison patents the motion-picture camera.

Cellulose photographic film is developed.

Ads appear in magazines.

1888

"Kodak" box camera makes picture-taking simple. The "snapshot" is born.

The first beauty contest is held in Spa, Belgium.

1889

Dr. Herman Hollerith receives first U.S. patent for a tabulating machine (first computer).

George Eastman places the Kodak Camera on sale for first time.

Universal Exposition opens in Paris, France; the Eiffel Tower is completed. Paul Poiret is charmed by an electrically lit fountain.

The brassiere is invented by Herminie Cadolle in France.

1890

Elsa Schiaparelli is born (d. 1973).

1891

An international agreement on copyright is established.

1892

Elbert Hubbard publishes the monthly magazine *The Philistine* to promote the Arts and Crafts movement in the United States.

The Magazine *Vogue* begins publication.

Le Figaro in Paris notes "stylish anarchism."

Anarchist attacks in Paris cause panic. Bomb explodes in Paris police station.

1893

Gabrielle "Coco" Chanel is born (d. 1971).

The Columbian Exposition in Chicago is a triumph for Beaux-Arts style.

Frank Lloyd Wright establishes his architectural practice.

Vaillant explodes a bomb in French Parliament. The "anarchist deed" is proclaimed to the ultimate political act.

1894

Debussy's revolutionary musical composition *Prelude à l'aprés-midi d'un faune* (*Afternoon of a Faun*) premieres. Considered a breakthrough piece of musical modernism, and a landmark in the history of music.

1895

Siegfried Bing opens a shop in Paris and names it L'Art Nouveau ("The New Art"). Bing sells exceptional works by many of the best-known designers, and the name of his shop becomes attached to their style.

Tchaikovsky's ballet *Swan Lake* premieres in Saint Petersburg.

National Association of Manufacturers organizes in Cincinnati, Ohio.

Anaheim completes its new electric light system.

First commercial movie performance (153 Broadway, New York) airs.

Charles Frederick Worth dies (b. 1825).

1896

Architect Frederic Louis Sullivan proclaims that "ever form follows function."

The magazine *House Beautiful* is founded. Its first issue is designed by Frank Lloyd Wright.

Paul Poiret is hired to the house of Doucet.

1897

The Boston subway opens, becoming the first underground metro in North America.

André Gide publishes *Les Déracinés* ("The Uprooted"), giving name to the proto-beatniks of Paris.

1899

The retrial of Alfred Dreyfus in Paris continues to divides the French. The case is the last gasp of royalists in France.

Economist Thorsten Veblen introduces the term "conspicuous consumption."

1900

Kodak's $1 Brownie puts photography in almost everyone's reach.

On Broadway, *Floradora* introduces what will become the chorus line.

Henri Matisse begins the Fauvist movement in painting.

Sigmund Freud's *The Interpretation of Dreams* is published. It describes his theory of the unconscious and introduces the id, ego, and superego. Freud's theories changed the perception of the human mind, and challenged traditional notions of "normalcy."

King Umberto of Italy is assassinated by an anarchist.

1901

President McKinley is shot and killed by a copycat anarchist.

Frank Lloyd Wright gives a speech "The Art and Craft of the Machine," in which he lays out basic principles of modern industrial design, as he sees them. He praises the Arts and Crafts Movement, but states that Morris's and Ruskin's time is over. " . . . that the machine is capable of carrying to fruition high ideals in art—higher than the world has yet seen!"

Paul Poiret hired to Maison Worth.

1902

In France, magician George Méliès's *A Trip to the Moon* tells fantasy in film.

Alfred Stieglitz publishes *Camera Work* to promote photography as art.

Edward VII crowned King of England. Jean Worth provides coronation robes. Poiret is appalled.

1903

Wiener Werkstatte (German for "Vienna Workshop") established in Vienna as an association of artists and craftspeople working together to manufacture fashionable household goods. They aimed to bring good design and art into every part of people's lives and establish a new art for the new century. Simplified shapes, geometric patterns, and minimal decoration characterize its products. Members also want to break with the past and bring new style to everything they produce. Emphasis is placed on the beautiful and unique as well as faultless craftsmanship. Besides furniture, the Wiener Werkstatte produces hand-painted and printed silks, leather goods, enamel, jewelry, and ceramics. It exerts an enormous influence on artists and Art Deco designers throughout the first part of the twentieth century.

Paul Poiret leaves Worth, opens his own shop in Paris.

London Daily Mirror begins illustrating only with photographs, not drawings.

The film *The Great Train Robbery* introduces editing, creates demand for fiction movies.

1904

New York City subway opens.

1905

Christian Dior is born (d.1957).

Albert Einstein first proposes the theory of relativity in a paper.

Isadora Duncan establishes the first school of modern dance in Berlin.

Paul Poiret marries Denise, who becomes his muse.

Les Fauves cause a sensation with their show of paintings at the new Salon d'Automne.

1906

Marcel Proust begins writing *Remembrance of Things Past* (*À la recherche du temps perdu*—literally, "in search of lost time"). It will later become the favorite reading of Yves Saint Laurent.

Paul Poiret hired to M. Doucet.

Reginald Fessenden invents wireless telephony, a means for radio waves to carry signals a significant distance.

1907

Deutscher Werkbund—Hermann Muthesius.

Frank Lloyd Wright completes the Robie House in Chicago.

Leo Baekeland invents the first fully synthetic plastic called Bakelite. Unveiled in 1909, Bakelite becomes so visible in so many places that it is advertised as "the material of a thousand uses." In 1924, a *Time* magazine cover story on Baekeland reports that those familiar with Bakelite's potential "claim that in a few years it will be embodied in every mechanical facility of modern civilization." This came to be very close to the truth. It was the material for an amazing number of products from cigarette holders and costume jewelry to radio housings, distributor caps, and telephones, until well into the 1950s.

Color photography invented by Auguste and Louis Lumiere.

With *Les Demoiselles d'Avignon*, the Spanish painter Pablo Picasso offends the Paris art scene in 1907.

1908

Henry Ford introduces the Model T car, an automobile meant to be affordable to everyone. It sells for $850.

Moviemakers set up shop in California at a place called Hollywood.

1909

The Futurist movement begins in Italy.

Les Ballets Russes causes a sensation in Paris, leading to a trend toward "oriental" dress.

The *New York Times* publishes the first movie review.

Gabrielle "Coco" Chanel opens *Chanel Modes* in Paris.

Margot Asquith, wife of British prime minister, invites Paul Poiret to exhibit his designs at the official residence. Scandal ensues.

1910

Rayon is developed.

Poiret branches out into scents and décor.

1911

Pablo Picasso's Cubist collages challenge traditional art.

Fifteen years before the artist's death, the Boston Museum of Fine Arts holds the first Monet retrospective in the United States.

1912

In May, Serge de Diaghilev presents Vaslav Nijinsky in a ballet treatment of Debussy's *Prelude à l'aprés-midi d'un faune.* The audience riots at its opening in response to its "indecency and savagery."

Photoplay debuts as the first magazine for movie fans.

1913

The Armory Show in New York brings "Modern Art" to the United States. Among other works, Marcel Duchamp's *Nude Descending the Staircase* and Henri Matisse's unconventional *Blue Nude* draw particular condemnation; both painters are attacked in the press as inept and unartistic. Nonetheless, the show, exhibiting more than 1,600 works, receives some praise and is heavily attended. In New York more than 70,000 people attend during the monthlong run. Even larger crowds turn out at the Art Institute of Chicago, where a smaller collection of works is displayed, despite the qualms of the director and the burning of Matisse in effigy by the students of the Institute. After a final stop in Boston, where it attracts small crowds and ignites no controversy, the show returns to New York, and the works go back to the artists or to new owners.

The novel approaches to color, motion, and form displayed at the Armory Show contrast strongly with the realistic works favored by many established artists. These innovations open up a new aesthetic for American artists, museumgoers, and collectors. The Armory show is now cited by many art historians as the most important American exhibition in the history of modern art.

Matisse coins the term "Cubism."

On May 29, 1913, in Paris, Les Ballets Russes stages the first ballet performance of *The Rite of Spring* (*Le Sacré du Printemps*), with music by Igor Stravinsky and choreography by Vaslav Nijinsky. The intensely rhythmic score and primitive scenario—a setting of scenes from pagan Russia—shock audiences more accustomed to the demure conventions of classical ballet. The unrest in the audience escalates into a riot. *The Rite of Spring* is now regarded as a path-breaking twentieth-century masterpiece.

Gabrielle "Coco" Chanel opens a boutique in Deauville, France; revolutionizes, modernizes, and democratizes women's fashion with tailored suits, chain-belted jerseys, and quilted handbags. She will become the most copied fashion designer in history, a title she will be happy to hold.

Poiret ejects the Baroness de Rothschild from his salon. She gets revenge by taking all her business to the unknown Chanel. Her friends follow.

1914

In Germany, the 35-mm still camera is developed, a Leica.

Federal Trade Commission regulates advertising.

Henry Ford's mass-production techniques of automation and moving production lines results in the price of a Model T Ford dropping to less than $300.

World War I breaks out. Military technology progresses rapidly and war becomes fully mechanized. Mass production is established as a prerequisite to victory in modern war. The side effects of the Great War are too numerous to count, but it extends to every type of manufactured goods. The increased capacity for production resulting from the war creates enormous potential for the manufacturing of household goods, once the war is over in 1918.

Poiret designs costumes for *Plus ça Change*. The future is black and white.

1915

Einstein formulates the general theory of relativity. The absence of an absolute frame of reference in the universe is disturbing to some but enters popular culture almost immediately.

1916

Hugo Ball recites the first Dada manifesto at the Cabaret Voltaire in Zurich.

The Coca-Cola bottle is introduced.

1917

Government offices are seized and the Romanov's Winter Palace is stormed in the Russian October Revolution.

First U.S. combat troops arrive in France as United States declares war on Germany.

Between 10,000 and 15,000 blacks silently walk down New York City's Fifth Avenue to protest racial discrimination and violence.

1918

Congress authorizes time zones and approves daylight saving time. The first daylight saving time in the United States goes into effect ten days later.

Regular airmail service (between New York, Philadelphia, and Washington, D.C.) is inaugurated.

First U.S. airmail stamps issued (24¢).

House of Representatives passes the nineteenth amendment to the U.S. Constitution, allowing women to vote.

1919

The Bauhaus School is founded in Germany.

1920

German film Expressionism is established with *The Cabinet of Dr. Caligari.*

Stanley and Helen Resor introduce psychological ad research.

1921

Cleveland Playhouse becomes first U.S. resident professional theater.

Chanel meets Russian composer Igor Stravinski.

1922

Paul Klee paints the *Twittering Machine*.

T. S. Eliot's *The Waste Land* considers the sterility of modern life.

Ludwig Wittgenstein's *Tractatus* argues that philosophy is meaningless and its pursuit should be abandoned in favor of the natural sciences.

A penniless Elsa Schiaparelli moves back to Paris from New York, where she meets and is dressed by Poiret.

1923

Neon signs begin appearing in cities.

Paul Poiret complains that his designs are being extensively copied in America.

1924

John Vassos designs a lotion bottle for the Armand company, introducing the plastic screw top. (The bottle becomes popular as a hip-flask.)

For the second year running, an exhibition in New York is packed with historical styles for homes, Queen Anne, Georgian, Elizabethan, Colonial (English and Spanish), Tudor, and Louis XVI. American style is clearly rooted firmly in the past.

André Breton writes the Surrealist Manifesto.

1925

Ben-Hur costs nearly $4 million, an unheard-of price to make a movie.

John Logie Baird demonstrates the first TV system, using mechanical scanning.

Warner Bros. starts experiments to make "talkies."

Women's fashion scandalizes as skirts are knee-length.

Exposition Internationale des Arts Décoratifs et Industriels Modernes is held in Paris and gives its name to the style now commonly known as Art Deco. One of the strongest and most influential reactions against the Art Deco movement comes from the Swiss architect Le Corbusier. His Pavilion de l'Esprit Nouveau at the Exposition is a forceful rejection of the use of expensive, exotic materials in the extravagant, one-of-a-kind objects that typified Art Deco. He defined the house as a "machine for living in," while furniture is "domestic equipment." The pavilion itself is a prototype for standardized housing, conspicuously furnished with commonly available items such as leather club chairs. Like members of the Bauhaus, Le Corbusier advocates furniture that is rationally designed along industrial principles to reflect function and utility in its purist forms, with a strict rejection of applied ornament. Other important movements positing avant-garde theories of design and architecture included De Stijl in Holland, which advocates a seamless unity of art and architecture, and Russian Constructivism, whose utopian projects embrace a combination of machine forms and abstract art.

Coco Chanel introduces her signature suit at the Paris Exposition.

1926

Rudolf Valentino's funeral hysteria, suicides, demonstrates the emotional power of film.

Don Juan, the first publicly shown "talkie," premieres in New York.

1927

Martin Heidegger publishes *Being and Time*. This will become one of the twentieth century's defining philosophical texts.

The film *Napoleon* tries wide-screen and multi-screen effects.

Elsa Schiaparelli opens "Pour la Sport."

1928

General Electric builds a television set with a 3-inch by 4-inch screen.

Walt Disney adds sound to cartoons; *Steamboat Willie* introduces Mickey Mouse.

1929

The Museum of Modern Art opens in New York.

Le Corbusier begins building The Villa Savoy. He presents the house as "a machine for living," appropriate for the new machine age.

Herbert Hoover thanks advertising executives for turning U.S. citizens into "happiness machines."

Brokers watch on an automated electric board as stock prices soar, then crash.

Les Paul, age 14, creates forerunner of the electric guitar.

Raymond Loewy opens his industrial design office in New York. Later it becomes nearly impossible to go through a day in the United States without encountering one of his streamlined designs.

Paul Poiret turns down a $16,000 licensing offer, is fired from his company. *Maison Poiret* is shut down by the board of directors.

1930

Broadway gets professional stage lighting.

1931

Chanel visits United States. She is not impressed with Hollywood but loves department stores.

1932

Disney adopts a three-color Technicolor process for cartoons.

Aldous Huxley's sci-fi classic, the dystopian *Brave New World*, is published.

1936

Yves Saint Laurent is born (d. 2008).

Schiaparelli debuts "Shocking."

Schiaparelli is part of a trade delegation to Soviet Russia, inaugurates first Soviet fashion boutique.

Spanish civil war begins.

1937

Pablo Picasso paints *Guernica*, showing the horrors of war.

German authorities present an exhibition of "degenerate art"; condemning amongst other movements: Cubism, Expressionism, Impressionism, and Surrealism. The Nazis' effort backfires, with over 3 million visitors coming to see and mostly appreciate, not sneer at, the works.

Theodore Geisel, "Dr. Seuss," begins writing and illustrating books for children.

J. R. R. Tolkien opens up a fantasy world with his novel, *The Hobbit*.

1938

Two brothers named Biro invent the ballpoint pen in Argentina.

More than 80 million movie tickets (65 percent of population) sold in the United States each week.

Christian Dior is hired as full-time designer by Robert Piguet.

1939

NBC starts first regular daily electronic TV broadcasts in the United States.

Schiaparelli designs "Tear" dress.

Germany invades Poland, beginning World War II.

Chanel closes her shop.

Nylon is developed.

1940

Germans take Paris. Very quickly raid the offices of the Chambre Syndicale, removing its archives. The Germans hope to move the fashion center of the world to Vienna.

British develop the "Utility Line" of clothing in response to wartime shortages. The clean, spare, tailored style becomes popular and influences fashion well beyond the war years.

The Disney film *Fantasia* introduces a kind of stereo sound to American movie goers.

1941

Orson Welles's film *Citizen Kane* experiments with flashback, camera movement, and new sound techniques.

The first television commercial, for Bulova Watches, is aired.

United States enters the war after Japanese raid on Pearl Harbor.

1942

American garment manufacturers invest $2 million in promoting American fashions.

Kodacolor Film for prints is the first true color negative film.

President Franklin D. Roosevelt puts pressure on synthetic fiber industry to produce materials for the war effort, by threatening to nationalize the companies. Rapid collaborative progress ensues, leading to rapid development of synthetic materials and textiles.

Albert Camus' existentialist novel, *L'Étranger* (translated as *The Foreigner*, *The Outsider*, and *The Stranger*) is published in France.

1944

Paul Poiret dies (b. 1879).

Scientists at Harvard University construct the first automatic, general-purpose digital computer.

The first instance of network censorship occurs. The sound is cut off on the Eddie Cantor and Nora Martin duet, "We're Having a Baby, My Baby and Me."

1945

The U.S. Air Force drops atomic bombs on the Japanese cities of Hiroshima and Nagasaki. The "atomic age" becomes a public perception, reinforcing the ideal of a Modern Age of new, and exciting—later frightening—technologies.

World War II ends.

Vannevar Bush conceives idea of hyperlinks, hypermedia.

In the Théâtre de la Mode, French designers display new apparel designs on artfully created scale mannequins in elaborate sets. The Théâtre tours Europe and the United States in the following years, reviving interest in French fashion design.

1946

University of Pennsylvania's ENIAC heralds the modern electronic computer.

Italian cinema counters Hollywood glitz with neorealism in *Open City*.

In France, the Cannes Film Festival debuts.

Postwar baby boom begins (ends 1964).

1947

Christian Dior introduces the line which becomes known as "The New Look," an opulent departure from the wartime fashions of the preceding years.

Bell Labs develops the first transistor, opening the door to the creation of all manner of miniature electronic devices.

Jean-Paul Sartre's play, *No Exit*, introduces the line "Hell is other people." Existentialism begins to enter popular culture.

Princess Elizabeth marries Philip Mountbatten in England, setting off wave of interest in royalty all over Europe.

1948

On TV, *The Ed Sullivan Show* debuts as *Toast of the Town.*

Artist Andrew Wyeth paints *Christina's World.*

1949

Network TV established in United States.

George Orwell's dystopian novel of a bleak, fascist future, *1984*, is published.

Italian neorealism continues with the film *The Bicycle Thief*, still a staple of film school curricula.

1950

Fourteen million television sets sold in the United States, increasing the number in service tenfold.

Acrylic fiber developed in the United States by E. I. du Pont.

1951

Alan "Moondog" Freed, a Cleveland disk jockey, emcees a rhythm and blues show on the radio. He begins referring to the music as "rock and roll." In September 1954 Freed is hired by WINS radio in New York. The following January he holds a landmark dance there, promoting black performers as rock 'n' roll artists. Within a month, the music industry is advertising "rock 'n' roll" records in the trade papers.

J. D. Salinger's *The Catcher in the Rye* is published. It will become a symbol of adolescent angst.

1952

First U.S. presidential campaigns on television.

On television, a UNIVAC 1 computer predicts the outcome of the presidential election, raising public awareness of computers.

Samuel Beckett presents his absurdist play, *Waiting for Godot.*

1953

A shy, lonely child, Yves Saint Laurent becomes fascinated by clothes and already has a solid portfolio of sketches when he first arrives in Paris at age 17. Michel de Brunoff, editor of *Vogue*, who was to become a key supporter, is quickly won over and publishes them.

1954

Coco Chanel, after a 15-year hiatus, returns to the world of apparel design. Over the next five years, lays the foundation of the "Chanel Look," which becomes a classic staple, copied and revived the world over for the remainder of the twentieth century. The French are less excited than the Americans.

1955

Disneyland opens in California.

Allen Ginsberg publishes the long-form poem *Howl*, which describes the destruction of the human spirit in the commercial media age.

1956

Foreign language films get an Oscar category. *La Strada*, by Frederico Fellini from Italy, is the first so honored.

Elvis Presley appears on TV.

1957

Russia launches the Sputnik 1 satellite into orbit, The "Space Race" begins.

Roland Barthes publishes *Mythologies*. His revealing discussions of popular culture foreshadow the discussion of postmodernism.

Christian Dior dies. (b. 1905).

Yves Saint Laurent, at 21, becomes a designer at Dior and is an instant hit.

Neiman Marcus opens a facsimile of Paris Dior boutique in Dallas, Texas.

Jack Kerouac's *On the Road* published (written in 1951).

1958

Playwright Harold Pinter's *The Birthday Party* is staged in London. Pinter's threatening, absurd plays are emblematic of modern angst and alienation.

Physicist Werner Heisenberg explains his uncertainty principle. The idea that not everything in the world can be determined by science is felt by many to be deeply disturbing.

1959

New York sociologist C. Wright Mills refers to a "postmodern period" in which conformity and consumerism have begun to replace the Modern Age of liberal ideals.

Frank Lloyd Wright's Guggenheim Museum in New York is completed.

Barbie dolls make their debut at the American Toy Fair. Life-sized, her measurements would be 39-18-33.

The microchip is introduced.

Xerox introduces the first commercial copy machine.

1960

Ninety percent of American homes have television sets. More than 500 American television stations are broadcasting.

John F. Kennedy is elected President of the United States. Jackie Kennedy becomes a style icon.

Oleg Cassini becomes Jackie's "court designer" at the White House.

1961

FCC Chairman Newton Minow calls television a "vast wasteland."

Yuri Gagarin of the USSR is the first man in space. President Kennedy responds by accelerating the U.S. space program.

1962

Telstar relays the first live transatlantic television signal.

The first video game "Space Wars" is invented by MIT student Steve Russell. It is soon being played in computing labs all over the United States.

Marshall McLuhan publishes *The Gutenberg Galaxy*, where he argues that the communications technology of the electronic age will re-tribalize humankind. He coins the term "global village" to describe this situation.

Andy Warhol's paintings of Campbell Soup cans are exhibited in New York. He becomes the foremost artist of the Pop Art movement.

Silent Spring, by Rachel Carson, is published. The book, a sharp critique of the use of pesticides, is credited with launching the environmental movement.

President John F. Kennedy calls attention to the abuse of the consumer. He declares four basic consumer rights, institutionalizing and expanding consumer expectations in the United States to include the right to safety, the right to be informed, the right to choose, and the right to be heard.

Yves Saint Laurent opens his couture house in Paris. Beatnik street style meets couture.

1963

Fans go wild after a Beatles concert in London. The *Daily Mirror* coins the term "Beatlemania."

President John F. Kennedy is assassinated in Dallas, Texas.

1964

The Beatles appear on the *Ed Sullivan Show*.

IBM develops a computer-aided design (CAD) system.

Doug Engelbart invents the computer mouse.

McLuhan's *Understanding Media: The Extensions of Man* proposes that "the medium is the message"—that the effect of a mode of communication far outweighs the effect of the content being communicated. Television would, for example, have the same effect on society, no matter what kind of programming took place.

Yves Saint Laurent shows Chanel-inspired collection in Paris.

An article in *Harper's & Queen* declares couture dead.

Baby Boom ends (begun in 1946).

1965

André Courrèges introduces the miniskirt.

Ralph Nader's book *Unsafe at Any Speed* attacks Detroit's auto industry, raising awareness about safety issues in automotive design and sparking a disillusionment with manufacturing in general.

The Beatles perform their first concert at Shea Stadium. This concert sets new world records for attendance (55,600).

San Francisco writer Michael Fallon applies the term "hippie" to the San Francisco counterculture.

Bergdorf Goodman, a New York upscale department store, hitches its wagon to youth culture and opens a store within a store, BiGi's, at its Fifth Avenue location. BiGi's caters to young fashions and is designed in a "pop" style. Many older customers protest this invasion to no avail.

Yves Saint Laurent designs "Mondrian Dress."

1966

Star Trek lands on TV.

Neorealistic style gives the film *The Battle of Algiers* a documentary look. Its influence is felt in films for decades.

Yves Saint Laurent opens his groundbreaking Rive-Gauche boutiques in Paris, the first ready-to-wear collections associated with a couture house.

The architect Robert Venturi attacks the modernist ideal, declaring "Less is a bore."

1967

"Be-in" held in San Francisco's Golden Gate Park; 30,000 people attend.

The Beatles release *Sergeant Pepper's Lonely Hearts Club Band*; pop music metamorphoses toward an art form.

The Beatles perform *All You Need is Love* on first worldwide satellite hookup. The audience is estimated at 400 million.

The Haight Independent Proprietors, an association of merchants in San Francisco declare the summer of '67 to be the "Summer of Love."

Riots in Detroit escalate into armed violence. President Lyndon B. Johnson defines the event as an "insurrection" and the Army is called in; 12,000 troops armed with tanks and machine guns pacify the area in 48 hours. Five other cities follow, with disturbances in at least 20 more.

"Death of Hippie, Son of Media" event in San Francisco.

Jacques Derrida's and Jean-Francois Lyotard's philosophies "deconstruct" Western rationalist thinking. Deconstructionist thinking points to a world in which there are no absolute viewpoints, and no narratives that are universally applicable. This begins immediately to cause rifts in academic circles and later begins to influence architecture.

A computer hypertext system is developed at Brown University.

1968

Iggy Pop and the Stooges appear at Detroit's Grande Ballroom. The band MC5 is also on the Detroit scene, celebrating the riots of the year before in their lyrics.

The "hippie" rock musical *Hair* opens on Broadway.

Martin Luther King is killed.

At the movies, *2001: A Space Odyssey* is a hit.

Andy Warhol predicts that "in that future, everyone will be world-famous for 15 minutes."

Student riots in Paris nearly bring down the government. Students at Columbia University in New York protest plans to build a gym in neighboring Morningside Park and take over administration buildings.

Robert Kennedy is killed.

1969

The Woodstock music festival is held in upstate New York, the high-water mark of hippie culture.

The Who release the album *Tommy*, the first musical work billed as a rock opera. It is later filmed.

1970

The Beatles break up, to fans' great dismay. "It's only a band," says John Lennon.

A demonstration at Kent State University in Ohio against U.S. bombings in Cambodia ends in the shooting deaths of four students by members of the National Guard.

1971

Coco Chanel dies (b. 1883).

Jesus Christ Superstar, a rock opera, released as an album the year before, opens on Broadway. Its London production becomes the longest-running musical. Authors Andrew Lloyd Webber and Timothy Rice change the world of theater and musical performance.

The New York Dolls create a new form of rock that presages punk rock and inspires the New York underground music scene.

ARPANET, Internet forerunner, has 22 university, government connections.

A Clockwork Orange is released in Britain. "Being the adventures of a young man whose principal interests are rape, ultra-violence, and Beethoven." The tagline for American director Stanley Kubrick's film makes headlines in Britain, where controversy erupts upon its release. Based on Anthony Burgess's 1962 futuristic novel of juvenile delinquency in London, the film depicts extreme brutality in a highly stylized, and heretofore unseen, manner. Kubrick's unpredictable camera techniques coupled with protagonist Alex's language (an English-Russian-slang hybrid invented in the novel) disrupt the narrative flow and disorient the viewer. Kubrick's opposition of ultraviolent acts with a mostly classical score also unsettles viewers.

1972

The Pruitt Igoe housing development, in St. Louis, Missouri is demolished. Charles Jencks asserts that its destruction signaled the end of the modern style of architecture.

David Bowie releases the album *Ziggy Stardust*. Concerts meld music with abstract theater. The Ziggy persona becomes an instant icon; glam-rock emerges.

1973

Elsa Schiaparelli dies (b. 1890).

Reggae music spreads out from Jamaica.

An American family, the Louds, comes apart on national television, presaging reality programming and proving Andy Warhol right.

Skylab, the first American space station, is launched.

A ceasefire is signed, ending involvement of American ground troops in the Vietnam War.

1974

People magazine debuts with Mia Farrow gracing the cover.

1975

Steven Spielberg's *Jaws* will be the first film to earn more than $100 million; sets the precedent for the "Summer Blockbuster."

1976

The Sex Pistols release their first single. They play their gigs in outfits designed by their manager's partner, Vivienne Westwood. They become the face of punk rock.

Yves Saint Laurent shows "Les Ballets Russes" inspired collection. *Vogue* responds that YSL has reminded us that "fashion, in its radical form of haute couture is costume."

IBM develops an ink-jet printer.

1977

Steve Jobs and Steve Wozniak incorporate Apple Computer.

Bill Gates and Paul Allen found Microsoft.

Disco music becomes the rage.

1978

Will Eisner's *A Contract with God* is the first graphic novel.

1979

Francois Lyotard publishes *The Postmodern Condition.*

The annual volume of plastic manufactured overtakes that of steel, the symbol of the Industrial Revolution.

George Lucas forms Lucasfilm, which will transform science fiction and fantasy films in general.

Sony introduces the Walkman, a portable, personal cassette tape player, changing people's relationship to their music and surroundings.

1980

Ettore Sottsass founds the Memphis Group of designers, which then goes on to create a sensation at the Milan Furniture Fair in 1981. The goal of the Memphis Group is to direct design away from the European functionalism of the late 1970s, by transferring "into the world of the Western home the culture of rock music, travel, and a certain excess." The group, always intended to be temporary, disbands in 1988.

1981

MTV begins broadcasting, with 120 videos to choose from.

IBM introduces first IBM PC.

The Center for Disease Control's first report on AIDS points to a growing epidemic.

1982

The Vietnam Veterans' Memorial in Washington, D.C., is dedicated on Veterans' Day. Maya Lin, a 21-year-old undergraduate at Yale's School of Architecture, has won the commission to design it. Her vision, a dark cut in the earth, with its emphasis on the chronological listing of the names of the fallen, has changed the way memorials are viewed and designed. She described it as follows:

"I went to see the site. I had a general idea that I wanted to describe a journey . . . a journey that would make you experience death and where you'd have to be an observer, where you could never really fully be with the dead. It wasn't going to be something that was going to say, "It's all right, it's all over,' because it's not."

Blade Runner, a film by Ridley Scott, presents a vision of future cities that is much darker and fragmented than ever seen before. It becomes the design standard of future vision for almost two decades.

Autodesk is founded and ships its first version of AutoCAD.

Time magazine names the Computer as its "Man of the Year."

1983

Yves Saint Laurent's work exhibited in a solo show at the Metropolitan Museum of Art in New York.

Sally K. Ride, age 32, becomes the first U.S. woman astronaut in space as a crewmember aboard space shuttle Challenger.

1984

William Gibson's *Neuromancer*, the first "cyberpunk" novel, introduces the term "cyberspace" and underscores the trend toward depicting the future in dark, chaotic terms, in a new type of science fiction.

The Macintosh computer is unveiled with an unprecedented ad campaign, featuring Orwellian imagery.

1985

Jean Baudrillard publishes *Simulacra and Simulation.*

Adobe PageMaker allows easy creation of professional-looking layouts on home and office computers.

1986

Comic books turn grim and violent with *The Dark Knight Returns.*

1987

From Japan, the "anime" cartoon film emerges.

1988

Who Framed Roger Rabbit mixes live action and animation.

Ninety-eight percent of U.S. homes have at least one television set.

Sally Fox, an entomologist, improves an ancient agricultural art and successfully breeds and markets varieties of naturally colored cotton she calls FoxFiber. Fox's cotton is naturally resistant to pests and naturally colorfast, so the fabrics don't fade. Manufacturers and designers respond enthusiastically and pale-colored cottons abound. Dye manufacturers and other cotton growers are less happy.

1989

The Berlin Wall is dismantled, hastening the disintegration of the Soviet bloc in Eastern Europe. To some, this is understood to mean that capitalism has won and is vindicated. Chaos follows in some areas, as Eastern Europe realigns.

1990

The World Wide Web originates at CERN in Europe. Tim Berners-Lee writes the program.

Adobe ships Photoshop 1.0. Photos can now be digitally manipulated on a home computer.

DuPont produces polyester microfiber.

1991

Operation Desert Storm begins. The United States leads a coalition to reclaim Kuwait from Iraq. "Stealth" aircraft and "smart bombs" become openly part of modern warfare. The B1 "Stealth" bomber's faceted look becomes a design inspiration over a wide spectrum of products.

In Europe, Internet sites more than triple in one year, pass 100,000.

Nirvana-mania sweeps the United States. MTV plays *Smells Like Teen Spirit* incessantly. Grunge, an outsider's style, is vaulted to the center of popular culture and fashion, negating itself overnight.

1992

Francis Fukuyama publishes *The End of History and the Last Man.*

Disneyland comes to Paris.

1993

National Center for Supercomputing Applications (NCSA) releases Mosaic, a graphical interface for the Internet, allowing the World Wide Web to be accessed by common users. The creators eventually form the company Netscape Communications.

HTML is introduced as the code for Web design.

1994

Netscape's first Web browser becomes available. The number of Web surfers increases exponentially.

1995

John Galliano, an Englishman, is appointed designer at Givenchy in Paris.

1996

Computer makers begin selling flat-panel displays.

1997

The Guggenheim Museum Bilbao is completed. The architect, Frank Gehry, brings his style of curved, clashing, free-form surfaces to fruition.

DVD technology is unveiled.

The first Weblogs, or "blogs," appear on the Internet.

The first point-and-shoot digital camera is introduced by Kodak.

John Galliano goes to Dior. Alexander McQueen takes over as designer at Givenchy. Two English graduates of St. Martin's School of Design are now heading two of the greatest French couture houses. ("Sad, very sad," says YSL's Pierre Bergé.)

Designer Gianni Versace is murdered outside his villa in Miami, Florida; Diana, Princess of Wales, dies in an automobile accident in Paris; and Mother Teresa, founder of the Missionaries of Charity, dies in Calcutta.

1998

Google Inc. opens for business. Its search engine will change how information is accessed and thought of.

Megapixel digital cameras become available at consumer level.

Apple unveils the colorful iMac computer.

1999

Gucci buys YSL.

The number of Internet users worldwide reaches 150 million by the beginning of the year. More than 50 percent are from the United States.

The Matrix presents moviegoers with a dark, postmodern vision. The movie's use of new visual effects and stylistic blend of influences sets a new tone for action films. The look of the film is extensively copied. The filmmakers tout Baudrillard's *Simulacra and Simulation*. Baudrillard claims they've misunderstood and distorted his work.

2000

The world celebrates the new millennium (a year early). Apocalyptic prophecies and computer virus scares prove to be groundless. The whole thing is a big yawn.

2001

Terrorists hijack four airplanes, flying two into the World Trade Center in New York City and one into the Pentagon in Washington, D.C. A fourth plane crashes into a field in Pennsylvania. A wave of patriotism arises in the United States, and the slide toward war in Afghanistan and Iraq begins. President George W. Bush urges Americans to go shopping to mitigate any economic effects the attacks may have.

From *Shrek* to *Harry Potter* to *Crouching Tiger, Hidden Dragon*, films are defined by their special effects. Cinematic realism is relegated to the "independent" genre.

2002

YSL couture house closes.

Black actors win top Oscars: Denzel Washington and Halle Berry win for *Training Day* and *Monster's Ball*, respectively.

2003

Hollywood releases heavy on special effects, violence, and sequels; typified by the third Matrix film, *The Matrix Reloaded*, which, in an ironic twist, due to extensive stylistic copying of the first release, looks like a copy of itself.

2004

The iPod becomes the "must have" gadget. It holds 10,000 tunes, but fits into a shirt pocket.

2005

Kyoto Protocol goes into effect. The international environmental treaty requires 35 industrialized nations to reduce heat-trapping gases such as carbon dioxide. Developing nations have promised to try to limit their emissions of such gases. The United States, which emits the largest amount of heat-trapping gases in the world, refused to sign the treaty.

2006

Chinese designers show ready-to-wear collections in Paris.

2007

Chanel, Lacroix, and Dior report double-digit growth in sales.

Versace accessories jumps to 40 percent of sales, up from 4 percent in 2005.

Valentino retires. His final show is a 1980s revival.

2008

Versace offers "designer" helicopters.

Polo Ralph Lauren is tapped to design U.S. Olympic costumes for opening ceremony. They go for 1920s *Chariots of Fire* look.

Yves Saint Laurent dies (b. 1936).

Ma Ke becomes first Chinese designer to exhibit a collection at Paris haute couture shows with her label "Wuyong" ("Useless").

2009

The global economy goes into a tailspin. Every market is affected, and deluxe goods flatline.

NOTES

Chapter 1

1. Edith Saunders, *The Age of Worth* (Bloomington: Indiana University Press, 1955), p. 65.
2. Karl Marx, *The Eighteenth Brumaire of Louis Bonaparte* (New York: International Publishers, 1963), 64.
3. Ibid., 110.
4. Alan B. Spitzer, "The Good Napoleon III," *French Historical Studies* 2, no. 3 (Spring 1962): 308–329.
5. James Laver, *A Concise History of Costume and Fashion* (New York: Oxford University Press, 1982), 113ff.
6. Roy A. Rappaport, "Ritual Regulation of Environmental Relations among a New Guinea People," *Ethnology* (January 1967): 26–27.
7. Victor Turner, *Dramas, Fields, and Metaphors* (Ithaca, NY: Cornell University Press, 1974), 17.
8. Quoted in Laver, 140.
9. Laver, 116.
10. Only held by the Sovereign, the Prince of Wales, and 24 others (generally sovereigns of other states, lords, prime ministers, and such) at any given time.
11. Alyn Brodsky, *Imperial Charade: A Biography of Emperor Napoleon III and Empress Eugenie, Nineteenth-Century Europe's Most Successful Adventurers* (Indianapolis: Bobbs-Merrill, 1978), 175–180.
12. "[She] assumes the manners and the style of a strumpet . . . she drinks, she smokes, she swears, she is ugly enough to frighten one, and she tells stories." (Quoted in Brodsky, 190).
13. Brodsky, 190.
14. Edward Legge, *The Comedy and Tragedy of the Second Empire; Paris Society in the Sixties, including Letters of Napoleon III, M. Pietri, and Comte de la Chapelle, and Portraits of the Period* (New York: Harper and Brothers, 1911), 142ff.
15. Gilles Lipovetsky, *The Empire of Fashion: Dressing Modern Democracy*, trans. Catherine Porter (Princeton, NJ: Princeton University Press, 1994), 55.

16. Marguerite Gardiner, "The Idler in France" *Project Gutenberg* (July 28, 2004), accessed June 29, 2008, from http://www.gutenberg.org/files/13044/13044-8.txt.
17. Ibid.
18. Lipovetsky, 84.
19. Turner.
20. Ibid.
21. Lillie De Hegermann-Lindencrone, *In the Courts of Memory 1858–1875: From Contemporary Letters*, Project Gutenberg, prods. Ann Soulard and Charles Franks (2004), accessed June 29, 2008, from http://www.gutenberg.org/dirs/etext04/8crts10.txt.
22. Lawrence H. Officer and Samuel H. Williamson, "Purchasing Power of Money in the United States from 1774 to 2006," MeasuringWorth.com, accessed June 29, 2008, from www.measuringworth.com.
23. Style.com shopping guide of December 12, 2007, shows this to be the price of a Badgley Mischka chinchilla bolero.
24. Turner, 266.
25. Roy A. Rappaport, *Ritual and Religion in the Making of Humanity*, Cambridge: Cambridge University Press, 1999, 24ff.
26. Ibid., 32.
27. F. Adolphus, *Some Memories of Paris* (New York: Henry Holt, 1895), 190.
28. Ibid., 190ff.
29. Rappaport 1999, 33ff.
30. See Ben Wilson, *The Making of Victorian Values: Decency and Dissent in Britain: 1789–1837* (New York: Penguin Press, 2007) for an excellent and entertaining book-length discussion of this development in England.
31. De Hegermann-Lindencrone.
32. Saunders, 135.
33. Rappaport 1999, 37ff.
34. Saunders, 137.
35. Ibid., 48.
36. Rappaport 1999, 6–7.
37. Saunders, 109.
38. Rappaport 1999, 321.
39. Lionel Trilling, *Sincerity and Authenticity* (Cambridge: Harvard University Press, 1997), 3.
40. Ibid., 10–11.
41. Guy Debord, *Society of the Spectacle*, (Detroit: Black & Red, 1983), 17.
42. Ibid.

43. Jean Baudrillard, *Simulacra and Simulation,* trans. Sheila Faria Glaser (Ann Arbor: University of Michigan Press, 1994), 6.

Chapter 2

1. Diana De Marly (1990) maintains that this was the first Worth gown brought to Eugénie. Edith Saunders (1955) places it later. Jean Worth's memoir (1928) backs up Edith Saunders and is presumably her source.
2. Edith Saunders, *The Age of Worth* (Bloomington, IN: Indiana University Press, 1955).
3. Diana De Marly, *Worth: Father of Haute Couture*, 2nd ed. (New York: Holmes & Meier, 1990).
4. Saunders and De Marley give conflicting accounts.
5. Edward Legge, *The Comedy and Tragedy of the Second Empire: Paris Society in the Sixties, including Letters of Napoleon III, M. Pietri, and Comte de la Chapelle, and Portraits of the Period* (New York: Harper and Brothers, 1911), 147.
6. Wagner would refer to Paris as the place "where all the pigs of Europe had come to wallow." See Alyn Brodsky, *Imperial Charade: A Biography of Emperor Napoleon III and Empress Eugenie, Nineteenth-Century Europe's Most Successful Adventurers* (Indianapolis: Bobbs-Merrill, 1978), 186.
7. Saunders, 134.
8. Ibid.,152.
9. David Duff, *Eugenie and Napoleon III* (New York: Morrow, 1978), 181ff.
10. The name changed when it expanded its affiliation to include ready-to-wear and men's wear in 1973.
11. Saunders, 165.
12. Apparently he did not die but was wounded. A number of articles refer to him as alive in later years.
13. Lillie De Hegermann-Lindencrone, "In the Courts of Memory 1858–1875: From Contemporary Letters," Project Gutenberg, prods. Ann Soulard and Charles Franks (2004), 187.
14. Jean-Phillippe Worth, *A Century of Fashion*, trans. Ruth Scott Miller (Boston: Little, Brown, and Company, 1928), 82.
15. F. Adolphus, *Some Memories of Paris* (New York: Henry Holt, 1895), 195.
16. Adolphus 1895, 197.
17. Paul Poiret, *King of Fashion*, trans. Stephen Haden Guest (New York: J. B. Lippincott Company, 1931), 21.

Chapter 3

1. Richard D. Sonn, *Anarchism and Cultural Politics in Fin de Siecle France* (Lincoln: University of Nebraska Press, 1989), 82.
2. Edward Lucie-Smith, *A Concise History of French Painting* (London: Thames & Hudson, 1971), 239.
3. Karl Marx, *The Eighteenth Brumaire of Louis Napoléon* (New York: International Publishers, 1963), 15.
4. Friedrich Nietzsche, *Thus Spake Zarathustra*, trans. Thomas Common. (Mineola, NY: Dover Publications, 1999), 81.
5. Sonn, 220.
6. Ibid., 196.
7. Paul Poiret, *King of Fashion,* trans. Stephen Haden Guest (New York: J. B. Lippincott Company, 1931), 30.
8. Ibid., 37.
9. Ibid., 61.
10. Sonn, 196.
11. Barbara W. Tuchman, *The Proud Tower* (New York: The MacMillan Company, 1966), 63ff.
12. Sonn, 185.
13. David Weir, *Anarchy and Culture: Aesthetic Politics of Modernism* (Amherst, MA: University of Massachusetts Press, 1997), 109.
14. Sonn, 192.
15. *Les Anarchistes: Bulletin de Quinzaine* (November 5, 1891), quoted in Sonn, 185.
16. Poiret 1931, 94.
17. Ibid., 67.
18. Ibid., 70.
19. Edith Saunders, *The Age of Worth* (Bloomington,: Indiana University Press, 1955), 208.
20. Pierre Bourdieu, *The Field of Cultural Production: Essays on Art and Literature* (New York: Columbia University Press, 1984).
21. Louis H Sullivan, "The Tall Office Building Artistically Considered," *Lippincott's Magazine* (March 1896).
22. Jean Worth in Winterburn 1914.
23. Paul Poiret in Winterburn 1914, 237ff.
24. New York Times, "New York Has No Laughter and No Young Girls," *New York Times*, October 19, 1913.
25. Ibid.
26. Palmer White, *Poiret* (New York: Clarkson N. Potter Inc., 1973), 110.

CHAPTER 4

1. Quoted in Juliet Nicholson, *The Perfect Summer: England 1911—Just Before the Storm* (New York: Grove Press. 2008).
2. Palmer White, *Poiret* (New York: Clarkson N. Potter Inc., 1973), 44.
3. The baroness is tactfully not identified by Poiret in his autobiography but is named as Diane ("Kitty") de Rothschild by Madsen (1990) and as Baroness Henri de Rothschild by White (1973). However, Diane was only six years old in 1913. Baron Henri's wife was Mathilde Sophie Henriette (1872–1926). If this was not Mathilde, then it is possible—and most likely—that this was "Kitty's" mother, the Baroness Nelly (née Beers) de Rothschild (1886–1945). A famous beauty and hostess, she was the wife of Baron Robert Phillippe de Rothschild. Poiret names Baron Robert as a friend in his autobiography. As a result of tossing out the Baroness, Baron Robert's mistress was free to shop at Poiret's establishment. This may have contributed to the baroness's rage.
4. Mary McLeod. "Undressing Architecture: Fashion, Gender, and Modernity." In *Back from Utopia*, eds. Hubert-Jan Henket and Hilde Heynen (Rotterdam: 010 Publishers, 2002), 312–325.
5. Benjamin, Walter, "The Work of Art in the Age of Mechanical Reproduction," in *Illuminations*, ed. Hannah Arendt, trans. Harry Zohn (New York: Shocken Books, 1968), 217–251.
6. This comes from a speech President Herbert Hoover made to a group of advertising executives shortly after taking office in which he stated, "You have transformed people into constantly moving happiness machines that have become the key to economic progress." (See *The Century of the Self*, written and directed by Adam Curtis, produced by Stephen Lambert and BBC Four, released by the Independent Feature Project.)
7. Mark Antliff, "Cubism, Futurism, Anarchism: The 'Aestheticism' of the 'Action d'art' Group," *Oxford Art Journal* 21, no. 2 (1998): 101–120.
8. White.
9. Paul Poiret, *King of Fashion*, trans. Stephen Haden Guest (New York: J. B. Lippincott, 1931), 68.
10. Rosalind E. Krauss, *Passages in Modern Sculpture* (Cambridge, MA, and London: MIT Press, 1996), 69.
11. Krauss, 106.
12. Elsa Schiaparelli, *Shocking Life* (New York: E. P. Dutton, 1954), 47.
13. Schiaparelli, 100.
14. Ibid., 108.
15. Poiret, 299.
16. Axel Madsen, *Chanel: A Woman of Her Own*. New York: Henry Holt, 1990), 163.
17. Quoted in McLeod, 321.

18. Ibid.
19. Marie-France Pochna, *Christian Dior: The Man Who Made the World Look New* (New York: Arcade Publishing, 1996), 38.
20. Peter Waldberg,. *Surrealism* (New York: McGraw-Hill, 1971), 66–75.

Chapter 5

1. Marie-France Pochna, *Christian Dior: The Man Who Made the World Look New* (New York: Arcade Publishing, 1996), 77ff.
2. Irene Guenther, *Nazi Chic*, New York: Berg, 2004), 209.
3. Ibid., 208–209.
4. Nadine Gasc, *Theatre De La Mode* (New York: Rizzoli, 1991), 90–91.
5. Guenther, 210.
6. Pochna, 84.
7. Ibid., 102.
8. Ibid., 104.
9. Ibid., 107.
10. Ibid.
11. Ibid., 95.
12. Christian Dior, *Talking about Fashion* (New York: G. P. Putnam's Sons, 1954), 109–112.
13. Roland Barthes, *Mythologies*, trans. Annette Lavers (New York: Hill and Wang, 1972), 32.
14. Axel Madsen, *Chanel: A Woman of Her Own*. (New York: Henry Holt, 1990), 191.
15. Ibid., 290.

Chapter 6

1. Jack Burnham, *Beyond Modern Sculpture* (New York: George Braziller, 1973), 73–74.
2. Paul Poiret, *King of Fashion*, trans. Stephen Haden Guest (New York: J. B. Lippincott, 1931), 93.
3. Ibid., 331.
4. Jean-François Lyotard, *The Postmodern Condition: A Report on Knowledge* (Minneapolis: University of Minnesota Press, 1984), 3.
5. Ibid., xiii.
6. Ibid., xxiv.
7. Suzi Gablik, *Has Modernism Failed?* (New York: Thames & Hudson, 2004), 127.

Chapter 7

1. Penelope Rowlands, *A Dash of Daring* (New York: Atria Books, 2005), 366.
2. Marie-France Pochna, *Christian Dior: The Man Who Made the World Look New* (New York: Arcade Publishing, 1996), 38.

3. Pochna, 48.
4. Rowlands, 361.
5. Ibid., 364.
6. Pochna, 144.
7. Axel Madsen, *Chanel: A Woman of Her Own* (New York: Henry Holt, 1990), 263.
8. John Clellan Holmes, "This Is the Beat Generation," *New York Times*, November 16, 1952.
9. Herb Caen, "Pocketful of Notes," *San Francisco Chronicle* (April 2, 1958): "Look magazine, preparing a picture spread on S.F.'s Beat Generation (oh, no, not AGAIN!), hosted a party in a No. Beach house for 50 Beatniks, and by the time word got around the sour grapevine, over 250 bearded cats and kits were on hand, slopping up Mike Cowles' free booze. They're only Beat, y'know, when it comes to work . . . "
10. Jack Kerouac, "Aftermath: The Philosophy of the Beat Generation," *Esquire* (March 1958).
11. Peter Coyote, *Sleeping Where I Fall* (Washington, D.C.: Counterpoint, 1998), 79.
12. San Francisco Chronicle, "Summer of Love: 40 Years Later," Peter Coyote. *San Francisco Chronicle* (May 20, 2007).
13. Ed Vulliamy, "Love and Haight," *Observer/Guardian (UK)*, May 20, 2007.
14. Coyote, 135.
15. John Holmstrom in *Punk Attitude*, directed by Don Letts, produced by Anouk Fontaine (Fremantle Media 3DD, 2005).
16. Chrissie Hynde in *Punk Attitude*.

Chapter 8

1. Richard Goodwin, *Remembering America: A Voice from the Sixties* (New York: Little, Brown and Company, 1988).
2. New York Times, "Mother of the Day," *New York Times*, November 26,1960, 8.
3. New York Times, "American Collections," *New York Times,* October 13, 1960, 32.
4. New York Times, "Mrs. Kennedy Sees New Spring Clothes," *New York Times*, March 23, 1961, 30.
5. Iggy Pop (James Osterberg), interview by Terry Gross, *Fresh Air*, NPR, Decenber 29, 2006.
6. Ibid.
7. Ibid.

Chapter 9

1. Gloria Emerson, "Chanel on the Styles of the Sixties: 'It is a Lousy Time for Women,'" *New York Times*, February 14, 1967.
2. See *New York Times*, July 22–26, 1967.
3. Laura Barton, "One Hell of a Nice Old Age," *Guardian (UK),* March 3, 2007.

4. Iggy Pop (James Osterberg), interview by Terry Gross, *Fresh Air*, NPR, July 14, 2006.
5. Henry Rollins in *Punk Attitude*.

Chapter 10

1. Axel Madsen, *Chanel: A Woman of Her Own* (New York: Henry Holt, 1990), 222.
2. Yves Saint Laurent, *Yves Saint Laurent* (New York: Metropolitan Museum of New York, 1983), 15.
3. George B Sproles, "Analyzing Fashion Life Cycles: Principles and Perspectives," *Journal of Marketing* 45, no. 4 (Autumn 1981): 121.
4. Robert Venturi, *Complexity and Contradiction in Architecture* (New York: Museum of Modern Art, 2002), first published in 1966.
5. Robert Venturi (with Denise Scott Brown and Steven Izenour), *Learning from Las Vegas*, (Cambridge, MA: MIT Press, 1977).
6. See Judith Thurman, "Swann Song; Yves Saint Laurent Bids Adieu," *New Yorker* (March 18, 2002): 134ff.
7. Dionne, *New York Times* December 12, 1983, 160.
8. Yves Saint Laurent (1977), quoted in *Yves Saint Laurent (New York:* Metropolitan Museum of New York, 1983), 39.
9. Horyn, Cathy. "Ending an Era in High Fashion, Saint Laurent Takes a Final Bow," *New York Times*, January 8, 2002, A1.
10. Independent, "*Adieu Yves: A Tribute to the Master of Couture, Independent*, June 3, 2008, accessed June 22, 2008, from http://www.independent.co.uk/life-style/fashion/features/adieu-yves-a-tribute-to-the-master-of-couture-838823.html.
11. Paul Bourdieu, "The Market of Symbolic Goods" in *The Field of Cultural Production: Essays on Art and Literature* (New York: University of Columbia Press, 1984).

Chapter 11

1. Francis Fukuyama, "After Neoconservatism," *New York Times*, February 19, 2006.
2. Friedrich Nietzsche, *Thus Spake Zarathustra*, trans. Thomas Common, Project Gutenberg, 1999.
3. Ibid.
4. Paul Tillich, "Nietzsche and the Bourgeoise Spirit," *Journal of the History of Ideas* 6, no. 3 (June 1945): 307–309.
5. Baudrillard, Jean. *Simulacra and Simulation*, trans. Sheila Faria Glaser (Ann Arbor: University of Michigan Press, 1994), 6.
6. Baudrillard.
7. Samantha Critchell, "Olympics Glory Days Inspire New Uniforms," wire story: Associated Press, June 11, 2008.

8. Stephen Koepp, "Selling a Dream of Elegance and the Good Life," *Time* (June 24, 2001).
9. William Gibson. *Pattern Recognition* (New York: G. P. Putnam's Sons, 2003), 17–18.
10. William Gibson, *William Gibson*, December 31, 2005, accessed June 24, 2008, from http://www.williamgibsonbooks.com/blog/2005_12_01_archive.asp.
11. Gibson.
12. Ibid.
13. Joelle Diderich, *Armani Brings Haute Couture to Masses,* wire story, Paris: Associated Press, 2007.
14. Ibid.
15. Hilary Alexander, "Armani on a Rainbow Trip," *Telegraph (UK)*, July 4, 2007.
16. Hilary Alexander, "Roland Mouret Returns with RM," *Telegraph (UK)*, July 4, 2007.
17. Cathy Horyn, "In Rome, Fashion Royalty Hails Its King," *New York Times*, July 8, 2007.
18. Jess Cartner-Morley, "Galliano Fires First Shot in Battle of the Couturiers," *Guardian (UK)*, July 3, 2007.
19. Paul Poiret, *King of Fashion*, trans. Stephen Haden Guest (New York: J. B. Lippincott, 1931), 299.
20. Marshall McLuhan and Quentin Fiore, *War and Peace in the Global Village* (New York: McGraw-Hill, 1968).
21. McLuhan and Fiore, 90.
22. Ibid., 126.

Chapter 12

1. Jess Cartner-Morley, "Out of Tragedy," *Guardian (UK)*, February 9, 2008.
2. Joelle Diderich, "Armani Brings Haute Couture to Masses," wire story, Paris: Associated Press, 2007.
3. Cartner-Morley.
4. Hilary Alexander, "Sarah Brown, Biba," *London Telegraph*, February 2008.

Chapter 13

1. Jess Cartner-Morley, "Fashion for All," *Guardian (UK)*, October 9, 2007.
2. Ray Kurzweil, *The Singularity Is Near: When Humans Transcend Biology* (New York: Viking, 2005).
3. Jessica Fellowes, "Credit Crunch: Why the Super Rich Are Different," *Telegraph (UK)*, June 26, 2008.

CHAPTER 14

1. See http://www.longnow.org (accessed July 26th 2008).
2. Maurice Merleau-Ponty, *Humanism and Terror: An Essay on the Communist Problem,* trans. J. O'Neil (Boston: Beacon Press, 1969), 203.
3. See, for example, Ged Davis, Shell International Ltd, "Creating Scenarios for Your Company's Future," presented at the 1998 conference on Corporate Environmental, Health, and Safety Excellence: Bringing Sustainable Development Down to Earth, New York, 1998.
4. Karl Marx, *The Eighteenth Brumaire of Louis Bonaparte*, trans. Daniel De Leon (New York: Labor News, Mountain View, 2003), 12 (online edition).
5. Ibid., 14.
6. Maurice Merleau-Ponty, *Signs*, trans. R. McCleary (Evanston, IL: Northwestern University Press, 1964). (Signe, Gallimard Paris, 1960)

BIBLIOGRAPHY

Adolphus, F. *Some Memories of Paris*. New York: Henry Holt & Co., 1895.

Alexander, Hilary. "Armani on a Rainbow Trip." *Telegraph (UK)*, July 4, 2007.

———. "Roland Mouret Returns with RM." *Telegraph (UK)*, July 4, 2007.

———. "Sarah Brown, Biba." *Telegraph (UK)*, February 2008.

Antliff, Mark. "Cubism, Futurism, Anarchism: The 'Aestheticism' of the 'Action d'art' Group." *Oxford Art Journal* 21, no. 2 (1998): 101–120.

Barthes, Roland. *Mythologies*. Translated by Annette Lavers. New York: Hill and Wang, 1972.

Barton, Laura. "One Hell of a Nice Old Age." *Guardian (UK)*, March 3, 2007.

Baudrillard, Jean. *Simulacra and Simulation*. Translated by Sheila Faria Glaser. Ann Arbor: University of Michigan Press, 1994.

Benjamin, Walter. "The Work of Art in the Age of Mechanical Reproduction." In *Illuminations*, by Walter Benjamin. Edited by Hannah Arendt. Translated by Harry Zohn. New York: Shocken Books, 1968, 217–251.

Bourdieu, Pierre. *The Field of Cultural Production: Essays on Art and Literature*. New York: Columbia University Press, 1984.

Brodsky, Alyn. *Imperial Charade: A Biography of Emperor Napoleon III and Empress Eugenie, Nineteenth-Century Europe's Most Successful Adventurers*. Indianapolis: Bobbs-Merrill, 1978.

Burnham, Jack. *Beyond Modern Sculpture*. New York: George Braziller, 1973.

Caen, Herb. "Pocketful of Notes." *San Francisco Chronicle,* April 2, 1958.

Cartner-Morley, Jess. "Fashion for All." *Guardian (UK)*, October 9, 2007.

———. "Galliano Fires First Shot in Battle of the Couturiers." *Guardian (UK)*, July 3, 2007.

———. "Out of Tragedy." *Guardian (UK)*, February 9, 2008.

Coyote, Peter. *Sleeping Where I Fall*. Washington, D.C.: Counterpoint, 1998, 79.

Critchell, Samantha. "Olympics Glory Days Inspire New Uniforms." Wire story. Associated Press, June 11, 2008.

Curtis, Adam. *The Century of the Self*. Directed by Adam Curtis. Produced by Stephen Lambert and BBC. Independent Feature Project, 2002.

Davis, Ged. Shell International Ltd. *Creating Scenarios for Your Company's Future*. 1998 Conference on Corporate Environmental, Health, and Safety Excellence: Bringing Sustainable Development Down to Earth. New York, 1998.

De Hegermann-Lindencrone, L. *In the Courts of Memory 1858–1875: From Contemporary Letters.* Project Gutenberg, 2004. Produced by Ann Soulard and Charles Franks. Accessed June 29, 2008, from http://www.gutenberg.org/dirs/etext04/8crts10.txt.

De Marly, Diana. *Worth: Father of Haute Couture*. 2nd ed. New York: Holmes & Meier, 1990.

Debord, Guy. *Society of the Spectacle*. Detroit: Black & Red, 1983.

Diderich, Joelle. "Armani Brings Haute Couture to Masses." Wire story. Paris: Associated Press, 2007.

Dionne, E.J. Jr. "The Man behind the Mystique." The *New York Times*, December 4, 1983, SM 160.

Dior, Christian. *Talking about Fashion*. New York: G. P. Putnam's Sons, 1954.

Duff, David. *Eugenie and Napoleon III*. New York: Morrow, 1978.

Emerson, Gloria. "Chanel on the Styles of the Sixties: 'It Is a Lousy Time for Women.'" *New York Times*, February 14, 1967.

Fellowes, Jessica. "Credit Crunch: Why the Super Rich Are Different." *Telegraph (UK)*, June 26, 2008.

Fukuyama, Francis. "After Neoconservatism." *New York Times*, February 19, 2006.

Gablik, Suzi. *Has Modernism Failed?* New York: Thames & Hudson, 2004.

Gardiner, Marguerite. "The Idler in France." Project Gutenberg. July 28, 2004. Accessed June 29, 2008, from http://www.gutenberg.org/files/13044/13044-8.txt.

Gasc, Nadine. *Theatre De La Mode*. New York: Rizzoli, 1991.

Gibson, William. *Pattern Recognition*. New York: G. P. Putnam's Sons, 2003.

———. Blog. December 31, 2005. Accessed June 24, 2008, from http://www.williamgibsonbooks.com/blog/2005_12_01_archive.asp.

Goodwin, Richard. *Remembering America: A Voice from the Sixties*. New York: Little, Brown, 1988.

Guenther, Irene. *Nazi Chic*. New York: Berg, 2004.

Holmes, John Clellan. "This Is The Beat Generation," *New York Times*, November 16, 1952.

Horyn, Cathy. "Ending an Era in High Fashion, Saint Laurent Takes a Final Bow." *New York Times*, January 8, 2002, A1.

———. "In Rome, Fashion Royalty Hails Its King ." *New York Times*, July 8, 2007.

Independent. "Adieu Yves: A Tribute to the Master of Couture." June 3, 2008. Accessed June 22, 2008, from http://www.independent.co.uk/life-style/fashion/features/adieu-yves-a-tribute-to-the-master-of-couture-838823.html.

Kerouac, Jack. "Aftermath: The Philosophy of the Beat Generation." *Esquire*, March 1958.

Koepp, Stephen. "Selling a Dream of Elegance and the Good Life." *Time*, June 24, 2001.

Krauss, Rosalind E. *Passages in Modern Sculpture*. Cambridge, MA/London: MIT Press, 1996.

Kurzweil, Ray. *The Singularity Is Near: When Humans Transcend Biology*. New York: Viking, 2005.

Laurent, Yves Saint. *Yves Saint Laurent*. New York: Metropolitan Museum of Art, 1983.

Laver, James. *A Concise History of Costume and Fashion*. New York: Oxford University Press, 1982.

Legge, Edward. *The Comedy and Tragedy of the Second Empire; Paris Society in the Sixties, Including Letters of Napoleon III, M. Pietri, and Comte de la Chapelle, and Portraits of the Period.* New York: Harper and Brothers, 1911.

Letts, Don. *Punk Attitude*. Directed by Don Letts. Produced by Fremantle Media 3DD. 2005.

Lipovetsky, Gilles. *The Empire of Fashion: Dressing Modern Democracy*. Translated by Catherine Porter. Princeton: Princeton University Press, 1994.

Lucie-Smith, Edward. *A Concise History of French Painting*. London: Thames & Hudson, 1971.

Lyotard, Jean-François. *The Postmodern Condition: A Report on Knowledge*. Minneapolis: University of Minnesota Press, 1984.

Madsen, Axel. *Chanel: A Woman of Her Own*. New York: Henry Holt & Co., 1990.

Marx, Karl. *The Eighteenth Brumaire of Louis Bonaparte*. Translated by Daniel De Leon. *New York Labor News*, Mountain View, CA, 2003, p. 12 (online edition).

Marx, Karl. *The Eighteenth Brumaire of Louis Napoléon*. New York: International Publishers, 1963.

McLeod, Mary. "*Undressing Architecture: Fashion, Gender, and Modernity*." In *Back from Utopia*. Edited by Hubert-Jan Henket and Hilde Heynen. Rotterdam: 010 Publishers, 2002, 312–325.

McLuhan, Marshall, and Quentin Fiore. *War and Peace in the Global Village*. New York: McGraw-Hill, 1968.

Merleau-Ponty, Maurice. *Humanism and Terror: An Essay on the Communist Problem*. Translated by J. O'Neil. Boston: Beacon Press, 1969, 203.

———. *Signs*. Translated by R. McCleary. Evanston, IL: Northwestern University Press, 1964 (Originally published as *Signe*, Gallimard Paris, 1960).

The *New York Times*. "New York Has No Laughter and No Young Girls." The *New York Times*, October 19, 1913.

———. "American Collections." The *New York Times,* October 13, 1960, 32.

———. "Mother of the Day." The *New York Times,* November 26, 1960, 8.

———. "Mrs. Kennedy Sees New Spring Clothes." *New York Times*, March 23, 1961, 30.

Nicolson, Julie. *The Perfect Summer*. New York: Grove Press, 2006.

Nietzsche, Friedrich. *Thus Spake Zarathustra*. Translated by Thomas Common. Mineola, NY: Dover Publications, 1999.

Officer, Lawrence H., and Samuel H. Willimson, "Purchasing Power of Money in the United States from 1774 to 2006." MeasuringWorth.com, 2007.

Pochna, Marie-France. *Christian Dior: The Man Who Made the World Look New*. New York: Arcade Publishing, 1996.

Poiret, Paul. *King of Fashion*. Translated by Stephen Haden Guest. New York: J. Lippincott Company, 1931, 21.

Pop, Iggy (James Osterberg). "Godfather of Punk." Interview by Terry Gross, *Fresh Air,* NPR, July 14, 2006.

Rappaport, Roy A. *Ritual and Religion in the Making of Humanity.* Cambridge: Cambridge University Press, 1999.

———. "Ritual Regulation of Environmental Relations among a New Guinea People." *Ethnology*, January 1967, 26–27.

Rowlands, Penelope. *A Dash of Daring.* New York: Atria Books, 2005, 366.

San Francisco Chronicle. *Summer of Love: 40 Years Later*, Peter Coyote. *San Francisco Chronicle*, May 20, 2007.

Saunders, Edith. *The Age of Worth.* Bloomington: Indiana University Press, 1955.

Schiaparelli, Elsa. *Shocking Life.* New York: E. P. Dutton, 1954.

Sonn, Richard D. *Anarchism and Cultural Politics in Fin de Siecle France.* Lincoln: University of Nebraska Press, 1989.

Spitzer, Alan B. "The Good Napoleon III." *French Historical Studies* 2, no. 3 (Spring 1962): 308–329.

Sproles, George B. "Analyzing Fashion Life Cycles: Principles and Perspectives." *Journal of Marketing* 45, no. 4 (Autumn 1981): 116–124.

Sullivan, Louis H. "The Tall Office Building Artistically Considered." *Lippincott's Magazine*, March 1896.

The Long Now Foundation. http://www.longnow.org.

Thurman, Judith. "Swann Song; Yves Saint Laurent Bids Adieu." *New Yorker*, March 18, 2002, 134ff.

Tillich, Paul. "Nietzsche and the Bourgeoise Spirit." *Journal of the History of Ideas* 6, no. 3 (June 1945): 307–309.

Trilling, Lionel. *Sincerity and Authenticity.* Cambridge: Harvard University Press, 1997.

Tuchman, Barbara W. *The Proud Tower.* New York: Macmillan Company, 1966.

Turner, Victor. *Dramas, Fields and Metaphors.* Ithaca, NY: Cornell University Press, 1974.

Venturi, Robert, Denise Scott Brown, and Scott Izenour. *Learning from Las Vegas.* Cambridge, MA: MIT Press, 1972.

———. *Complexity and Contradiction in Architecture.* New York: Museum of Modern Art, 1966.

Vulliamy, Ed. *Love and Haight. Observer* (*Guardian UK*), May 20, 2007.

Waldberg, Peter. *Surrealism.* New York: McGraw-Hill, 1971.

Weir, David. *Anarchy and Culture: Aesthetic Politics of Modernism.* Amherst: University of Massachusetts Press, 1997.

White, Palmer. *Poiret.* New York: Clarkson N. Potter Inc., 1973.

Wilson, Ben. *The Making of Victorian Values: Decency and Dissent in Britain: 1789–1837.* New York: Penguin Press, 2007.

Winterburn, Florence. *Principles of Correct Dress, by Florence Hull Winterburn; including chapters by Jean Worth and Paul Poiret*. New York: Harper & Brothers, 1914.

Worth, Jean-Phillippe. *A Century of Fashion*. Translated by Ruth Scott Miller. Boston: Little, Brown, 1928.

CREDITS

Frontispiece Cecil Beaton © Condé Nast Publications
1.1 Library of Congress
1.2 The Granger Collection, New York / The Granger Collection
1.3 Library of Congress
1.4 The Art Archive / Eileen Tweedy
1.6 Jeremiah Gurney/Picture History
2.1 Roger Viollet Collection/Getty Images
2.2 The Metropolitan Museum of Art, Gift of Mary Pierrepont Beckwith, 1969. (C.I.69.33.4a-d) Image © The Metropolitan Museum of Art
2.3 Hulton Archive/Getty Images
2.5 The Art Archive/Blenheim Palace/Eileen Tweedy
2.6 Fine Art Photographic Library, London/Art Resource
2.7 Lady Agnew of Lochnaw, c.1892-93 (oil on canvas) by John Singer Sargent (1856-1925) © National Gallery of Scotland, Edinburgh, Scotland/The Bridgeman Art Library
3.1 © The Bridgeman Art Libarary
3.2 Central Art Archives / Hannu Aaltonen.
3.3 © Réunion des Musées Nationaux / Art Resource
3.5 Mary Evans Picture Library
3.6 Library of Congress
3.7 The Art Archive/Bibliothèque des Arts Décoratifs Paris/Dagli Orti
3.8 Library of Congress
3.9 Hulton Archive/Getty Images
3.10 The Metropolitan Museum of Art, Purchase, Friends of The Costume Institute Figts, 2005. (2005.207) (C.I.69.33.4a-d) Image © The Metropolitan Museum of Art
3.11 © Musee Galliera/Roger-Viollet/The Image Works
3.12 Photo by Paul Thompson/Topical Press Agency/Getty Images
4.1 ©ARS, NY/Snark/Art Resource, NY
4.2 Hulton-Deutsch Collection/CORBIS
4.3 © Man Ray Trust/ADAGP/Telimage–Paris, 2009
4.4 George Hoyningen-Huene © 1928 Condé Nast Publications
4.5 © Rue des Archives/The Granger Collection
4.6 © The Bridgeman Art Library
4.7 ©Alinari Archives / The Image Works
4.8 Collection of Kunsthaus Zurich
4.9 © Hulton-Deutsch Collection/CORBIS
4.10 Bettmann/CORBIS
4.11 Frank Driggs Collection/Getty Images
4.12 Sasha/Getty Images
4.13 © Swim Ink 2, LLC/CORBIS
4.14 © Philadelphia Museum of Art/CORBIS
4.15 V&A Images (left)
5.1 Sasha/Getty Images
5.2 John Rawlings © 1943 Condé Nast Publications
5.3 Hulton-Deutsch Collection/CORBIS
5.4 Courtesy Fairchild Archives
5.5 Horst P. Horst © 1946 Condé Nast Publications
5.6 Horst P. Horst © 1946 Condé Nast Publications
5.7 Nat Farbman/Time & Life Pictures/Getty Images
5.8 Photo by Pat English//Time Life Pictures/Getty Images (left)
5.8 Courtesy Everett Collection (right)
5.9 Reprinted through the courtesy of the Editors of TIME Magazine © 2009 Time Inc.
5.10 Walter Sanders//Time Life Pictures/Getty Images
5.11 Courtesy of The Advertising Archives
6.1 Madame Poiret in a dress by Paul Poiret (1879–1944) 1919 (b/w photo) by Delphi Studio (20th century) Private Collection/Archives Charmet/The Bridgeman Art Library
6.2 © The Museum of Modern Art/Licensed by SCALA/Art Resource, NY
6.3 © Mary Evans Picture Library 2008
6.4 REUTERS/Dario Pignatelli
6.5 © Adrian Boot/Retna UK
6.6 Courtesy of The Advertising Archives
7.1 Savitry/Picture Post/Getty Images
7.2 AP Photo

7.3 Express/Archive Photos/Getty Images (left)
7.3 Alfred Eisenstaedt/Time & Life Pictures/Getty Images (right)
7.4 Central Press/Getty Images
7.5 Central Press/Getty Images
7.6 Ralph Crane//Time Life Pictures/Getty Images
7.7 Bettmann/CORBIS
7.8 Lynn Goldsmith/CORBIS
8.1 Kennedy Library Archives/Newsmakers
8.2 Reprinted through the courtesy of the Editors of TIME Magazine © 2009 Time Inc.
8.3 AP Photo
8.4 AP Photo
8.5 Bettmann/CORBIS
8.6 Wally McNamee/CORBIS
8.7 Courtesy of Fairchild Publications
8.8 Larry Ellis/Express/Getty Images
8.9 Photo by Leni Sinclair
9.1 Keystone/Getty Images
9.2 Bert Stern © 1967 Condé Nast Publications
9.3 Lynn Goldsmith/CORBIS
9.4 Tony Frank/Sygma/Corbis (left)
9.4 Bettmann/CORBIS (right)
9.5 Neal Preston/CORBIS
9.6 Bettmann/CORBIS
9.7 Bettmann/CORBIS
9.8 © CORBIS SYGMA
9.9 Robin Platzer/Twin Images/Time Life Pictures/Getty Images
10.1 Courtesy of the author
10.2 AP Photo
10.3 Steve Schapiro/Corbis
10.4 H. Armstrong Roberts/ClassicStock/Corbis
10.5 Bettmann/CORBIS
10.6 AP Photo
10.7 The Metropolitan Museum of Art, Gift of Yves Saint Laurent Rive Gauche, 2003. (2003.443) Image © The Metropolitan Museum of Art
11.1 AP Photo
11.2 Hulton-Deutsch Collection/CORBIS
11.4 Courtesy of Fairchild Publications, Inc.
11.5 © Erin Fitzsimmons
11.6 AP Photo
11.6 Courtesy of Fairchild Publications
11.7 Courtesy of the author
12.1 Courtesy Everett Collection
12.2 Collection of Kunsthaus Zurich
12.3 Courtesy of Fairchild Publications, Inc. (left)
12.3 Courtesy of Fairchild Publications, Inc. (right)
12.4 AP Photo
12.5 Veer
12.6 Reuters/CORBIS
12.7 Courtesy of the author
12.8 Jason Lee/Reuters/Corbis
13.1 Photo by Mike Marsland/WireImage
13.2 Courtesy of The Advertising Archives
13.3 Bettmann/CORBIS
13.4 Guido Baviera/Grand Tour/Corbis
13.5 Emmanuel Faure/Getty Images
13.6 Hulton Archive/Getty Images
14.1 Hulton Archive/Getty Images
14.2 George Hoyningen-Huene © 1932 Condé Nast Publications
14.3 Photo by Eric Ryan/Getty Images
14.4 Anwar Hussein Collection/ROTA/WireImage
14.5 © Artists Rights Society (ARS), New York/ADAGP, Paris
14.6 Keith Bedford/Reuters/Corbis
14.7 The Long Now Foundation/Rolfe Horn
14.8 Neal Preston/CORBIS
14.9 Kevin Mazur/WireImage

Color Insert

p. 1 Massimo Listri/CORBIS
p. 2 © Musee Galliera/Roger-Viollet/The Image Works
p. 3 Georges Goursat/Getty Images
p. 4 Philadelphia Museum of Art/CORBIS
p. 5 John Rawlings © 1941 Condé Nast Publications
p. 6 Loomis Dean/Time Life Pictures/Getty Images
p. 7 Bettmann/CORBIS
p. 8 Ted Streshinsky/CORBIS
p. 9 STAFF/AFP/Getty Images
p. 10 Photo copyright Mick Rock 1972, 2009
p. 11 Tim Jenkins © 1977 Condé Nast Publications
p. 12 Giovanni Giannoni © 2006 Condé Nast Publications
p. 13 SAJJAD HUSSAIN/AFP/Getty Images
p. 14 Marcel Thomas/FilmMagic
p. 15 STR/AFP/Getty Images
p. 16 Mary Evans Picture Library/The Image Works

INDEX

N

O

P